SECRET
SLAVE

SECRET SLAVE

Kidnapped and
abused for 13 years.
This is my story
of survival.

Anna Ruston
with Jacquie Buttriss

BLINK
bringing you closer

Published by Blink Publishing
3.25, The Plaza,
535 Kings Road,
Chelsea Harbour,
London, SW10 0SZ

www.blinkpublishing.co.uk

facebook.com/blinkpublishing
twitter.com/blinkpublishing

Paperback – 9781911274100
Ebook – 9781911274117

A CIP catalogue of this book is available from the British Library.

Typeset by seagulls.net
Printed and bound by Clays Ltd, St. Ives Plc

13

Papers used by Blink Publishing are natural, recyclable products made
from wood grown in sustainable forests. The manufacturing processes
conform to the environmental regulations of the country of origin.

Every reasonable effort has been made to trace copyright holders of
material reproduced in this book, but if any have been inadvertently
overlooked the publishers would be glad to hear from them.

Blink Publishing is an imprint of the Bonnier Publishing Group
www.bonnierpublishing.co.uk

To Jamie, his mum and our four children

CONTENTS

CHAPTER 1

THE CLEANSING

'Would you like to come and meet my family? My mother likes having visitors. She would love to meet a nice English girl like you.' Malik's friendly smile gave me a warm feeling. He was a stocky man, overweight, not good-looking and about twice my age, but he seemed kind, and I wasn't doing anything special.

'Well ...' I hesitated, looking across the taxi office towards Val, to see what she thought. But she was deep into a prickly phone conversation with someone, so I couldn't interrupt.

'It's time for my break. I can drive you there now to say hello. We needn't be away long.' He stood up. 'Come on, just a cup of tea with my mum?'

'OK.' I nodded. It was a bit claustrophobic in the taxi base, and smelt of the kebabs the drivers had been eating that evening, so I could do with some fresh air. I'd probably be back before Val even noticed.

Malik ushered me to his taxi and opened the front passenger door for me.

'Where does your mum live?' I asked, in a moment of uncertainty. I didn't want to be away too long.

'Not far, just a few streets away.'

As we drove along, I looked out at all the lights in the windows of houses that we passed. Why did other people's houses always look so warm and inviting, like my great-grandma's used to be? I had always been happy living there with her, until she died when I was ten. I had never even slept in a bed on my own until the night after she died. Now I didn't really have a home. Rejected by my mother and abused by my violent father, I was a naive, unloved runaway, staying on Val's sofa. She was kind to me, but nobody really cared or loved me, like my great-grandma used to do.

'How was school today?' Malik asked as we turned onto the ring road.

'All right.' I shrugged.

'What lessons did you have?'

'Lots of lessons, mostly boring ones,' I sighed. 'Art was good.'

'Is art your favourite subject?'

'Not usually, but it was good today.'

'So, what subject do you like best?'

'Mmm …' I wasn't used to being asked about my day. Having just turned 15, I was a typical teenager, so I wasn't into conversations about school lessons. But Malik seemed to take a genuine interest in me. His smile warmed me at a time when I craved affection – that made me feel good.

'I like gym,' I said. 'And dance.'

He glanced at me with a grin. 'I can see you have a good body for dancing,' he said. 'In Pakistan, we love dancing – the women do some beautiful dances. Maybe my sister could teach you to dance the Sammi.'

'Maybe …' I nodded. 'Are we nearly there?'

'Yes,' he answered, turning into a side street. 'Only two more minutes.'

Sure enough, two minutes later he pulled into the driveway of a large semi-detached house.

'Here we are.'

'It's a big house.' I could see the dark outline against the starry sky.

'Yes, it's two houses made into one.'

'Do you live here too?'

'Yes, nearly all my family lives here. My mum, some of my brothers, their wives and children, and my sister and her family too.'

'Wow!'

I couldn't see much detail in the darkness, but there were lights on in most of the windows. It looked a welcoming house.

'Come on.' He led me to the front door. 'Take your shoes off.'

'Why?'

'Because we always take our shoes off when we go inside the house.'

'What for?'

'To keep it clean, and because that's our way.' He smiled as he unlaced his shoes. 'Come and meet the family.'

I took my shoes off, left them next to his in the porch, and stepped into the hallway. He put on some flip-flop sandals, but there was nothing for me so I walked barefoot.

He took me into a large living room with three long settees arranged as three sides of a square. On the fourth wall there was a gas fire and a hole built through the wall, with a badly fitting door that seemed to lead into the adjoining house, behind the fireplace. There were a lot of people, watching a tiny TV in the corner, showing a Pakistani film.

'Come and sit down,' he said, leading me to a settee. Several of the women got up to make space and went to the kitchen but an old lady sat still and gave me a half-smile. 'This is my mother, Farhat Aziz.' He pointed to me and said, 'Anna.'

'Hello,' I said, sitting down next to Malik.

Next, he turned to the men in the room. 'And these are my brothers.'

They all smiled and looked pleased to see me.

A sad-eyed young woman, about ten years older than me, came in with a tray.

'This is Muneeza. She is my brother Khalid's first wife.'

I gave her a smile as she passed me a cup of milky tea.

'Get some chapattis,' Malik ordered her with a stern expression. I hadn't seen this side of him before. I had a moment's hesitation: maybe I shouldn't have come. But then Malik flashed a smile at me and I felt fine again. 'I expect you're hungry?' he asked.

'Yes,' I nodded.

Muneeza came back with a large plate of buttered chapattis. They looked a bit different to the one I ate when Val and I had a takeaway a few days before.

'They're home-made,' Malik explained, as if reading my thoughts.

'Yes, it's very good,' I agreed.

Just then, Muneeza brought a bowl of minced meat with a strange scent and put it down on the table in front of me, along with a bowl of oranges, cut into quarters. They all looked at me, so I took a spoonful of meat to taste. It stung my tongue, but I tried not to pull a face.

'Do you like it?' asked Malik. 'It's lamb with Punjabi spices.'

I nodded my head. 'Not bad.'

Malik and his brothers all laughed.

I hadn't realised how hungry I was, so I helped myself to another chapatti, partly to take the taste of the spices away, and sucked an orange quarter, which tasted quite bitter to me, but I wasn't really a fruit eater.

After I'd eaten, his mother, tried to talk to me, but I couldn't understand anything she said. Her smile vanished and a look of contempt took its place. The brothers were talking amongst themselves, so I ate a third chapatti and fidgeted as the time passed.

'I need to go to the toilet,' I whispered to Malik.

'Muneeza,' he called, then some strange words I didn't understand. 'We speak Punjabi here,' he explained. 'Muneeza will show you to the bathroom.'

When I came out, Muneeza and another woman were waiting with a mop, some bleach and other cleaning things. They went straight in and scrubbed everything. To me this seemed rather a strange thing to do, but I had realised by now that this was a strange family – well, strange to me anyway.

'Can we go now?' I asked when I came back into the living room.

'Soon.' Malik nodded, then carried on talking to his brothers in their language. I sat down next to him and listened, but it was just a jumble of sounds. I didn't know what they were saying, but they kept looking at me and smiling. They could have been talking about me, but I couldn't tell. So I just sat there and looked up at the images of women in long, wafty clothes on the silent TV screen, then at the wooden elephant clock ticking slowly on the mantelpiece. I kept staring at that clock, thinking he'd better take me home in a minute.

Finally, Malik seemed to notice. 'What's wrong with you?'

'It's getting late: I'd like to go now.'

'Not yet,' he insisted, then carried on talking with his brother, Eshrat.

'Please will you take me home?' I pleaded, a few minutes later. 'Don't you have to get back to work?'

Malik turned and put his arm lightly around my shoulders, his dark eyes sparkling. He hadn't done anything like that before, so it felt a bit odd, but it was like he was showing me affection and I wasn't used to that. I was confused, but glad he liked me. Perhaps he wanted me to be his girlfriend.

'No, you stay here,' he insisted. 'Stay the night with us. It's late and you look tired. I'm sure you will sleep well here. I have to go back to work now, but I will take you straight home in the morning.'

'Well …' I hesitated. 'All right.'

He got up, checked everything was locked and went out through the front door. I was left alone, feeling nervous, in a room full of strangers.

What's going on here? I wondered. *What do I do now?*

The old lady started talking to me again, but I couldn't understand a word she said so I just smiled at her. At that moment two children came running through the room. They stopped when they saw me and pointed, shouting '*Gori, gori!*' Nobody told them off. That's when I started to feel uneasy.

Before long, taking no notice of me, the family went off in different directions, putting the lights out.

'What about me?' I asked one of the women. I found out later she was Malik's sister, Bushra. She gave me a kind look and led me up the stairs to an open doorway.

'You sleep,' she said, in her broken English, pointing into the room.

I was quite tired, now that I had eaten, and the milky tea made me feel very sleepy. Looking back, I don't know why I agreed to stay, but I thought Val wouldn't mind. It would only be for one night. She would assume I'd gone to stay with a school friend, which I sometimes did, or maybe back to my dad's. She hated him, so she wouldn't check. Nobody would miss me.

I looked around me. It was a big room, facing the stairs, with a bed against one wall, already made up. It would be fine for tonight. Malik would come back in the morning and take me home ... But where *was* home? Where should I go? Should I go back to my dad's house and put up with his physical and possibly sexual abuse, as he had threatened? No, that was why I'd run away. I couldn't go back there. Or should I go to my mother? I hadn't seen her for a couple of years, which was a good thing. She always told me how much she hated me and showed it in every way she could, not to mention all her boyfriends. Val had been very kind to let me stay on her sofa since I ran away from Dad's but I knew I was in the way there. I would have to think of something ... somewhere to go on a Saturday morning.

I had only a small purse with me. Inside were a few copper coins and Val's door key. I should have had my dad's key as well, but I'd thrown it into a hedge when I ran away – I never wanted to use that key again.

The only other things I had in my purse were my school bus-pass for ID and a small photo of Jamie, the boy I'd been out with a few times before he joined the army. I liked him a lot, but he was being posted abroad. The only person alive who really cared about me, I would miss him. I was supposed to go with his parents to see him off at the station the day before, but I didn't – I don't know why. Maybe it seemed a bit serious, meeting his parents, but I wish I'd gone. Jamie would have been so pleased. Maybe I could get Malik to take me to Jamie's parents' house? Although I hadn't met them, Jamie must have told them about me. Perhaps they would take me in. I yawned – I could decide where to go in the morning.

I had no toothbrush or anything. Never mind, I thought. I was so tired it wouldn't matter for one night.

The big double bed, with its old-fashioned eiderdown, looked very inviting so I just undressed down to my underwear, put out the light, slipped under the sheet and drifted off to sleep.

I had no idea when I woke – no watch or clock. But the light was shining in round the edges of the curtains and I heard sounds downstairs, so I got up and dressed.

Malik was back from work and came up the stairs to collect me.

Good, I thought. *Now at last he will drive me away from here.*

He took me down to the living room, to sit on one of the settees. I could hear the women preparing food, through the archway in the kitchen.

OK, I thought. *I'm going to have breakfast before we leave.*

They gave me a cup of 'tea'. But I didn't like what they called tea. Sickly sweet, it was made of boiled milk, with a lot of sugar in it. I knew I'd have to drink it, or they might think me rude. I gulped it down quickly to make sure the taste wouldn't linger. But it did.

I turned to Malik and gave him a smile, hoping we could get going at last. But he ignored me.

'Can you take me home now, please?' I asked.

That was when it started. His whole face clouded over with anger.

'You're not going home,' he spat out, sitting up and confronting me. 'You're not going *anywhere*, you're mine now!'

I was only a few days past my fifteenth birthday. *What does he mean?* I wondered. *I'm not going home? What can I do now?*

'You're *mine*,' he repeated, grabbing my arm and pulling me up.

'Ow, you're hurting me!' *Why was he being so rough?*

'*I'll* show you where you're going!' He dragged me to the stairs, pushed me up the first few, then took hold of my long blonde hair and dragged me up the rest. 'That's the only place *you're* going.' He gave me one last shove, back into the bedroom, where I floundered on all fours.

'Don't say a word,' he ordered me. 'Don't look out of that window.' He pointed to the front window, overlooking the street, its curtains still closed. 'Don't go near it, I will know if you've even touched the curtains. Just sit on that bed and don't move.' He turned and left, slamming the door behind him and turned the key in the lock.

I couldn't believe it. What had happened to me? *Why*? All I'd said was I wanted to go home ... even though I didn't know where home was. Already I'd stayed too long at Val's. And now I couldn't remember Jamie's parents' address, so I couldn't go there either. Well, it would have to be my mother's. But now what would I do? What *could* I do? Malik had been so angry with me, so forceful, that I didn't dare disobey him. Maybe, if I did as he said, he would change his mind and let me leave when he got back.

I sat on the edge of the bed, in this barren room, sobbing silent tears. But I couldn't shake his menacing image out of my mind. His black eyes glazed with evil, clenched face and lips stretched taut as he ground his teeth.

There I sat, cold to the bone and shivering with fear. How long did I sit like that? Long enough to cry myself dry – several hours, I'm sure. Why hadn't I worn a watch that day? But if I had, it wouldn't have accelerated the slow, heavy pace of time. I willed him to return if he was going to take me home, but I didn't want him to come and threaten me. The longer I sat there, the greater my apprehension.

There was nothing to look at in the room. The curtains were drawn, almost closed, and I didn't dare open them after what he had said. There was no TV, no pictures on the walls, no books or magazines; nothing to take my mind off my fears.

I sat still, on the edge of the bed, and watched the door. Perhaps someone, one of the women maybe, would come and unlock it, let me out, wave me goodbye. But nobody came. I had no food, nothing to drink: I couldn't even go to the toilet.

I panicked. Suppose nobody came? I might starve to death. Had they forgotten me? Unable to sit still any longer, I started banging on the door. Lightly at first, then harder and louder, shouting and yelling, 'Let me out! I need the toilet.'

Still nobody came. The only response was the sound of angry voices from downstairs. The women were shouting foreign words at me. I couldn't understand any of it, but it sounded like swear words.

Sitting back on the bed, I felt drained, powerless; I was a prisoner without even the most basic facilities. Unable to hold it in any longer, I squatted in the far corner, opposite the old-fashioned wardrobe, and peed on the floorboards. I felt so ashamed, but I couldn't help it.

I think it must have been late afternoon when Malik finally came home. With every loud footstep I flinched. *Would he still be angry?* I heard the key turn and he flung the door open, quickly closing and locking it again.

'My back hurts,' he complained, putting something down on the floor and taking his shirt off. 'Massage it for me.' He lay down on his front across the bed.

For a moment I hesitated.

'Come on,' he urged, 'massage my back.'

Too frightened to refuse, I didn't have the first idea how to do massage, except what I'd once seen in an American film, where the woman rubbed the man's shoulders and each side of the neck. I tried that on him, revulsed by his fat body and sweaty vest.

'No, you stupid bitch! I said my *back*.'

Trembling, I moved my hands down his back to his waist.

'Yes, there,' he ordered, lifting his vest for me.

I had to do what he said: I was too afraid not to. I did some rubbing movements outwards from the middle of his back, then upwards and downwards, making sure I stayed above his low-slung trousers.

Suddenly, he turned over and almost sent me flying.

I shall never forget what came next.

As he got off the bed, he picked something up from the floor and stood over me. At first my gaze was fixed on the demonic leer that contorted his face. Then I noticed it: the stiff bottle-brush he triumphantly held up as he watched the horror flooding my face.

'You're a dirty, f***ing bitch!' he snarled. 'You're a filthy white slut and I'm going to clean you, so you can be mine.' A sadistic smile crossed his face.

What did he mean? How was I dirty? Why the bottle-brush?

'How many f***ing, filthy Englishmen have you been with?'

'I haven't …' I pleaded.

'Don't lie to me. All English girls are slags, *white* slags! I need to cleanse you.'

With a wide grin of excitement he pushed me down on the bed, tore down my pants and pulled my legs apart. I was filled with terror as he forced the rough-bristled brush inside me, tearing my skin to shreds as he pushed it in and out, up and down, round and round. At this I screamed out in agony – I couldn't help it – the pain was excruciating.

'Shut the f***up!' he yelled.

'Stop. *Please* stop!'

'You're enjoying this, aren't you?' he jeered, relishing my pain. 'This is an Englishman inside you.'

But I couldn't speak, I couldn't think … Terrified of the damage he had caused me, I feared every slightest new movement of the brush.

With one sudden jerk, he tore the brush right out of me. I almost fainted from pain.

'You're *mine* now,' he snarled. 'You'll do what I say.'

I was in cold shock.

'*Won't* you?' he shouted, holding the brush near me again, while his eyes lit up at the sight of my fresh red blood running out.

'Yes,' I sobbed, barely able to hear my own voice.

It seemed to please him.

'Turn over, white bitch!' he ordered me and stood back to watch my discomfort. He gave me a push, so I lay flat on my tummy, hardly daring to peer over my shoulder in fear.

With a sigh of satisfaction, he pointed the sharp, plastic handle of the brush towards my backside.

'*No!* I shrieked in desperation. '*Please* don't …'

But it was too late.

As he forced the handle in and out, the searing pain cut through me. The more noise I made, the more frenzied he became, his heavy hand over my mouth and nose, pulling my head back and stifling my screams, almost choking me. I struggled desperately to breathe. Within minutes, he had split my anus and there was blood everywhere.

Now at last he was satisfied, it seemed. He calmly put on his shirt, picked up the brush and walked out of the room, locking the door behind him.

I didn't want to stay on that bed, so I pulled the bloodied eiderdown around me and crawled over to the corner, next to the wardrobe, leaving a dark red trail. Shamed and degraded, I curled up on the floor like an injured fawn, sobbing.

Why did I agree to come here? What had I done to deserve this?

CHAPTER 2

PUNISHMENT

I don't know how long I sat, with the bedcover wrapped around me, rocking painfully on the bare floorboards in the corner of the room. My past hadn't all been happy, but nothing had prepared me for the horrors in this house. I wanted to stop myself rocking, but I couldn't. After a while, when it was beginning to get dark, I heard footsteps coming up the stairs and flinched, rigid with fear. I heard the key turn in the lock and watched as the door was pushed slowly open. I held my breath ... then let out a deep sigh of relief as one of the women came in, carrying a mug of something.

She was a big woman, years older than me. Later, I found out that this was Surayya, the wife of Malik's brother Eshrat. I wondered whether she had heard my screams, whether she knew, or guessed ... But I couldn't tell anything from her stern expression.

She plonked the mug down on the chest of drawers near the bed. Then, without even a glance in my direction, turned towards the door and walked out, locking it behind her. I listened to her footsteps fading away, then the door at the bottom of the stairs being closed and locked as well. She must have been told to make sure I couldn't get out.

Was this it? Was I now a prisoner?

I could see the mug was steaming, so I assumed it was tea. I'd had nothing to eat or drink since the previous night. I wasn't hungry at all, with the shock, I suppose, but my mouth and throat were parched from all the crying. Leaning into the corner, I pulled myself up, one painful step after another. My whole body cried out for a drink of some kind, but when I looked into the mug, I felt sick. It wasn't tea, or even water, just a murky fluid with bits floating in it. I couldn't even guess what it was, and I didn't want to drink it – I couldn't. I just dipped the tip of one finger in and used it to wet my lips.

Afterwards I sat on the edge of the bed in a sort of trance. For a time I no longer felt the pain – I was numb, disoriented. I don't know what I was thinking. I can only remember sitting there, silently weeping. I didn't dare make a sound in case someone heard me and came. I didn't want to see anybody.

For a long time I sat there, desperately lonely, craving attention, yet knowing this was impossible and, above all, I was petrified of Malik's return. I hadn't been to the toilet since the day before and I didn't know what to do, so I went over and banged on the door. The only response was angry women's voices, shouting at me again in a language I didn't understand. It sounded as if they were swearing at me to stop the noise.

But at least something came of it. A few minutes later, Surayya came back again, this time with a glass of water, which she put down on the chest of drawers, and a wide, low, empty barrel with a lid on it. Written across the front was the word 'ghee'. She carried it across the room and put it down on the floor, away from the bed. Without saying a word, she went back out again and locked the door behind her. At first I didn't realise what it was, but when I'd gulped down the water, it wasn't long before I needed a wee. That's when I guessed and used it, because I couldn't wait any longer.

The next problem was when I wanted to poo. I couldn't do it in the barrel – that would be too shameful, and it would smell so bad.

There was a large, wooden chest of drawers by the bed, so I looked in there to see if I could find anything, but it was mostly full of linen and men's clothes. Next, I opened the doors to the old-fashioned wardrobe and rooted around the pile of stuff on the floor. That's where I found a zipped white handbag. It didn't look like it had ever been used, so I opened it up and used it to poo in, then zipped it closed again and replaced it in the wardrobe.

It was the evening when Malik came back. I heard his deep voice booming down below, and moments later his heavy footsteps trudging up the stairs, deliberate with intent. He unlocked the door and stormed in, slamming and locking it behind him. There I sat, rigid with fear, still on the edge of the bed. I hadn't turned the light on, so his great bulk loomed against the shadows. He was grinding his teeth as if he'd riled himself up. The light from the street lamp outside filtered through the curtains and illuminated the rage in his face, the evil in his black eyes. Lunging towards me, he grabbed my hair in one fist to lift me up. He rammed me up against the wall, holding my head against the cold, hard plaster with his other hand.

'You ever tell anybody about this,' he snarled, 'You *ever* look out of that window, and your head's going to go through this wall!'

That's when he grabbed my hair even more tightly, pulled my head a few inches away and smashed it against the wall. He let go and I folded, dazed, to the floor, feeling as if my head would explode. As he strode back towards the door to put the light on, I gazed up at the wall, where I could see the blood trickling down. When I put my hand to my scalp, I felt the wetness of blood oozing through my hair.

He smirked with satisfaction as he saw the blood. 'You're my property now and you'll do as I say,' he told me. Then he paused. 'Whatever I say, you do, or else you know what the consequences will be, don't you?'

I gave a slight nod.

'*Don't* you?' he demanded loudly, pulling my head up by my hair again and putting his face right in front of mine.

'Yes,' I replied shakily, stifling a sob.

'*Good*, you'd better believe it.'

'Would you kill me?' I dared to ask.

'Well, you just try me,' he replied, letting go of my hair as he pushed my head down.

That's when I knew. *I'm in real trouble now*, I thought. *Serious trouble*. Realisation of the danger I was in set me off into uncontrollable weeping. I just couldn't stop. He watched me for several seconds, then, whenever a sob came out, I got a smack in the face from the back of his hand.

'Shut up your bleating,' he demanded. 'You're a weak, white slag, with nothing to cry about! Nobody wants you, nobody misses you – you're lucky I've taken you in and now I'm looking after you so I don't want any of your white trash emotion.'

Nodding, I did my best to stifle my tears.

'All you have to do is whatever I say, and you'll be all right.' He pulled me roughly from the floor to sit me back on the edge of the bed. 'Now do it,' he demanded, undoing his trousers.

'Do *what?*' I asked. I had no idea what he meant.

'Do what all you white slags do.'

He took hold of my hair again and forced my head forward to give him oral sex, really hard. Horrified, I didn't dare struggle – he was so big and so forceful that he was choking me. He pushed and pushed inside my mouth and made me stay there until he ejaculated at the back of my throat. It made me violently sick, all over him, which led to more backhanders across my poor, bruised face. Then I had to do it all over again … and again.

Finally, I lay back on the bed to try and recover. But this was just what he needed. Breaking out into a huge grin, he put his hand in his pocket and pulled out a disposable razor. He waved it at me and its sharp edge glinted under the light, causing me to tremble uncontrollably. As I tried to pull myself away across the bed, he put his weight against my legs, pulled up my skirt and pulled my pants down around my thighs.

'Don't hurt me!' I shrieked. '*Please* don't hurt me.'

'Look at all that dirty hair,' he smirked. 'Pubic hair is *very* dirty, I have to make you clean.' He grinned as he took the razor slowly down to my pubic area.

I screamed. He seemed to enjoy that, as he sat himself across my thighs and held me down. He moved the razor across and back, to and fro, then downwards between my legs and pressed harder as he reached my clitoris, crossing it roughly several times, deliberately nicking the delicate skin to draw blood. For me it was exquisitely painful and horrifying whereas he was euphoric and the more anguished I became, the more excited he was.

Unable to contain himself any longer he raped me as viciously as he could, hurting me badly, reopening my bottle-brush wounds from that morning, the blood running down my legs, raising his excitement to fever pitch so that he raped me all over again. I was in agony, and petrified of what he was doing to me – the damage to my insides, the shame. But the worst thing was, as he penetrated me, thrusting repeatedly and painfully, he muzzled me. He put his large, fleshy hand over my nose and mouth so tightly I couldn't shout or scream ... or breathe. It suffocated me, and that was an added feature of his pleasure. Even more distressing for me, it was also a traumatic reminder of the first time I had been raped, when I was 11.

'You've been with different men, you white slag! I have to punish you, I'll make sure you never do that again.'

'I've not been with anybody,' I protested. 'I'm only 15 years old.'

Could he read my thoughts? Of course I was not going to tell him about that earlier rape, by Val's ex-husband. Although I knew that was not my fault, I had never really got over it. But this was so much worse.

'Fifteen-year-olds are the worst slags,' he continued. 'I know English girls, I'm a taxi driver.'

As I struggled to pull myself up to a sitting position he pushed me back down again and climbed on top of me once more, bruising every part of my body with his rough movements, making me cry out, which excited him into another rape. More desperate struggles to breathe … He would not leave me alone.

'I'm going to make you suffer for what you've done,' he explained, his eyes gleaming with pleasure.

'I've done nothing,' I sobbed.

'I know you've been with other taxi drivers,' he insisted, 'so it's for your own good. I have to punish you.'

Finally, he stopped.

'I own you now,' he announced, triumphantly. 'You'll never be anybody else's, you're mine.' Then he lay on the bed. Satisfied at last, he turned over and went to sleep next to me.

I was so frightened that I didn't dare move. Soon he was snoring loudly enough to shake the ornaments, if there had been any. Very gently I tried to roll a little away from him, so that I didn't have to smell so much of his strong body odour, though I realised that I had not been permitted to have a wash since I'd arrived, nor any change of underwear. At least that was not my fault.

I lay there in the darkness, wounded, throbbing and burning with pain. My mind was in turmoil, all the while I was wondering, *will I be permanently damaged? Is it possible for me to survive this ordeal and stay sane? How?* I tried to separate my mind from my body, to distance my thoughts, but I was hurting too much. How had I got myself into this hell? Was it all my fault? Was I somehow to blame? But then a glimmer of hope: was this a nightmare that I would wake up from in the morning?

I tried to think of a way out, but my brain was shaken, confused. Somehow I forced myself to concentrate for a few moments. *What can I do? Is there any way to escape from this monster, to rescue my body ... and my sanity?*

If only I could find where he'd put the key – I knew he'd taken it out of the lock. The bed was up against the wall, and I was lying on that side. I wondered if I could wriggle gently down, or clamber lightly over him to try and find the key. But I trembled at the thought. That would certainly wake him and send him into a frenzied attack, which might be the death of me so I knew I couldn't risk waking him. I had to stay where I was all night.

Every inch of my body felt bruised and battered, assaulted by sharp pangs of pain, as if I was being stabbed. I had nothing left, my resistance spent, I couldn't help it ... That night I wet the bed for the first time since I was a toddler. I couldn't get up to change the sheets, so I lay in the cold and wet all night, wallowing in misery.

Perhaps now that he'd had his pleasure, he might just open the door in the morning and let me go. It was the only thing I could hope for, as I lay awake in the darkness, my head throbbing loudly, ears full of white noise and my whole body on fire, listening to his rumbling snores. If only I could put my pillow over his face and smother him ... but he would be much too strong for me.

When Malik woke up in the morning, he snarled something at me, but I didn't understand as he was speaking in Punjabi.

I just knew from the way he said it that it must be something bad. I started to tremble, but he didn't seem to notice.

He sat on his side of the bed with his back to me, muttering. I didn't know if it was something to do with me, or with someone else. Whoever it was, he seemed angry, so I kept as still as I could and closed my eyes, so that he might think I was asleep.

He got up and got dressed and was about to leave the room when he noticed the barrel and turned to look at me. I didn't shut my eyes in time so he saw I was awake and I took my chance.

'What is that barrel for?'

'That's what you get to piss in,' he replied with a shrug.

'Why have I got to wee in the barrel?' I asked. 'Why can't I go to the toilet?'

'Because you're a dirty, f***ing bitch!' He looked at me with disgust. 'I don't want you using my toilet, you're dirty.' Then he leant across, smacked me round the head, adding to my massive headache from the previous day, pulled me by the hair out of the bed and left me sprawling on the floor.

'That's what you get for asking stupid questions,' he sneered, then turned and walked away, locking the door behind him as he went.

CHAPTER 3

SEEKING SOLACE

Finally, I could remove the wet sheets, which I bundled up and hid under the bed. I found some clean ones in a drawer, so I could put those on instead when the pain subsided ... *if* it ever would. It was still early morning, I thought, and I'd been awake all night, so I lay on a dry part of the mattress and tried to get as comfortable as I could. Exhausted, I fell asleep.

I woke to the sound of the key turning in the lock. What time was it? Somebody was coming in. I got out from under the covers and sat up, just as the sad-looking woman, Muneeza, crept into the room. Thin and pale, she was at least ten years older than me, with hunched shoulders, red eyes and blotchy skin. For some reason I immediately felt sorry for her. I don't know why – she looked as if she suffered.

Perhaps a kindred spirit, I thought. *Maybe she understands.*

'Tea,' she said, with a nervous smile. My mouth was still very sore, but I tried to smile back. She had a chapatti on a plate and a mug of steaming hot, milky liquid, which she put down on the chest and removed the watery stew I hadn't drunk from the day before.

'Thank you,' I said.

It was 36 hours since I'd eaten anything and, despite my troubles and pains, I was hungry and desperate for a drink.

Just as she was about to turn, she shook her arm and a small white packet fell out of her sleeve, onto the rug. I didn't know what it was, but it looked as though she had done that deliberately.

She hesitated, as if watched, and my gaze darted to the door, unlocked and ajar … Could I escape? But just then, it opened slightly and one of the brothers, the one called Eshrat, stepped forward and barked an order at Muneeza in a hostile voice. She quickly scurried out and he took a step back onto the landing to lock the door again. Was I being guarded to prevent my escape? It felt like it. How long would I have to stay here?

The packet had fallen close enough to the bed for me to lean down and pick it up. When I opened the end flap, I saw that it had four foil strips of tablets inside. Then I gazed at the packet, printed with strange writing that I could not read … until one word caught my eye, a word written in English letters: 'Paracetamol'. I'd heard of paracetamols; I knew they were painkillers. I felt quite overwhelmed at that small gift; it was the first kind thing, the *only* kind thing, anyone had done for me in that house. Perhaps Muneeza knew more than she let on.

I popped out two of the tablets and gulped them down with the milky liquid.

The chapatti was still warm and spread with butter. I was grateful it was something soft that I could eat and it was a relief to put something in my stomach at last. The milky tea didn't seem as sweet today. Perhaps they had put less sugar in, or maybe my body was in shock, craving more sugar.

Alone again, and the pains slightly numbed, I slid gently off the bed and went back over to the corner where I'd sat and rocked the day before. It was a hidden-away spot, in the gap between the end of the wardrobe and the wall. From there, if I pulled right back, I couldn't see the locked door, or the bed, or even the front window, only the woodchip wallpaper, the bare wooden floorboards and the frayed end of the rug. I was so scared, sitting there alone. What was happening to me? Why hadn't anybody come and found me? But who was there to find me? Nobody would care.

I curled myself up, as far as I could, and tucked myself into the angle of the walls, rocking to a silent rhythm, which seemed to calm me. In this corner I felt safe – at least as safe as I could be in this room. If he did come in and attack me, I felt I could defend myself here. I could put my hands up to protect my head, or my feet up to try and fend him off. I think I sat in that corner all day, rocking to and fro.

As I rocked, I spotted a broken biro sticking out from under the wardrobe, and I stopped and picked it up. There was a jagged piece of the plastic, so I used the pen to pick at the wall. Gradually I scraped a groove in the dingy brown woodchip, which encouraged me to chip further into it. This was my project, something useful to do; something I could make progress with. I don't remember what I was thinking, if I was thinking anything at all. Maybe I could slowly make a hole in the wall itself, a hole to escape through, or at least to get help. Yes, I think that was it, making a hole to freedom. I carried on for a while, chipping away, but it was not easy to do as it must have been quite thick. Gradually, I picked off a few flakes and they added to the pile of dust that had dropped onto the floorboards. So I had to flatten the dust across and try to push it down the gaps between the boards. I noticed one of the floorboards was loose, so I lifted that a little, until it squeaked and pushed the rest of the dust down into the void underneath, before replacing it. I hoped no one had heard the squeak downstairs, or I would be in trouble.

When I paused to have a rest from the scraping, I suddenly realised the small area of wallpaper I had managed to get off looked really obvious from there. I stopped. If Malik ever saw what I'd done, I was convinced he would beat me to death. I desperately hoped he wouldn't notice it, beyond the wardrobe.

There was nothing else to do, no TV, no books or magazines. I must have been feeling a bit hyper and depressed – my head was buzzing. The day dragged on and I was so bored that I started to bite my fingernails, just as I had done when I was younger – biting them off and eating them, chewing them down to the quick. I tried to do it slowly, to fill the time.

I curled up on the floor in my corner and fell asleep for maybe an hour or two. When I woke up again, I edged forward and looked round the room. But there wasn't much to look at, with the windows and curtains closed so that there was no sunlight and no fresh air. I was so scared, sitting there; I didn't know which way to turn, what to do. I daren't touch the curtains to look out of the window – he had forbidden me to do that on pain of smashing my head through the wall. But as the afternoon wore on, I was tempted to have a peek, maybe to wave and attract somebody's attention, but then I noticed something balanced across the top of the curtains, along the curtain rail, that looked as if it would fall if I moved even a corner of the curtain, and I was too frightened to take that risk. I wouldn't have been able to reach to put it back again.

I tried to think about where this room was, remembering the evening Malik had brought me there, when we arrived and got out of the car. It was dark then, but he had parked in front of a sort of tunnel between two houses, under the first floor. The room I was in now was only one flight of stairs up and it felt like it was at the front of the house, maybe over that tunnel.

There was just one window – a wide one at the front with old-fashioned, swirly-patterned curtains drawn across it. I went over and sat on the bed so that I could take a closer look at the swirls, following them with my eyes, in and out of each other, across the material. Gradually, I started to see, or to imagine I could see, shapes of people dancing, children playing and clowns jumping. I'd never been to a circus, but I once visited a fairground with my great-grandma Mavis. There were clowns there, juggling clubs and jumping about.

I loved my great-grandma and she loved me. She was such a happy person; everyone loved her. She used to call me 'My Angel' and I called her 'Nana'. She was the only person in the world who had ever really loved me. It gave me a warm feeling, just thinking about her.

I know I was born in the front room of my grandmother's house and straightaway taken up to Nana's cottage. I don't know why, except my mother didn't want me and my father wasn't my real father. It was a decision made before I was born that my great-grandma would have me. There were two bedrooms in the cottage: I slept with Nana in the bigger one and Great-Grandpa was in the other. So it was just Nana, Great-Grandpa and me.

We lived in the stone cottage at the top of a hill in the village of Allerback. It had two outside toilets and a well in the back garden. I remember we had to lift off the wooden cover and turn a big handle to bring the water up to the top in a bucket. Sometimes Nana used to let me have a go, but she was always worried in case I fell down the well. It was quite a big hole and she was very protective.

Nana was a small lady – I think she shrank as she got older. She always wore a bandage on her knee, all the years I remember. And she used to wear a blue overall every day, because she was always working – cleaning or washing or cooking. I could picture her in her blue overall with silvery buttons down the front and a massive grey bun on the top of her head, with pins in it. A hard worker, she had worked all her life. She used to cook doves and pheasants for a well-off lady in the village and she cleaned for her as well.

I remembered Nana's tin bath that she used to do the washing in. I would watch her light a fire underneath it, then sprinkle in the soap-flakes, and she used to shave a big bar of something over it too. Then she put all the washing in and scrubbed it by hand. Afterwards she doused the fire and added some cold water from the well. Finally, she would take all my clothes off, lift me into the tin bath and wash me too. My favourite part was when she pulled out the mangle and let me turn the handle as she fed the sheets and everything through, between the rollers. I loved watching them come out flat, like long pieces of paper. Finally I helped her pull down the airer from the kitchen ceiling and she put all the washing to dry on that, over the cooking range.

Such a lovely woman she was, my Nana. If only she was here now. She always showed me love and affection. I used to sit on her knee and she played with me, mostly with the dolls when I was little. She even used to take me down to the village chemist to buy baby food for my dolls. Nana was an amazing woman. Any money she had, she would go and buy me a second-hand pram to push my dolls in. She once bought an old 'Silver Cross' pram. It wasn't immaculate, but I loved it. We used to go down the bottom of the garden together and pretend I was the mum – I think I always wanted to be a mum, from my earliest memories. I especially loved my 'Tiny Tears' doll that she bought me for my birthday.

My favourite time of day was bedtime. Every night, Nana boiled some milk and stirred in a spoonful of 'Camp' coffee and we drank it together. Then we had a wash and cleaned our teeth at the kitchen sink before we went into the bedroom. When it was time to get undressed, I always had to help Nana undo the suspenders on her thick stockings and the hooks on her whale-boned corset – I loved helping her.

Both in our nighties, we climbed into her big bed and she made me say prayers with her. There were three prayers, and we always had to say them in the right order. Every night we said these prayers, and I think they helped us both to get to sleep.

Just thinking about Nana, while held captive in this prison room, helped me to remember I once mattered to somebody. I still mattered to me, and to her too if she could see me now, so I had to try and survive this torment but it was so hard.

* * *

What little light there was in the room was slowly dimmed. It must have been evening and nobody had come since first thing that morning. I didn't dare switch on the light in case it attracted anyone to come up and complain at me so I just found the packet, pushed out two more paracetamols from their foil strip and, as I had nothing to drink, gulped them down.

As I slowly made up the bed with the clean sheets I had found in a drawer, I hoped I might be left alone tonight, alone to sleep and for my wounds to heal. The paracetamols certainly helped. I had done nothing much all day, but I was dead tired. As soon as I lay down in the bed, I fell fast asleep.

The turn of the key in the lock roused me and I opened my eyes in dread to see Malik lumbering into the room. He switched on the light and made straight for me. Leaning across the bed and grabbing a handful of my hair, he yanked me off and through the doorway, but all my aches and pains made me stiffer now and I couldn't move quickly enough for him.

'I want eggs on toast,' he growled, letting go of my hair and pushing me across the landing from behind. Going from one step to the next was too painful for me, so I had to try and slither down the stairs on my side, every bump jarring my tender insides. Somehow, I managed to pull myself upright again in the kitchen, while he got out the eggs and bread. He disappeared through to the living room, leaving me to cook them. I had to search for a pan and some oil. He hadn't told me how he wanted his eggs, so I did them fried and toasted the bread under the grill. As I waited for the toast to brown, I noticed the clock on the kitchen wall: 4:25am. No wonder the house was so quiet.

'Is it ready yet?' he rasped as he came back to the kitchen.

'Yes.'

I put it all on a plate and handed it to him.

He carried it upstairs, while I had to crawl the whole way up and watch him eat, sitting on the edge of the bed. After all that exertion, I couldn't find a way to sit comfortably. In the past, the smell of food would have made me hungry, but I wasn't now.

'Stop fidgeting,' he barked at me. 'Move over!'

I tried to keep still, but I couldn't stop trembling. Would he attack me again tonight? Surely he couldn't inflict another onslaught so soon?

He smacked his lips as he finished off his meal and turned to look at me. He must have seen me shaking. 'So, white slag, you're frightened of me, are you?' he laughed.

I tried to slide myself backwards, away from him, but it was no use.

'Come here and do it,' he demanded, pulling me across the bed by my arm. I did what he wanted, retching and choking as he pushed himself hard, into my mouth, to the back of my throat, again and again. When it was over, he lay down, panting. Well, I thought it might be over, but no.

'Come on, you white bitch!' He tore off my clothes and forced his hand between my legs, grabbing and squeezing me much too hard, then scraping his rough fingernail across my clitoris, re-opening last night's wound and making me cry out. 'Shut your mouth!' he roared as he punched me in the face and climbed on top of me, his heaviness squashing the air out of my lungs. As I turned my head sideways to avoid his foul smell, I could feel the blood trickling from my nose, but I had to try and ignore it. The fresh blood excited him into a frenzied rape, his hand pushing down my wounded nose and blocking my mouth so hard I struggled for breath. The more noisily I gulped for air, the harder he thrusted inside me, tearing open the previous wounds so painfully that I cried out, which only goaded him on more fiercely.

Finally, he was done. I gulped great, desperate breaths of air as I curled up my wretched body in an instinctive attempt to ease the pain.

After rolling his big-bellied bulk over, within minutes he was snoring loudly. I lay as close to the wall as I could, weeping quietly. How could I bear this torture? Surely it would end soon.

I was hurting badly, but I didn't dare climb out of the bed to reach the paracetamols, for fear of waking him. Had he broken my nose? I lay down and tried to sleep, but I couldn't relax in such a tormented state.

Then it came to me: I would say Nana's prayers. Maybe she would hear them and come to my aid, or perhaps God would help me.

The tears rolled down my cheeks as I forced myself to concentrate. How did that first one go? I started to whisper it inside my head:

In my little bed I lie,
Heavenly Father, hear my cry.
Lord protect me through the night,
And bring me safe to morning light.
Amen

I imagined Nana saying it with me and putting her arms around me. She always told me she loved me. At the end of this prayer I felt strangely calm. My tears slowed and the warmth of those years with Nana lulled me to sleep.

CHAPTER 4

THE BOY IN THE PHOTO

Only a few hours later, when the sun was up and shining round the edges of the thick damask curtains, Malik snored himself into a coughing fit, rousing me as well. I stayed as still as I could and closed my eyes, hoping desperately that he might leave me alone. He heaved himself out of bed and I risked a glance as he got dressed in the same clothes he wore the day before, turned and unlocked the door.

'What time is it?' I asked, rubbing my eyes. I knew it must be early morning as by now, I'd realised the room was always brightest then, so the window must be facing east. The sunbeams danced on the big, patterned rug that covered most of the wooden floor.

He glanced at his watch and grunted: 'Eight o'clock, time I went to take over the shop.' So off he went, locking up and leaving me alone again. Relief flooded my whole body. He had told me when we chatted at the taxi base that as well as driving cabs, he took turns with his brothers to run the family shop in a nearby street, where his eldest brother lived. That meant he would probably be out all day.

I didn't particularly look forward to another day locked in this barren room, with nothing to do but grieve for my lost freedom and pick off more wallpaper flakes to pass the time. It was a lonely prospect, but at least I would be free from harm for a few hours.

Once again, as I sat up and tried to move, pains shot through me from my various injuries. I gingerly reached for my paracetamols and gulped down two more with the water left in Malik's glass, relishing the cool, soothing liquid as it first moistened my lips. Then I swilled it round my mouth and let it run down my throat.

For a while I rested with my feet up on the bed, watching the dust dance in the sunbeams. I was drawn to the thin snatches of bright sunshine that leaked round the edges of the curtains. If only I could just lift one corner slightly, very gently, to see the outside world – people walking freely by, trees swaying in the breeze, children playing games. I was very tempted but if anyone heard the curtain move, or saw me looking out, well, I'd be better off dead. I knew some of Malik's brothers had houses in this street and there were a lot of Pakistani families in the town, so there were probably other families and relatives living nearby, maybe in the houses opposite.

As I sat there, on the bed, I found myself rocking again; I don't know why. I tried to think of something to take my mind away from there. As I looked once more at the patterns on the curtains, the swirling lines and shapes, the variations of colour, I saw clowns leaping and juggling on the hillsides, slender women dancing on clouds, fish swimming and weaving about in streams, where reeds swayed and sunlight glinted on ripples and eddies. In my head I started to make up stories about the clowns, imagining them putting on their make-up, practising their acts, making people laugh … After all, I was only just 15 – still a child. How cruel life could be, but maybe I would soon find a way to be free again.

Thinking about the clowns took me back to the fairground where I had first seen them with Nana on a big field, near my school. It was the first and only time I had ever visited a fair. We left Nana's cottage and walked there together. I don't know how old I was – maybe six or seven. We walked around to look at all the rides and Nana bought me some sticky candyfloss on a stick, which I loved. I went on a cup-and-saucer ride and a little roundabout, waving at her every time I passed, and I can remember her cheery, rosy-cheeked laugh as she waved me on. After that we went into a round tent and sat on a bench to watch the clowns. They made me laugh so much as they pretended to trip over and throw buckets of water over each other, only the water was bits of paper.

Next, Nana took me to a stall where they gave me a stick with a metal ring on the end and I had to try and hook a plastic duck in a cardboard pond. I was so excited when I caught one that I jumped in the air and nearly fell over. The man handed me a plastic bag with a real live goldfish in it. I couldn't stop grinning – I never thought I would have a pet of my own.

'He looks a bit lonely,' said Nana. 'Let's see if I can win him a friend.'

'Yes, *please*!' I squealed.

Sure enough, Nana hooked a duck as well and won her own fish, and then another … Soon we had six of them to take home! She always spoilt me when she could, and I loved it. I gave all the fish names and put them in a tank we found in one of Great-Grandpa's out-houses, then I fed them all myself. Sometimes I would go and talk to them and I wondered whether they could understand. I think I must have overfed them though because they didn't last very long.

One morning I got up and had my cod liver oil and malt that Nana used to make me swallow every day before breakfast, and sometimes syrup of figs – eugh! The cod liver oil and malt mixture was really thick stuff and I hated it, so she used to give me a sugar lump afterwards.

'It's very good for you,' she would say when I protested. She was strict about having it every day without a break, but I knew it was because she wanted me to grow strong and healthy.

While Nana was making breakfast, I used to go and feed the fish before school. One morning I found them all floating on top of the water. Maybe that was something fish did, I thought, but they were very still and Nana had to tell me they were dead. I cried and cried.

'Never mind,' she smiled, lifting me onto her knee and giving me a big hug, 'you can stay home today and help me make jam. Would you like that?'

'Yes, please,' I said, considerably cheered.

She got up on the little step-stool and reached down a huge metal pan. I can still remember cutting up all the fruit and stirring the steaming mixture in the pan until it began to set. Then she let me spoon some of it into jars and we put tops on and labels. Even though I've never really liked jam, that one tasted so good – I ate some of it on my toast because it was *my* jam.

But I didn't usually like missing school because I enjoyed it, especially my friends and the lunches. I was quite a sunny child then. We used to have chocolate sponge and custard for afters once a week, my favourite. It was green custard and it tasted minty with the chocolate pudding.

I had been quite happy for the half-hour or so that I had been leafing through my memories of Nana. It was the one thing that helped me forget for a while how awful my life had now become. But I was stirred from my remembrances by the sound of the key in the lock. It must still be morning, surely he couldn't have returned already?

The door slowly opened and in stepped an old woman – Malik's mother. Well, I suppose she wasn't really old at all, probably only in her fifties, but she looked old to me. I wondered if that's what marrying young and having lots of children did to a woman.

Her face looked angry and she spat out some words at me, but I didn't understand. She put up a clenched hand and beckoned me to go with her. I was confused. Malik had told me not to leave the room, but now his mother ordered me to. Was I his prisoner, or hers? I knew the answer of course, but I was anxious that whatever I did would be wrong, so I meekly followed her downstairs, gently placing my feet to avoid too much of the pain I still had.

When we reached the hallway, she repeated the words she had said and I guessed she was insulting me. Later, I would find out she was castigating me for being 'an English slut' and sleeping with her son (even though he was the paedophile who had kidnapped and raped me). She took me into the living room and made me sit down on the hardest sofa, then brought me a cup of weak, milky tea. As before, it had sugar in it, but it was not sweet enough for me. Usually I hated sugar in drinks, but now my body craved it. She put on the tiny television, high up on a wall-bracket, and it was the start of a Pakistani film. I didn't have a clue what it was about, so I just watched the pictures to keep sane. This woman, who obviously didn't like me, seemed to be trying to be kind in her own rough way.

At lunchtime one of the younger women brought me two chapattis and a bowl of curry. It smelt very strongly spiced and garlicky, which I'd never liked, so I only had a small spoonful, with one of the chapattis. I'd lost my appetite and wasn't really hungry any more but I did drink the glass of water they gave me.

When the film finished, Malik's younger brother Eshrat came and sat on the settee opposite me. He spoke good English. It appeared to be only the men who could speak English: why not the women? To me that seemed very strange.

Eshrat started asking me questions – 'Where do you come from?', 'How old are you?', 'Where do you live?', 'What is your mother's name?', 'What is your father's name?', 'How long have you been going down to the taxi base?', 'How do you know Val?', 'What do you like doing?' … It was a whole chain of questions with very little time in between for me to reply. I felt slightly battered by all of these questions, but he wasn't being nasty with it. In fact, he was smiling at me and seemed like a nice, friendly person. I thought maybe he would protect me against Malik, so I gave him all the answers he wanted.

After that, his wife Surayya came to sit with us (she was the one who had come up to my room the first morning with the ghee barrel). There I was, an immature 15-year-old, now being raped and assaulted daily by Eshrat's brother. Surely they would know this was wrong? But they didn't seem at all concerned about the situation. In fact, I later found out that some of the men in that family had sex with much younger children – mostly their own nephews and nieces.

I wanted to ask Eshrat and Surayya some questions of my own, like when could I go home? But I didn't dare. So all I asked was where Malik was.

'I don't know,' replied Eshrat. 'He is here, there and everywhere.'

'What time will he be back?' I continued, in trepidation.

That was when he suddenly turned. 'Why are you asking? Why do you need to know?'

'Because I want to go home.'

'This is your home now,' he snarled, as he stood up and strode off into his side of the house. What he said really frightened me.

I'll never get out of here, I'm stuck in this hell forever, I thought.

Meanwhile, Surayya had gone into the kitchen. When she realised her husband had left me on my own, she came and asked me in the two English words she knew: 'You help – *pakora*?'

I nodded. After all, I had nothing else to do. She started to show me how to make pakoras and I tried to copy her. She wasn't particularly friendly, but she was all right and at least I

41

was learning something. When she pushed up her loose, flowing sleeves, I could see the faded bruises on her arms, so I knew that perhaps she was being badly treated too. But I couldn't ask her, for fear that her husband, Eshrat, might tell Malik and I didn't dare think what he would do to me.

My head and my body still ached as I stood with Surayya, so I was glad when I was allowed to go and sit down again, this time watching Muneeza, the one who had brought me the paracetamols. She was doing the biggest pile of ironing I had ever seen, with a heavy iron on a rickety board. She looked very frail and overburdened. I wanted to help and give her a rest, but I knew I couldn't. I hoped she might look up at me and I could give her a smile, but it seemed she was the lowest of the low in this family and she kept her head down all the time I was there, with the mother and Surayya barking what sounded like insults or swear words at her.

Suddenly, the front door opened and in marched Malik. Ignoring the others, he immediately pulled me up by the hair and pushed me upstairs so roughly that I kept stumbling. Each time he kicked me and swore at me. He threw me into the room, so that I hit my shoulder on the end of the bed and sprawled across the floor, then slammed and locked the door behind me. At least he had gone and left me there, which was a huge relief.

As I went back to sit in my haven, the corner beyond the wardrobe, I nursed my bruised shoulder and wished anew that Nana was with me. I tried to conjure up an image of her in my mind. I used to have a photo of her, in her blue overall, her hair up in a bun and a big smile across her face, but I didn't know where it was. Perhaps it was thrown out with the rest of her belongings. I had not seen it for years.

If only I had that photo with me now, I thought.

That reminded me: I *did* have a photo with me. It was the one Jamie had given me when he was about to join the army and had to go off for his training. I had kept it all those months and only saw him two or three times after that, when he came home on leave. He always came to pick me up and paid for me on the bus and everything. I found where I'd hidden my purse, in the back of the wardrobe. This was my only reminder of Jamie and it was even more precious to me now; a link with freedom and normality. I tried to think what I felt about him and I realised that I had quite strong feelings, but we'd not been going out for long and we were very young, so we hadn't yet talked about how we felt. If we had, I might have told him I liked him very much, or even that I loved him. Somehow I knew he felt the same way about me.

I held that photo in the palm of my hand and willed him to think about me at this moment, just as I was thinking about him. He would be with the army in Germany now. Did he ever think of me? Did he wonder what I was doing? He probably wouldn't know yet that I had disappeared. I don't suppose any of my friends would have realised yet either, as I often had to skip school when my father had beaten me too badly, or after I had run away.

I wanted to keep that photo safer than just in the wardrobe, but where could I hide it? Then I remembered the perfect place

– under the loose floorboard I had found the day before. I prized the board carefully up again. I gave Jamie's picture a kiss and slipped it down into the hollow, before replacing the board as quietly as I could, this time without a squeak. It was a great comfort just to know the photo was there, safe. And like Nana, he was always with me.

CHAPTER 5

A FACE ON THE CARPET

As the afternoon wore on, I picked away some more of the wallpaper, right into the corner, where it would not be visible without a torch. This was where I would make my hole in the wall. I knew it would take a long time, but it didn't look like anyone was in a hurry to let me out, especially Malik. Just thinking his name made me shudder, so I turned my thoughts back to Nana and the happy years.

People were always friendly to Nana, wherever we went. I remembered the first time I went to church with her. I felt safe being in the church, especially with Nana – she had been there lots of times. Going out, nearly everyone said hello and, even though I was little, the priest leant down and shook my hand.

'Welcome to our church,' he said with a smile. 'I hope you will come again?'

'Yes, please,' I agreed.

I did go quite often with Nana after that. Uncle Bert, Nana's son and my great-uncle, came as well sometimes. He used to visit us at Nana's cottage, after he came to live at my Grandma and Grandad's house, in another part of the village.

Uncle Bert wasn't quite right; he went a bit funny. Thinking back when I was older, I realised that he must have suffered some kind of trauma in the war or something. One day, when I was about five and at Grandma's, I was watching *Play School* on TV and Uncle Bert came and watched it with me.

Grandma's TV was quite old-fashioned and it had slits around it for decoration. On *Play School*, they were making a box and they said it was to collect money for charity, so Uncle Bert must have thought they were collecting through the television. He got all excited and wanted to put money in the box, so he kept going over to the TV and posting coins through the slots so that they could go into their collection box.

'I gave it to them,' he said proudly, 'them on the telly.'

At the time I didn't really understand why he was like that, so I just laughed and he laughed with me.

Another time when we were watching a cowboy film, the cowboys started shooting the Indians and Uncle Bert hid behind the sofa.

'Don't shoot me! Don't shoot me!' he yelled at the television. I realised he was serious. I don't know whether it was the noise that frightened him, or he thought they really could come out of the telly and shoot him. He wouldn't come out from behind the sofa for ages, until I went to get Grandma and she sent for the doctor.

I remembered too the time when we were in the lounge. Uncle Bert's pipe went out, so he got out his wallet and took some £20 notes to light it with – his pension money, I suppose. I didn't know the value of money then, but I thought it was funny so I laughed. But when I told Grandma, she said it was dangerous because he could have set fire to himself and she phoned the doctor again. The next time I visited, Uncle Bert had gone.

'He wasn't very well,' she explained. 'So the doctor called an ambulance and they took him away.'

'Where is he now?'

'He's in a safe place, where he can't hurt himself and he's being looked after.'

I just accepted that, I suppose, at the age of five.

* * *

Back at Nana's cottage, when Great-Grandpa was in a good mood he used to play games with me. I remember playing marbles with him, and sometimes with Nana too, when I was about seven. It was Great-Grandpa's game so he sat in his rocking chair and I had the bag of marbles.

I used to shake it up and show him the bag. 'Guess how many marbles,' I asked him, and he had to say a number. The trouble was, he always wanted to win.

'OK, Great-Grandpa, let's see if you're right.' I had to make sure that I only emptied the right number of marbles out of the bag, so that he could see he had won. But once I emptied too many out by mistake.

'You cheated!' he yelled and grabbed the bag, put all the marbles back in and threw it at me.

'Ow!' I cried out, more with surprise than injury, as I don't think they hit me and I knew he never meant to hurt me.

Nana heard my cry, came rushing in and saw what had happened.

'That's enough!' she told him.

He got up out of his chair, grabbed Nana and pulled her

right out into the garden, where we had just had a standpipe installed to save having to use the well. Then he forced her head under the standpipe, with her face upwards, and turned on the tap at full tilt. I remember how frightened I felt – I thought he was going to drown her. When I screamed at him to stop, he did. I didn't know it, but Nana knew: he had dementia.

Gradually Great-Grandpa became more and more aggressive. He came into our bedroom one night and attacked Nana, but she managed to fend him off. Every night after that, I had to help her push the wardrobe across the door to stop him coming in when we were asleep. Eventually, he wasn't safe for any of us and had to go into a home. I never saw him again because soon after that he died.

Things got easier after that because we could go out more. I think Nana used to worry about Great-Grandpa hurting himself when he was at the cottage but now she could take me out to new places, a bit further away. We could do what we wanted but this new freedom didn't last for very long.

Nana's health started to deteriorate. Every night she had me place a tablet under her tongue for her – I think it was for her heart. Her faculties were all there, but she kept having to sit down, and sometimes she passed out. Obviously, I wasn't old enough to look after her, so we couldn't stay in the cottage and when I was eight we moved to Grandma Kathleen's house, down the hill. Nana kept having flutters in her heart, so we lived in the front room – that way she wouldn't have to climb any stairs. It was a large room, with a telly and a settee as well as the double bed.

'You were born in this room, in that same bed,' said Grandma Kathleen.

* * *

It was odd how all those loving memories came flooding back as I sat there in the corner of my heartless prison room. But I had nothing else to do, other than conjure up the stories of my childhood. I was a happy, much-loved, smiling child for the first ten years of my life, while Nana was alive. She could not have been a better great-grandmother, grandmother and mum, all rolled into one: we loved each other to bits.

It had been just the two of us – Nana and me, in her cottage on the hill for a couple of years since Great-Grandpa died – so it seemed strange to be in a large, modern house, with inside toilets and water on tap, with Grandma and Grandad *and* their dog.

Bruce was Grandad's Alsatian. I've always loved dogs and I used to cuddle Bruce whenever he would let me. He always protected Grandma and Grandad, and now he protected us as well. I think he must have sensed Nana was poorly, so he used to sit right next to her on the settee, or on the bed. Whenever she went to the downstairs toilet, he would sit outside, waiting for her. At first, if I even put my arm round Nana, he used to think I was attacking her, but he soon got used to that.

'Why don't I live with my mum?' I asked Grandma Kathleen one day, when I was helping her with the washing-up. 'Why am I with Nana?' I was conscious all my friends at school lived with their parents and I didn't.

Grandma hesitated. She dried her hands and turned to face me.

'Well, pet, your mum didn't want you,' she told me.

That was a bombshell. 'Why not?'

'She couldn't look after a child,' Grandma explained, 'but your Nana could. She wanted to have you, so that's why you lived with her. She looked after you for your first eight years, and now we look after you.'

'Yes, and you look after Nana too,' I added.

'That's right.' She smiled, as she turned back to the sink.

It was fun living at Grandma Kathleen's. I used to help her with the shopping and she was a good cook. One of my favourites was bacon, tomato and crusty cobs, and on Sundays, we usually had chitlins, brawn and black pudding.

In the afternoons Grandad always watched the horse racing, and at weekends he loved the wrestling, watching Giant Haystacks or Big Daddy and egging them on.

'Would you like to take Bruce for a walk?' Grandma Kathleen asked me one day, when I was about nine.

'Yes, *please*!' I was so excited, because I had never taken a dog for a walk on my own. I took him down the road to the shop and tied his lead to the ring in the wall outside, while I went in to spend my pocket money. But when I came back out, Bruce was gone. I had to go back and tell Grandad that his dog had disappeared. The house was like a morgue. Grandad went out for hours and hours, walking the streets and driving round the neighbourhood, looking everywhere for Bruce, his baby.

We all thought Bruce had gone forever but two weeks later there he was, back in the place I had left him, with his lead tied to the ring. Grandad was overjoyed when I took him home with me; we all were. But not for long: Bruce came back with a nasty side to him. Maybe he wasn't fed properly, or somebody was cruel to him. He bit me one day when I was playing with him.

'Bruce bit me,' I wailed as I held up my hand to Grandma Kathleen, who washed it and put on some antiseptic cream and a plaster.

'You're lucky, pet. It's not a deep wound,' she said with a sympathetic smile. 'But you'll have to be very careful when you play with him.'

One thing didn't change though – he remained very protective of Nana and a few nights before she died, he wouldn't leave her side for more than a minute or two so he was allowed to sleep in the front room with us. I think he still had that sixth sense.

* * *

The night I remember most clearly was the night Nana died.

'You're not sleeping with Nana tonight,' said Grandma Kathleen.

'Why not?' I demanded.

'Her heart is racing too fast and she's very poorly.'

I made a big fuss and kicked off, but Grandma Kathleen wouldn't change her mind, so I went to see Nana and I told her what Grandma had said.

'Come on,' she said with a weak smile on her grey face. 'Get in.'

So I did. I got in and cuddled up, with my thumb in my mouth for comfort. She put her arm round me and I put mine round her. That's how we fell asleep. At seven or eight in the morning, I woke up. I tried to wake her, but she didn't move.

'Come on, Nana. Wake *up*!'

When I tried pushing her, she still didn't move. I don't think I realised she had died – I just thought she was soundly asleep.

So I shouted: 'Grandma, *Grandma*, come down *quick*!' I still had my arm round Nana, and I couldn't pull it out – I didn't want to, anyway.

Grandma was in the front bedroom, next to the stairs, and she came running down in her nightie. She took one look at Nana and she knew. I was puzzled by her expression.

'Come on, you've got to get up, get dressed and get out,' she told me.

'No, I'm stopping with Nana,' I insisted, ignoring the look on Grandma's face, and the cold stiffness of Nana's body.

I think Grandma must have pulled me out of the bed eventually and she called the doctor. When he came, he confirmed that she had died, and then I really believed it. I burst into tears.

'I think she must have died at about one in the morning,' the doctor told us.

I was with Nana when she died, in the same corner of the room where I'd been born, ten years before. Ten years of carefree happiness … the only years of joy I had known. And she died in my arms.

They opened the windows and made me leave the room.

'Out you go,' said Grandma Kathleen.

'Why do I have to go out?' I asked.

'Because you've been such a great help to Nana, but you can't help any more now,' said Grandma, gently ushering me out of the room.

I turned at the door and looked at the doctor. He just nodded his agreement. So I took one last look at Nana, and then I left the room. It was the last time I saw her.

Finally, two men in black suits and shiny shoes arrived with a trolley and took Nana away in a bag.

I think I must have known for a while there was something seriously wrong with her, and I seem to remember worrying about it. I was always very careful, putting that tablet under her tongue, to make sure she had it.

Grandma Kathleen took down the bed and I had to sleep upstairs after that. I had never slept alone before, so I just lay there, on the crisp white sheets, crying. I missed Nana lying next to me; I missed her so much. I missed her lovely smell – she always smelt of lily of the valley, I think it was talc. I cried and cried, under the sheets, thumb in my mouth, thinking of Nana. I imagined her in her coffin under my bed.

It seemed like I cried all night.

* * *

Various relatives came to visit Grandma Kathleen and Grandad, but I thought it was odd that neither of my parents came. My mother was Nana's granddaughter, but she didn't come until the next day. I didn't know who the stranger was.

Grandma had to whisper to me: 'That's your mother.'

With some curiosity I looked at her, but she didn't seem to notice me, or perhaps she didn't want to look. I had no memory of her at all – I didn't think I had ever seen her before. When she finally looked at me, I tried to smile, but she just turned away. Never having had a mother, other than Nana, I wasn't bothered. But I was pleased to see Uncle Jack, who had come down from Thirsk, still in his army uniform. It was my Grandma and Grandad, Uncle Jack and my mother who all sat around talking, but I wasn't included, so I played with my 'Etch A Sketch' in the kitchen, in between tears – I still couldn't stop crying.

That day was the day the case went missing. It was a brown leather suitcase with a clasp on it. Nana always had it and I thought it must be years and years old. The leather was peeling and flaking in places and the clasp had lost its shine. Nana always kept this case under her bed. She got it out at least once a week, because it had her pension book in it. There was money too – lots of cash, bank books and I don't know what else. All her treasures and savings were in that case.

'You'll have some of this one day,' she would say, as she showed me her bank book. I remember it had lots of noughts in it, but I didn't really know what that meant.

Grandad was the one who first realised the case was missing. 'Did you see her go out when she left?' he asked Grandma and Uncle Jack but they both shook their heads. Then he asked me and I said, 'No.'

'Well, there you are then,' he said.

Grandma Kathleen made a face and said, 'Surely you don't think …'

'Well, she's gone, and the case has gone …'

Grandma Kathleen had to tell all the family about the case disappearing because everything Nana wanted to leave to me and my cousins had gone with that case, wherever it was. I remember the terrible family arguments that followed its disappearance and a cold atmosphere, but that might have been because I missed Nana so badly. I didn't care about the case then, just about Nana having left me.

None of us ever saw the contents of the case again. Grandma Kathleen made the arrangements and there was a funeral with lots of family and quite a few of the neighbours too, because everyone loved Nana. Uncle Jack was there because the army gave him compassionate leave, but my mother was not invited, and the funeral people were told not to let her in if she came.

I can't remember the funeral, so I don't think I was allowed to go, but I do remember spending time with Uncle Jack. I always liked him and he used to spoil me because I was the only girl in my generation.

* * *

Grandma and Grandad thought they were too old to keep me.

'But where will I live if I can't stay here?' I asked, the day after the funeral.

'You can go back to your mother and father, they're the ones who should be looking after you.' Grandad looked pretty fed up when he said this, so that made me worry.

I turned to Uncle Jack. 'Can't I come and live with you?' I pleaded.

He smiled kindly as he sat me down next to him on the settee. 'I wish I could have you,' he said. And I thought he meant it, the way he said it. 'But I can't.'

'Why not?' I felt deflated, and the tears came to my eyes again.

'I'm in the army, you see. And I wouldn't be allowed to have you with me at the barracks, so I can't.'

There was no choice – I had to be shipped off to Mum's. It was Uncle Jack who took me to my mother's bungalow, where she still lived with my dad. I couldn't remember him either.

When we got there, Dad was in. He saw us arrive, but he didn't even say hello, he just went out to the garage. My mother wasn't there – I think she must have been at work. Uncle Jack came in with me and we put my bags down in the hall, then went into the living room. We didn't know what to do, but Uncle Jack didn't want to leave me like that. He sat with me for two hours – we talked a bit and turned the television on to watch *Blue Peter*. But then he stood up.

'I've got to go,' he announced.

'No, *please* don't go,' I pleaded, hanging onto him because I didn't want him to leave me there on my own.

'I have to, I'm afraid.' He paused. 'I've got to catch the train back to Thirsk this evening.'

He left and I just carried on sitting there, all alone, in the living room. I didn't know what to do or where to go; I didn't even know if I would have a bedroom or anything.

I don't know how many hours I sat there, but it was night-time when my mother came in. She didn't say anything, just picked up my bags and took them upstairs, so I followed her.

'You can unpack,' she told me, 'but don't come down again tonight.'

I sat on the end of the single bed in the poky bedroom and cried. Luckily I had eaten at lunchtime, but I got nothing to eat or drink that first evening. Already I hated it there.

As I opened my window, turned out the light and got into the narrow bed, I lay there, whispering to Nana.

'Why did you leave me, Nana? Why did you have to go? Why didn't you take me with you?' I knew she couldn't answer, of course, but it comforted me to talk to her. 'Come through the window, Nana. Come and fetch me.'

* * *

In the corner of my prison room, I closed my eyes and I could still remember Nana's lily-of-the-valley scent, the blue overall she wore and the bandage on her knee.

'Come and help me now, Nana,' I whispered.

If only I could open the window, I thought, *she might come through.*

I suddenly got cramp in my foot, so I stood up and stretched until it went, then I had nothing else to do, so I sat on the rug to trace the patterns on it with my fingertips. That was when I noticed a shape that looked just like the side of Nana's face. I traced round her chin, her nose and up to her forehead. Then I saw there was a round bulge at the top, just like her bun. I traced all round her head and down to her neck, talking to her.

'*Do you remember when I used to brush your long hair for you at bedtime? You would say I made it shine. I had to count the brush-strokes up to a hundred.*'

The harder I looked, the more detail I could see, or perhaps I imagined it. There was a spot for her eye; she could see me. I felt calmer now – I couldn't change anything that might happen to me tonight, or tomorrow, but at least I could talk to Nana and I knew she was with me.

CHAPTER 6

CONVERSION

It was the first night that Malik hadn't come to torment me. The first good night's sleep I'd had. He might have had to do overtime at work, or maybe he'd been in an accident that put him in hospital ... or perhaps he had other women. Anything that kept him away would be a huge relief, even if I had to stay in captivity a little longer, but I knew he would almost certainly storm into the room today and make up for lost time, tearing me apart again. How I dreaded his heavy footsteps on the stairs.

Already I had started to lose count of how long it was since I'd arrived. I had nothing to write with, but I wished I'd started to count the days by scratching notches on the skirting board in my corner. Perhaps I should start doing that now.

As I sat up in bed, numbed by tedium and the fear of what this day would bring, I heard footsteps on the stairs. I flinched and held my breath ... then let it out again. The footsteps didn't sound like Malik's, so perhaps they were his mother, or his little brother, 12-year-old Asif, both of whom Malik had told me had their bedrooms on this floor.

Then I realised they had stopped at the top of the stairs and there was a shrill sound right outside the door. I watched as the door itself started to vibrate, then a metallic point came through and moved along in a straight line, followed by a blade with a grating, sawing sound. It gradually made a hole in the bottom of the door, about six inches square. I heard voices speaking words I didn't understand – it sounded like Eshrat's voice, and his mother's. Within moments, they had gone back downstairs, and that was it.

So, what was the hole for? I feared the worse – rats to taunt me, or … I didn't dare think. I held my pillow round my head and over my ears, as if that would stop me thinking. It didn't, of course. If only the hole had been a bit bigger, large enough to squeeze through. Even if I couldn't get out of the house, I was desperate to use a proper toilet in a bathroom rather than this disgusting barrel, which they only emptied once a day.

How much longer would I have to stay? What if Malik tired of subjecting me to so much pain? He loved it now, but he might get bored in the end. Would he throw me out on the streets?

For a moment, I had hope … But then I remembered how much it excited him to shame and hurt me, to cause my warm, red blood to run; to make me cry out and to see me desperately gulping for breath when he stifled my breathing with his huge hand. He loved the power to cause me pain, and especially the complete control he had over me. I hadn't realised that at first, but now I was beginning to understand: I had nothing. He wanted to keep it that way, to dominate me. But I did have my memories – he couldn't take those away. They were my own, and they kept me going in those early days – memories of Nana, my hidden photo of Jamie, and the fact that I still had a germ of hope, as long as I thought there might be a possibility of release.

Just then, I heard footsteps again. *What now?* Again, they stopped at the door – one person this time. I could make out some shadowy movement on the dim landing through the hole. As I watched, whoever it was began shoving stuff through – something in a bowl, plus a glass and a small jug of water. A hand came through the hole, a woman's hand, then a small plate was pushed through with a chapatti on it, or maybe there were two. Then, without a word, she put something across the hole, a piece of material, before returning downstairs.

For a little longer I sat still on the bed, looking at that food. I dreaded to think what was in the bowl. I wasn't so hungry now as I had been the first couple of days – I didn't really feel like eating much, and choosing not to eat was the only choice I had. But I was still thirsty, so I slid myself off the bed and went over to the door to pick up the water, hoping there might be some cereal in the bowl to tempt me, but no. It was half-full of slop – thick white liquid, with long, thin leaves and seeds in it. Just looking at it and smelling it made me feel sick, so I pushed it back through the hole. I ate one of the buttered chapattis and drank some water.

* * *

I can't remember whether it was that evening when Malik came back, or the next night. He stomped up the stairs, burst into the room, locked the door and put the key in his trouser pocket. Seeing I wasn't on the bed, he put the light on and smirked to see me cowering in the corner. Perhaps it wasn't such a good place, after all – it seemed to give him more of a sense of power to see me looking so afraid and subservient.

'Come here,' he ordered.

I didn't dare refuse. He aimed a hefty, flying slap at my head with the back of his hand and I fell on the bed. Then he got hold of my hair and pulled me further up, parting my legs and pulling my pants off. I tried to cover myself, but he tore my hands away and smacked my head again. He stood there for a few seconds, which seemed more like minutes to me. Though I knew what was coming, it didn't make it any easier to bear.

I felt so ashamed and humiliated as he leered at me, his gaze on the space between my legs, taunting me and not letting me move, goading himself into a frenzy, holding back his lust until it overpowered him. That night was the worst yet: he was relentless. I screamed and wailed, but nobody came to save me. He loved all that. It only energised him more, but I couldn't help it.

I don't know whether he had been on drugs, but he was demonic. He just wouldn't stop, other than for breaks to beat me physically, punching me about the head and body, pulling me by my hair onto the wooden floorboards by the end of the bed, where the rug didn't reach, to rape and assault me again. It came in waves that night, his lumbering weight squashing me flat, his heaving body, his painful thrusts as he smothered me, pushing my chin away so that I felt as if I was being stretched on a rack, like I'd seen in my school history book, unable to breathe except in tiny gasps between his movements.

I don't know how long it was before he dropped onto the bed with exhaustion, a big smile on his ugly face. Completely spent, I was still on the floor. I stayed there all through the night, hurting and bruised all over, ashamed of what I had become, of what he made me do. It was a hot, stuffy night and the thick, foul-smelling air was filled with his snores. I inched painfully across the floor to the rug and lay curled up round the image of Nana, tracing it lovingly with my hands and whispering under my breath to her.

'Why did you leave me, Nana? Come to me now, please. I'm your angel. I need you, Nana. Come and save me.'

Just saying those words calmed me. I think I must have talked to her in my head most of that night, thinking of those childhood memories and repeating her prayers. There were always three of them, including the Lord's Prayer. The bit I kept on repeating was towards the end.

'Deliver me from evil ...'

If I said it often enough, and really believed it, maybe it would protect me from more harm. I did believe in God, like Nana taught me, though I didn't think of Him much, so I hoped He heard my prayers anyway.

* * *

It was just getting light when Malik roused himself and got dressed. I don't know whether he even noticed me, lying on the floor. He just grunted, unlocked the door and left, locking it behind him as usual.

Maybe one day, he'll forget, I thought, pulling myself back up onto the bed. *Maybe one day …* At last I must have fallen asleep.

The next thing I knew was the key in the lock, followed by a voice. I opened my eyes: it was Eshrat's voice.

'Come downstairs,' he said roughly. 'Today, my wife will teach you to make chapattis and samosas.'

I followed him, leaning heavily on the banister, taking it very slowly, one step at a time, down the stairs.

'Hurry up, you white bitch!' he snarled. 'There's nothing wrong with you.'

But when I got down to the hallway, I glanced in the mirror. It was the first time I'd looked at myself since my arrival in this house of horror. I was shocked – I had never been so pale, the colour of an almond kernel. The thing that stood out, of course, was my black eye, closed up with a little pink showing. There was bruising and swelling down the left side of my face, and another bruise spreading from my chin, down my neck on the right. I ached with bruises all over; even my teeth and the roots of my hair were sore.

I stumbled into the kitchen to find Eshrat's wife Surayya rolling out some dough. The sad-faced woman, Muneeza, was there as well, scrubbing pans. I looked at her, but she kept her head down, as if frightened to make eye contact.

Surayya was all right with me: she showed me how to mix the ingredients to make more dough, knead and roll it out, and then I rolled some more myself. It didn't look as good as hers, but she finished it off for me, to neaten the edges. Some we cut in two and put a spoonful of curried mince on every half to make samosas, folding them together and sealing to cook in the oven, while we baked chapattis on the hotplate.

When Eshrat left the room, Surayya let her veil slip – I'm not sure if she did it accidentally. I saw a big bruise on her neck, as if someone had tried to strangle her. She quickly re-arranged it, but shot me a sympathetic look that suggested she knew what had been going on.

Eshrat came back and shouted something at Muneeza. She immediately stopped what she was doing to obey him. But as she followed him out of the kitchen, she briefly raised her head a little as she passed, a slight smile in her eyes. I was sure she was badly treated and probably beaten too but I didn't yet know her story. I pitied her because she was so downtrodden. Would I get to be like that too? Who was her husband? Was he as cruel as Malik? I couldn't imagine anyone else being that perverted, that sadistic. After all, I was only just 15, so Malik was a paedophile.

Surayya boiled some milk to make what they called 'tea'. Sure enough, it did have a dip of a teabag in the milk while it was heating. She stirred in the sugar, then took the tea and the samosas on a tray into the living room and motioned for me to help myself.

I wasn't hungry, but it would have been rude to refuse so I took a samosa to try. At first I nibbled it and it wasn't bad, so I managed to eat the whole thing, then I sipped the 'tea'. She encouraged me to eat more, but I couldn't.

Next, she stood up, so I did too. But she gently pushed me down again and went to the bathroom. Now alone in the living room, I could hear Eshrat shouting and a child crying in the next-door room, through the hole in the wall.

Just then, Surayya returned with a silver thing that looked like a thick pen – she called it 'kohl'. She made me sit sideways and she sat down next to me on the settee. First, she used this silver stick around my good eye. Then, very gently, round my injured one. When she'd finished, she took me to the mirror: I looked awful, like a panda in reverse! My bad eye still wouldn't open properly – she'd obviously tried to hide the bruising and put too much on.

'Thank you,' I said with a smile. After all, she had tried to help. I would have preferred that everyone could see what he did to me, but it seemed I wasn't the only victim in that house.

The mother came into the living room and when she saw me she started shouting what I think were probably swear words – I heard the word 'English'. Surayya took me back upstairs and locked me in again.

* * *

Over the coming weeks the violent rapes and beatings continued, every day passing into the next in a blur of pain and distress. I think I was gradually becoming more depressed and perhaps a bit mentally ill. Each day I thought I couldn't take any more; it was so relentless, but I had no choice.

I had been captured in April 1987, and the longer daylight round the edges of the curtains showed it was summer. I had suffered so much at the hands of Malik – cruel rapes, assaults and beatings most nights, and sometimes daytimes too, and still, his sadistic craving for my blood was as much a feature of his attacks as the way he deliberately choked me, making it so difficult and painful to breathe that I had to struggle for air. He loved it when I struggled – that was far worse than the injuries and the shame. I had never been allowed out of the room since the day I learnt to make samosas with Surayya – that must surely have been at least two or three months ago now. Time slowed down and I slept a lot, so I lost track of the days and months.

All that time in the same stuffy room, with nothing to do but survive each day, each hour in fear, and nurse my wounds as best I could. It seemed to have stunted my brain. I think I wasn't quite right, somehow – I just tried to do whatever Malik demanded, knowing he might then leave me alone.

The only other people I ever saw during this time were Surayya, who brought me food and water, sometimes coming into the room with it, and the sad-faced woman, whose name I now knew was Muneeza. Treated as the skivvy of the house, she was tasked with the disgusting job of taking my barrel to the bathroom, emptying it out, bringing it back and scrubbing the bathroom each day. I pitied her.

One day, Surayya came up to the room to collect me and take me down to the bathroom. Waiting for me was Malik's only sister, Bushra. That was the day they dyed my blonde hair black, which involved a lot of standing and leaning over the basin. Afterwards, when I looked in the bathroom mirror, I looked like a ghost, with my hair black and my white face.

Suddenly I felt faint and at the same time I felt as if I'd wet myself. I pointed to the toilet so they stood around me as I sat down. Almost immediately, there was a rush of lumpy blood into the bowl, splashing all around. The two women looked shocked and I must have passed out.

When I came to, lying on the tiles, surrounded by blood, Muneeza was trying to clean up. I don't think I was having periods yet – I had once had a 'show' of brownish-red stuff, but I didn't think this was it. The women's shocked expressions confirmed to me that I'd had some kind of haemorrhage.

I think I must have been slipping in and out of consciousness.

'Hospital,' I said when I was awake. But they shook their heads.

At that point, Malik arrived and Bushra brought him into the bathroom.

'I don't feel well,' I told him. 'I've lost a lot of blood.'

He was looking around with a big grin, loving this.

'Please take me to the hospital.'

'No, you don't need any f***ing hospital!' he swore. 'You just need to lie down, I'll take you upstairs.'

For once, he carried me up the stairs. I was grateful for that. Then he gently laid me down on the bed. I could tell he was in two minds: all fired up, he desperately wanted to rape me, but hesitated. I pretended to lose consciousness. He shook me a couple of times, but I didn't flinch. I could sense him standing there, next to the bed, watching me. Once he was convinced, he just walked out and locked the door. I breathed a huge sigh of relief, but the room was whirling around my head and that's when I really did lose consciousness, for several hours. It was dark when I came to. There was a little more blood on the eiderdown, but it blended into all my previous stains and I was relieved to find the bleeding had stopped.

I was very frightened by what had happened; I didn't understand it at all. Maybe I'd find out one day, but for now, I just needed to sleep.

The next day, Malik and Eshrat came up to my room with a glass of some murky-looking liquid.

'You have to drink this,' Malik insisted. 'It will be good for you and make you stronger.'

He helped me to sit up a bit and I sipped the green liquid: it was bitter.

'It's horrible,' I complained, gagging at the acrid taste it left in my mouth.

'It's herbal medicine from Pakistan,' explained Malik. 'You must drink it up, to make you well again.'

I could see I had no choice, so I drank it all. They let me have some water afterwards, then left me in peace.

For the next few days I had cramps in my abdomen and whenever I went to the toilet in the barrel, I lost a little more blood. It worried me that I must be very ill, or perhaps it was the severity of the rapes I suffered so often. But gradually I began to feel better again.

* * *

One day, Surayya, Bushra and Muneeza came to dress me in a new, heavily embroidered Pakistani outfit and a long scarf. It felt swishy and strange, very different to Western clothes. I had never worn loose trousers before, so that felt very odd.

Using their few English words, they explained the rules.

'Head down, scarf down on face,' Bushra told me, showing me with her own scarf.

'Eyes down,' added Surayya. 'No look men.'

Muneeza said nothing.

'Come,' said Surayya.

We all trooped down the stairs and stood in the hallway with the rest of the family and some other people I didn't know. I found out later from Malik that they were his other brothers, their wives and children. One of his brothers, Khalid, had three wives there, including Muneeza. She was the first woman he had married, whom he seemed to have discarded now. She had just one child, who was handicapped, but I couldn't tell what was the matter with him. Apparently, they all blamed her for the child being born ill, and everyone but Muneeza ignored him, including his father.

There were quite a lot of other children, all dressed up and running around, playing, until Malik's mother said something to him and he shouted angry words at them. They stopped straightaway.

The doorbell rang and Malik let in an old man with a big, silk turban on his head. When they all bowed their heads, I did so too. Everyone went through to the big prayer room at the front of the house and the old man started to do this long, monotonous speech. Suddenly, he was asking me to come forward. I looked around, but they were all pushing me and Malik stood next to the man, whom I guessed must be some sort of holy man.

What was going on?

The holy man said something in Punjabi and looked at me, though I only noticed this because I forgot the rule and took a quick glance through my thin scarf-veil. I said nothing. Then the man repeated what he had just said.

Malik stepped forward and grasped my arm tightly.

'Say the words after him,' he barked at me. So I did. I had no idea what I was saying, but Malik's grip on my arm tightened painfully whenever I hesitated or stumbled. They had to tell me one word at a time, so that I could try to repeat the sounds of it.

Somehow I got through it, but I didn't know any of what I had said – I knew nothing of their religion. I was glad when it was all over and everyone gathered in the living room to join in the feast. I wasn't hungry at all, just desperately worried.

What had I said? What had I done?

Bushra was the woman with the most English, so I decided to ask her.

'What words did I say?'

'You say Punjabi words, that our tradition.'

'But what did they mean?'

'Mean you Muslim now,' she explained.

'I don't want to be Muslim,' I whispered to her in a panic.

'You Muslim, not change now.' She patted my arm, as if to reassure me. 'Muslim good.'

But it was not good to me; it was not even all right. I was horrified. They should have told me. Did it mean I was no longer a Christian? How could that be? Would I have to be a Muslim forever?

So this was another way they had trapped me. But they couldn't stop me believing in God and Jesus if I wanted to, I thought. Nana had always read me stories about Jesus and Noah and Moses out of the big Child's Bible she bought me – I used to love looking at the pictures. I knew Nana would be cross with me if I stopped believing in God.

'You change name,' added Bushra, as an afterthought.

'No,' I replied nervously. 'My name is Anna.'

'You Muslim name Yasmeen,' she informed me.

I shook my head, but decided to say nothing more. They could call me whatever they wanted, I knew I couldn't stop them, but it was not my real name – I would have to keep remembering that.

* * *

They soon took me back to the room, while the family and the holy man continued eating and celebrating. I sat on the bed and repeated my name over and over to myself.

'My name is Anna, I am a Christian.'

And when I finally lay down to sleep in bed that night, I said the prayers Nana taught me. If I said them enough times, surely that would stop me being a Muslim.

CHAPTER 7
BANISHED

After the conversion ceremony, they began allowing me to spend time downstairs some days. Perhaps they thought that now they had turned me into a Muslim, I wouldn't make any trouble. But the mother, Farhat, was the real troublemaker. I had been in the house several months now, and I had started to learn a few of their Punjabi words. So now I could tell some of what they were saying about me, especially the nasty words they used when making fun of me. I hadn't heard the young women do that, but the brothers did it quite a lot, not realising that I could understand any of it.

The mother was the worst one. She was a horrible woman – what my grandma would call a 'nasty piece of work'. I once heard her telling Malik lies about me, making up things I'd done, just to provoke his anger against me. I didn't know all the words, but she used her hands a lot, so I could often fill the gaps.

'That white s**t told Surayya you smell,' Farhat told Malik, pinching her nose while making a disgusted face. 'And she called you a bad English word.' She paused with a smirk to let that sink in. 'You need to beat that slut every day, my son.' She swept her hand down, as if using a cane. 'You must put her in her place.'

Sure enough, Malik led me straight upstairs and gave me a beating until he drew blood, which led to the inevitable rape.

She must have heard my cries, and I could imagine her malicious smile – I'm sure she got a lot of satisfaction out of that.

To her, I was always 'white trash' and I suspect she resented my presence. But, although she had quite a say in things, and she was the only woman who did, Malik was the boss ... and I was his wretched punchbag.

One day, when I was allowed downstairs, sitting alone in the living room, I could hear some kind of argument going on through the doorway cut in the wall. At first, it was Eshrat and Surayya, but then it sounded as if he turned on Muneeza, who was always in trouble, like me.

In the few times I had been allowed downstairs, I had gradually learned more about the sad-faced woman who had come up to my room soon after I arrived and dropped the paracetamols for me. Of course I had used them all up long ago now, but she was the only one who had been kind to me at the beginning.

Muneeza had an odd existence, being the cast-off wife of Khalid. He didn't want her, or her child, and neither, it seemed, did anyone else. The butt of everyone's abuse, especially Eshrat's, she lived in both houses. She had no room of her own, not even a bed – she had been given one blanket, for both summer and winter, and was told to sleep on the hardest settee in either house, her handicapped child's cot beside her.

Muneeza was very small and frail; extremely thin, with long hair, like they all had. She was so thin that she didn't look more than about five stone. When I first met her husband, I was told he had two other wives, but later I discovered he actually had five wives in all. Three of them lived in different houses in this street, and the other two lived in Pakistan, where he went to visit them every few months.

Muneeza was the least important wife. Eshrat was always finding something to beat her up for, when Khalid wasn't there, which was most of the time. Once I saw him lash out at her with the chapatti rolling pin, when we were in the kitchen – I didn't know why. He just kept saying horrible words to her as he hit her on the back of her neck and across the back of her waist. She went down on the floor, crying, clasping her neck. I gasped. He shouted at her, pointing to the living room and gabbling some Punjabi words – I think he was telling her to go and lie down, or even get lost. She crawled away.

Eshrat then turned to me. 'I'll teach you for making that f***ing face!' he said and lashed out at me with the rolling pin, catching my shoulder. I tried not to show how much it hurt, but I don't think he hit me as hard that time as he did her.

Sometimes Muneeza and I tried to communicate, if no one else was near, but we couldn't understand each other much as she didn't know any English words. The only thing we could do was smile at each other, but neither of us felt like smiling most of the time. I did feel a bond with her, though. I'm sure she must have been as deeply depressed, and maybe mentally ill too, but she had a son to look after. I think it was Malik's sister, Bushra, who told me one day about him.

'Hassan,' she said, pointing at him, playing with a faded plastic mobile on his cot. 'Heart,' she added, pointing towards her own heart in case she'd chosen the wrong word.

'How sad,' I replied. 'Will he live?'

'Live? Yes, live a little long.'

'Poor Hassan.'

'Yes, poor boy,' she nodded, with sympathy.

Although Eshrat's wife, Surayya, was all right with me, I noticed she was always rude to Muneeza and bossed her about. She seemed to tell tales about her to Eshrat, to get him to shout at her, or beat her. I decided I must not trust anyone in this house, except maybe Muneeza herself, but she was the lowest in the pecking order, perhaps even lower than me, so she could not help me.

* * *

I was supposed to stay in the same place Malik had told me to sit when he brought me down. I don't know how long I'd been there – I must have been in some kind of trance, sitting there with nothing to do, not even helping in the kitchen. The television wasn't on that day. There was a crumpled newspaper on the table, but I couldn't read their alphabet. I had no idea what was going on in the outside world, and no one outside this house had any idea what was going on inside.

I thought about whether my father or mother ever wondered where I was. Somehow I doubted it – no love lost there. Malik had probably told Val in the taxi base some story about what I was up to. My grandmother was still alive, as far as I knew, but I hadn't seen her since Nana's funeral, five years before, because of my mother stealing all Nana's savings. If only I could contact someone to let them know …

That was when I had the idea. It was too dangerous for me to use the phone in the hall, as I could hear people moving around the house, but the argument in Eshrat's house sounded far enough away that maybe I could creep through the open doorway to try his phone, which was almost within sight of where I was sitting.

Within seconds, I had picked up Eshrat's phone and checked for the dial tone. But I hesitated – I didn't know my grandmother's phone number, so I was trying to remember my mother's ...

Suddenly, Eshrat walked into the room, stormed across, grabbed the receiver from me and slammed it down. He turned and gave me an almighty wallop across the head with the back of his hand. Something flashed in my eye and I fell to the floor with a scream of pain. One of his rings had a diamond sticking out of it, so that must have cut my eye. He kicked me repeatedly and shouted at me.

'You whore! You are forbidden to use the phone. If you think I'm cross, just you wait until Malik comes home. I'm calling him now!'

He dialled the number and ranted about me to Malik in such gabbled Punjabi that I could barely understand any of it, except for a few swear words and the name they had given me, the name I hated – Yasmeen.

I lay there, curled up on the floor, and cried with pain.

'Shut up!' yelled Eshrat.

'You've hurt my eye!' I wailed. 'I can't see with it ...'

'That's your own stupid fault,' shrugged Eshrat, and he kicked me again.

I could feel my eye swelling up. Soon it was completely closed. Inside, it was agony. I feared I might be permanently damaged.

'Please take me to A&E,' I begged him. '*Please!*' I wailed. 'I don't want to lose my sight.'

'No *way*! You should have thought of that sooner.' He bent down and pulled me up into a chair, where I slumped, tearful. 'Malik is on his way home and he's angry!'

I could do nothing now but sob in fear of my fate.

Malik arrived within minutes. Eshrat ranted at him and Malik then turned on me. I got the full brunt of his fury that day. He pulled me up the stairs by my hair, got me into the room, then slammed me up against the wall.

'*I'll* show you not to disobey me again!' he shrieked.

After a few punches to my body, with me trying desperately to protect myself, he ground his teeth and threw me onto the bed, with a triumphant glare.

He spent all his fury on me that morning, raping me with full force. I was in such agony with my eye that I could barely cope with this onslaught. All I could do was concentrate on trying to survive. He finally stopped and lay back with a satisfied grin. I tried to keep still beside him – I should have hated him with a vengeance, but I didn't have the physical or mental strength to feel anything but pain. I couldn't stop crying.

'Shut up, you stupid snivelling, *my avi*!'

I found out later that those words meant 'mother-f***er'.

'You're nothing but a white slut,' he added. 'A whore.'

'My eye hurts,' I whimpered. 'Eshrat cut my eye with his ring, when he slapped my face. I need to go to hospital.'

He got up off the bed and shot me a look of contempt. 'That was your fault, you should not have been so disobedient. If you can't behave yourself, this is what you get. Now you are forbidden from leaving this room until I say so. And that won't be for a long time. Do you understand?'

'Yes.' My bottom lip trembled.

'That will teach you. You're nothing but a piece of s**t!'

He stormed out of the room, slamming and locking the door behind him.

After his footsteps died out and I heard the door being locked at the bottom of the stairs, I curled up in the foetal position. I didn't know whether there was a word for someone like Malik, a mental illness perhaps – a man who was always angry and loved inflicting pain. He craved a reaction, and was always fired up to make me cry, to hear me scream and especially to draw blood. The more blood there was, the more excited and ferocious he became. I'd heard the word 'sadist' – was that it? Yes, I thought he must be a sadist – but why, and why me?

* * *

Alone again, with endless empty time, I sat in my corner, chipping off some more of the woodchip; rocking to and fro. As always, I thought of Nana. I really thought she could see and hear me, so I often talked to her. I told her about what had happened downstairs and about Muneeza and her son.

I thought back to the day Nana died and how abandoned I felt when I wasn't allowed to go back in her room, or to say goodbye. I don't know why they didn't let me attend the funeral.

Maybe that would have helped me feel more ready to leave her and move on. But I was only ten years old. I suppose they thought I was too young and, even though I couldn't stop crying, nobody really bothered with me, apart from Uncle Jack. I remember the day he took me and my bags to Mum and Dad's house and they didn't even welcome me or offer me anything to eat.

I hated it there. It was a cold house; nobody wanted me there. My mother ignored me as much as she could – she never kissed me, never hugged me, never smiled at me or said 'goodnight' to me. Instead she kept her distance and only talked to me when she had to. She was a manipulative woman with no love to give – not to Dad or me anyway. He didn't want me either, it seemed. I didn't know my parents and they didn't know me, so that was the end of my happy childhood.

My mother always wore the latest fashions, with lots of make-up, and she was constantly changing her hair colour too. It was all about her. She worked as a barmaid and she used to go out with boyfriends, which my father hated. I think she did it to annoy him. My dad was quite violent towards her. I remember once when he deliberately trapped her arm in the door, and there was blood everywhere. The paramedics came and took her to hospital. He had damaged some tendons, so she had to stay in hospital for a couple of days. She tried to hide it when she went out.

One day she just left with her latest man. We didn't see her again, but we heard that she'd bought a bungalow. So that's where Nana's savings went – the money she wanted to be shared between my cousins and me.

Then it was just Dad and me. He looked like Grizzly Adams, with his black beard and moustache, short-shaved hair and stocky build. If anyone came to the house, he'd be Mr Nicey-Nicey.

'Your dad's really nice,' my new school friends used to say.

'Oh, I don't think so!'

'Oh, he *is*! He's lovely.'

I just shrugged.

Dad always smiled at other people, but not me. He had no sense of humour. He was always very sour with me, I wouldn't have dared try to joke with him. He was very old-fashioned and strict. His only pleasures in life seemed to be punishing me and watching *Blake's 7* on TV – he loved it.

I always had to be careful what I said, but I couldn't please him. He was a man who had to have things the way he wanted and he always had to have the last word ... or action.

'Dad, could I have the telly on, please?' I would ask.

'What have I told you?' he replied in his rough, aggressive voice. 'Don't ask me again.'

'*Please!*'

He would whack me across the face with the back of his hand. That marked me – I think he wanted to leave his handprint on me, so he got his own way, as usual.

I used to bite my nails all the time and I sucked my thumb when I went to bed, to help me get to sleep. While living with Nana I had stopped doing it, but I started again at my dad's house. He didn't like it and tried to stop me.

'Stop biting your nails!' he barked at me. 'You've got to let them grow, or the punishment will happen.'

In the daytime he started using a bamboo cane to rap me hard across the knuckles. It was a sharp, stinging pain: once for each finger, five times on each hand.

'That will stop you,' he told me.

But it didn't. After I went to bed, he used to storm up the stairs to check up on me. I usually heard him and pretended to be asleep, without my thumb in my mouth, but that didn't work – I couldn't hide my nails. I heard him take his belt off and pull it straight so that it made a 'thwack' sort of noise and a click, which was the sound of the clasp.

'Sit up,' he used to say, looking at my chewed fingernails. 'Put your hands out.'

Holding the clasp end, he raised his belt and whacked it down five times across the palm of each hand. That really hurt. Later, he hit me with the clasp end instead, which often drew blood. I tried not to show it hurt, but that made him even angrier and he would do it again. I used to try to make myself numb and think of Nana – that always helped.

When he caught me sucking my thumb, he would yank it out and hit it with the cane, always the same thumb, several times, until I started to cry.

Soon he got so bad-tempered that he would pull me out of bed every night, pull up my nightie and whack my bottom twice with the cane. It didn't usually cut me, but I always had bruises. I used to hide under the cover when he'd finished so that I didn't have to see the pleased look on his face.

As I remembered my father's punishments, I suddenly realised the similarity with Malik: was my dad a sadist too? Was there something about me that made people punish me when it wasn't my fault?

* * *

I went and sat next to the part of the rug where I could see the picture of Nana, tracing gently round her face with my fingertip.

'Are you watching over me, Nana?' I asked. But I didn't need an answer – I knew she was with me. I could feel her cuddling me, it made me feel warm and loved. 'You're always in my heart, Nana, and in my mind. That's what keeps me going,' I told her.

I know it sounds odd, but it didn't seem strange to me. Talking to Nana was the only thing that gave me strength – that and saying her prayers. They were my only way to stop myself going mad, the only thing that gave me comfort … and maybe a chink of hope.

CHAPTER 8

CHICKEN HEADS

From the light round the edges of the curtains, the sun was rising earlier so I knew it must be spring again. That meant I had been a prisoner in the house for a year. It felt like a terrible nightmare that had lasted forever. Nearly every day and night filled with the horrors inflicted on me by this tyrant, every one of which had to be endured, somehow. And it was getting worse.

One afternoon, when I was not expecting Malik to come home, I heard his heavy footsteps and cowered in my corner, ready to try and defend myself, as I knew I was in for trouble from the way his feet stomped on each step and the fury on his face when he came in through the bedroom door.

'What the f***ing hell did you tell my mother?'

'I didn't tell her anything.'

'Don't you *dare* lie to me!' He grabbed hold of my hair and dragged me out of the corner, kicking my legs away from under me, so that I was helpless. Then he pulled me upright again and took his other hand from behind his back, brandishing the chapatti rolling pin at me.

'I'm not lying,' I protested. 'Please don't hurt me.'

But I could see from his expression that it was no use.

He lunged at me with the rolling pin.

'This is for your f***ing lies!' he snarled as he crashed it down across my back. 'And this is for swearing at my mother.' He lifted the rolling pin again and started to beat my head with it, while I fell to the floor, screaming and curled up, my hands trying to cradle my head and protect my skull. After raining several blows, he suddenly stopped and stepped back, out of breath, perhaps realising at last that he had gone too far.

I didn't dare move. The pain was pounding in my head and both my hands felt broken, but I kept them in place, in case my skull was damaged too. The room reeled around me. I was ice-cold, dizzy and nauseous.

He got down on the floor, laid me out, semi-conscious, and raped me with vicious energy. For once, I didn't feel anything; I passed out, oblivious.

I must have been unconscious for a long time. It wasn't until the next morning that I woke up on the bed, where he must have laid me. I opened my eyes to see fresh blood on the eiderdown and my poor swollen hands, stiff and misshapen. Gently I tried to move the fingers, but it was too painful to move them, other than gently raising one hand to my head, which also felt swollen in places and tender too. My vision was blurry and I was very anxious about the shooting pains inside my skull – I'd heard you can die from bleeding on the brain. But what could I do?

I don't know how much later it was that Muneeza came in to empty the ghee barrel, but I saw the shock on her face as soon as she set eyes on me. She came over and very gently stroked my cheek, then ran out of the door without even locking it, down the stairs, calling out in Punjabi as she went.

I saw the open door, but I couldn't have moved if I'd tried.

Within seconds Muneeza came back with Bushra and Surayya. Even the mother, Farhat, came up behind them to see what all the fuss was about. Bushra took charge, telling Surayya to go down and phone Malik.

'Tell him Yasmeen is hurt. Can we take her to hospital?' Then she turned to Muneeza. 'Get a bowl of warm water and a cloth. And bring some paracetamols as well.'

I only heard some of the Punjabi words they spoke, but enough to understand their concern. Muneeza gently sponged the blood from my scalp and where it had dripped down my face, as well as my painful hands. Then she helped me to sip some water to take two of the painkillers and slipped the rest of the packet into the top drawer. The pills weren't strong enough to touch the pain this time, but at least I had a packet now to take when I needed them.

'Malik says no hospital,' reported Surayya. 'He is coming back. He will call the doctor to come here and see her.'

They tried to tidy up my clothing and prop me up with extra pillows they brought in, but I was very agitated about them moving my head, even slightly.

I remember Malik bringing the doctor into the room. As he studied my injuries, I was surrounded by the whole family.

'How did this happen?' he asked me.

'She's very clumsy,' Malik butted in. 'She fell down the stairs.'

'That would explain the head injuries, but how did you damage your hands so badly?' he asked me.

Again, Malik answered before I could say anything. 'She was protecting her head when she fell,' he explained.

'Mmm, I see,' the doctor nodded.

'We've sponged her head,' added Surayya.

'Well, she will need more than that,' explained the doctor. 'I will call for an ambulance to take her to hospital. I'm pretty sure she has some broken bones in her hands, and I want them to X-ray her skull as well.'

'No X-rays needed, she has a phobia about hospitals,' Malik lied. 'My sister is a trained nurse. She will splint Yasmeen's fingers and bathe her head. We'll make up a bed for her downstairs in the living room, so that we can keep an eye on her and look after her properly.'

'Well …' murmured the doctor, uncertainly.

'Thank you for coming, Doctor. I'll show you out.'

So that was that: Malik got away with it.

* * *

Fortunately, over the next two or three months, Malik managed to be less fierce with his assaults on me and I gradually recovered from my injuries. This was helped by the fact that he seemed to have two full-time jobs, most days now. He was still driving his taxi every night. Then there would be the dangerous time, before he had a short sleep and went off to do a day shift at the family shop. The evening and his early morning 'lunch break' were the other times I spent my days dreading.

This was usually the routine, so life was at least a little more predictable and I had some periods of time when I didn't have to quake with fear at every footstep on the stairs. However, he could take time off whenever he wanted, so I was never completely safe. And when he had whole days off, he would either go out somewhere, or more often than not stay at the house and make my life hell.

On the rare occasions when Malik had a whole day off, he would sometimes fetch me from the room.

'Come on, you f***ing c***,' he said one day. 'I want you downstairs.' Then he grabbed hold of my upper arm so tightly that I was afraid he was blocking off the blood flow. He pulled and pushed me down the stairs to the living room, where he plonked me down on the hardest settee, the one where they made Muneeza sleep when they didn't want her next door.

'Sit here and don't move.'

I had to do as he said. I couldn't move off that settee, even to go to the toilet, without begging him. He liked to keep me waiting as long as possible, of course.

It must have been a Thursday, because that was their slaughtering day. It was a large family and all the brothers came over that day, while two of the wives ran the shop. All the children were there too so it must have been school holidays, I suppose, which was good for me as the children often spoke to each other in English, which they had learnt at school.

At first I didn't know what was going on when the men all went down the garden to the garage until I heard the loud squeals. I asked one of Bushra's children what the awful sounds were.

'Chickens,' he said, giggling at the fact that I didn't know.

'Why are they making that noise?' I asked in all innocence, thinking they were being moved or put in cages, or having their claws clipped. I had always been frightened to death of any birds, so I shuddered to think.

'They are chickens being killed,' said one of the younger girls, with a big grin.

'The men are wringing their necks,' added a boy of about ten, using his hands to mime the killing, while the girls and a little boy started imitating the shrieking.

'Oh no!' I gasped, putting my hands over my ears.

They thought this very funny and carried on, dancing around the room, miming the wringing of necks and the squeals. Even worse, I could hear the real chickens' shrieks piercing the air.

'Can't they stop that noise?' I wailed, horrified at the thought of all those chickens so close to the house, both alive and dead – I didn't know which was worse. My whole body was on edge, trembling at the shrill sounds that pierced my brain and echoed round my head. Now that the children had told me, I could not rid myself of the mental image of what the men were doing to those poor birds.

I thought that was bad enough, but the worst horror was when they started bringing all the dead chickens back to the kitchen. The women plucked them and passed them on to the men to clear out their insides, which they sloshed into a bucket – eugh! Then they chopped off their feet and their heads with a huge cleaver and tied them up with string.

By now I was having panic attacks: I couldn't breathe properly and I felt my heart was beating at least twice as fast as it should.

I was desperate to get away from there, upstairs if I could, where I could put a pillow over my head to deaden the sound. But I had to stay there and sit still; I didn't dare move. The only thing I could be grateful for was that they didn't make me help them, but I suppose that was only because I didn't know how.

Finally, the slaughter ceased, but the production line in the kitchen was going at full pelt and the poor, naked, trussed chickens were being stacked on a wide shelf along one wall. I knew I would have to walk past the kitchen archway, right next to that shelf, to get back upstairs. How would I manage it? I'd have to try and shut my eyes. I couldn't wait to get away from it all.

One of the children went into the kitchen and came out holding a milk bottle, which he brought across to me. It was only when he put it in my lap and I saw it had the head and two claws of a small chicken inside that I couldn't help it: I screamed and leapt to my feet, wetting myself all over the red rug, which now developed a dark stain. The children saw it and I was so ashamed. The bottle had fallen onto the rug and I ran across the room, screaming, in shock.

I could see that Malik was furious when he heard me from the kitchen. He stormed out to punish me, but just then the phone went and he had to go out in a hurry, so he slapped me hard round the face three or four times and left. I asked Bushra if I could go and use the toilet and she nodded. But as soon as I went in to clean myself up, I felt more warm liquid running down my legs. When I looked, this time it was a gush of bright red blood. Was this like once before? Bushra came to get me and I told her about the blood. She went off to get some scraps of material, which she gave me.

'Period,' she said. 'Use rags.'

'Too much blood,' I explained, as I didn't think it seemed like an ordinary period. But she just shook her head.

She took me back upstairs and locked me in. *Phew!* I was so relieved to get away from those chickens, the noise and everything. My cheeks stung from Malik's slaps, and I felt a bit faint from the blood loss, but at least the sounds of the chopping in the kitchen were now very faint. Yet I could not rid myself of the piercing squeals and shrieks that continued to echo in my head.

The children must have told the grown-ups because about half an hour later, I heard several light sets of footsteps skipping or walking up the stairs. I wondered what was going on – I'd never heard the children being allowed to come up these stairs before. Now I could hear them giggling as they reached the top. Then the horror accelerated for me, as they started to push one chicken head, slowly, beak first, through the hole cut out of the door. As soon as I saw what it was, I screamed. Another head followed, then two pairs of legs with claws on. They lay on the floor, dead eyes staring at me. Horrified, I screamed and screamed, and yet I couldn't stop looking at them.

'Go away, take them away! *Leave* me alone!' I pleaded. But it just made them giggle all the more.

Finally, I heard an adult voice.

'Come on, children,' said Surayya. 'We've had our fun, now it is time for ice creams.'

'*Yes!*' I heard one of the children shouting, and they all skipped off, laughing down the stairs, and left me alone again. But the horrifying claws and the heads with the staring eyes were still there. All I could do was to pray that Muneeza would come up to empty the barrel and get rid of them for me, or that it would soon be dark. If I kept the light off and couldn't see them, perhaps I could ignore them. I desperately hoped so.

* * *

Late that night, when he got back and came up to the room, Malik had great fun taunting me with those chicken parts, tracking one of the pointed beaks up inside me, watching my face for a reaction. I don't know whether I screamed because it was the chicken or because of the pain, but he loved it. Then he saw the blood continuing to trickle out of me.

It was time for the regular shave he used to give me, removing any trace of pubic hair. As on the first ever occasion he did it, more than a year before, and many times since, he deliberately let the razor stray back and forth across my clitoris, drawing blood and causing me to cry out. It was the start of a long and protracted evening of repeated rapes, but somehow that night I found a way of shutting out the worst of the pain. I found that if I concentrated really hard, I could remove myself from all this and numb the effect it had on me. It was almost as if I was hanging up above the scene.

But my lack of extreme reaction angered him, so he became even more ferocious. He made me sit on the edge of the bed and pulled my head up by my hair to give him the oral sex he craved, forcing himself inside my mouth and thrusting as hard and often as he could, ramming the back of my throat so much that I threw up before he had even ejaculated, which infuriated him. I got an extra bout of hitting and kicking for that.

But, although I could learn to numb the pain, the smothering during rapes was a different matter. That always terrified me and left me gasping desperately for breath every time. I really thought that one day he might stifle me too long and kill me.

The only thing that saved me that night was the time. He had to go to work at the taxi rank, leaving me lying, bloody and exhausted, across the bed.

As I lay there in the darkness that night, I said one of Nana's prayers, the one that ended: '*Lord protect me through the night, and bring me safe to morning light.*'

I couldn't count how many times we must have said that prayer together, but the final time was the night when Nana died peacefully in her sleep, so she didn't get to see the morning light.

Perhaps it would be a good thing if the same happened to me.

CHAPTER 9

TEETERING ON THE BRINK

It was winter now, so I had been held prisoner in this house of hell for over 18 months. Despite all the injuries I had suffered from the relentless physical and sexual abuse, and eating very little food, I had not had any illnesses during that time.

But now things changed: I didn't feel right. I was always tired and was often sick, which meant I had to use the ghee barrel to vomit in, so the foul smell permeated the air in the room. Even Malik found it hard to bear and had a go at poor Muneeza for not emptying the barrel often enough. But it wasn't her fault. I felt sure that all the beatings, assaults and rapes had weakened my resistance so much that it was slowly shutting down. Morning after morning when I woke up, and day after day for weeks, I was so nauseous that I retched into that barrel repeatedly, but there was very little for me to sick up so I suppose it was mainly bile.

I couldn't think what was wrong with me. Terrified, I began to believe I might have leukaemia, or something like it.

'Please take me to see a doctor,' I begged Malik. 'If you want to keep me alive, let me see a doctor.'

'Stop being so f***ing dramatic,' he replied, ignoring my pleas. He didn't stop finding reasons to beat me, mainly for being sick, and that drove him on to the fierce rapes that inevitably followed every time. However, during those weeks he rarely stayed in the room for long, with it smelling badly. Even though I was so bored and depressed, I preferred being left alone. And I got used to the smell, I suppose – I had no choice.

* * *

As Muslims, they didn't celebrate Christmas and New Year in that house, so I had no marker as to when it was that the sickness ceased. Maybe I didn't have anything too serious after all. But there was another thing which, being so young and naive, I didn't twig what it meant. I just thought that for such a thin person, as I had become, it was strange that my tummy seemed to have swelled, and I often felt odd flutters and twinges inside. Now I convinced myself that I must have a cancer growing in my tummy. But I couldn't see a doctor and I had nobody to ask. I was petrified that I was dying, yet glad of the chance to end my torments. Perhaps it would be the only way out of my captivity. And by now I didn't suppose anyone outside the house would ever find out.

Finally, it dawned on me. I was feeling quite well again, but my tummy was still swelling and I could feel definite movements, almost like someone was inside me, kicking. Ah, so that's what it was: I must be pregnant. With so much bleeding caused by Malik and the fact I'd never had regular periods anyway, I hadn't realised they had stopped. Pregnant! I was elated. Now I would not be alone – I would have someone to love, who would love me back.

I wanted to tell somebody, to announce it ... But who would want to know? Almost certainly not Malik and the family – another mouth to feed. Though there could be one great bonus, I thought. Surely, once I'd told Malik, at least he might be gentler with me, unless he wanted me to get rid of it. No, I wouldn't tell anyone until I had to. None of them had noticed so far – the loose clothes and long scarf they had given me to wear helped to hide my tummy. Not even Malik, who mostly didn't even stop to look at me before the onslaught.

This was my secret, something I could keep to myself – a germ of happiness amid the terror. I couldn't stop smiling. At last, this was one aspect of my life that Malik couldn't control, at least until he knew about it. This would be a real, living human being, who would depend on me. I was sure I would depend on him or her as well, in a way – we could make each other happy. The knowledge lifted me out of my morbid depression, but the downside of that was the utter realisation of my helplessness and shame.

* * *

Every night or day, Malik continued his sadistic campaign. By now I knew the signs. He would stomp heavily up the stairs, unlock and fling open the door, lock it again and turn towards me, grinding his teeth, clenching his fists and glaring with lust as he forced himself on me. Always he would hurt me to make me bleed and provoke reactions that fired him up for another onslaught, and another.

Surely it was unnatural constantly to have so much sex, for me to be always in so much pain? I had heard the term 'sex maniac' and I assumed that must be what he was. He could never have enough of it – he always wanted more.

Now, whenever he was beating me, I tried to cradle my arms round my tummy, to protect my unborn baby, but that sometimes meant more cuts and bruises to my arms and my back.

Every time now that he wanted oral sex he pulled my head back by my hair. He did the same when raping me, and at the same time his other hand pressed as hard as he could on my nose and mouth to make me struggle for breath and increase my pain. The more I struggled, the stronger he became. He wanted to make me bleed or vomit so that he could beat me for it and start the whole thing all over again. It was a vicious circle, a battle I could never win.

On one particular occasion while ramming himself inside me he was so frustrated by my attempts to distance myself that he took revenge. He pulled me off the bed, got hold of my arm and held it up behind my back, towards my neck, gradually twisting it until he heard it snap. I screamed as the pain shot through me.

'That will teach you, white whore!' he gloated, pushing me back on the bed. 'Now you can feel my anger, can't you?' He sneered in triumph. 'You are *mine*! You do what I say, don't forget that.' With that he turned and stormed out of the room.

I lay back on the bed, nursing my misshapen arm, sobbing in agony. Could the baby feel all this? What harm would Malik's cruelty, my pain and distress have on my unborn child? I wished I knew it was safe from harm. But Malik still hadn't realised. To me it was astonishing, given he could see my naked body every day, that he didn't notice.

I sobbed aloud with the pain, needing somebody to come and find me. Somehow I knew my arm was badly broken and would need a plaster cast.

Malik's little brother, Asif, slept in the next-door room and sometimes, after my screams had stopped and he heard Malik leaving, he would shout through the wall to check I was all right.

That night he must have heard me sobbing.

'Are you OK?' he shouted.

'No, I need help,' I wailed. 'My arm is broken.'

Asif must have gone downstairs and told the family. Malik was still there, doubtless chatting with them as if nothing had happened. He came up with Eshrat, Bushra, Surayya and his mother, Farhat.

Bushra took one look at my arm and knew I needed help.

'How did that happen?' she asked, glancing at Malik.

'She must have fallen after I left,' he said.

Telling lies was obviously second nature to him but I didn't care, as long as they took me to hospital.

'She will have to go to A&E to have it X-rayed and put in a cast,' said Bushra.

'Shall I call an ambulance?' asked Surayya.

'No, I'll take her,' Malik replied, always the one in control.

The four of us squeezed into the back of Malik's taxi – Bushra, Surayya, the mother and me, with Eshrat in the front passenger seat and Malik driving. It was a horrendous journey to start with; every slight movement of the taxi, or the people on either side of me, jolted my fragile arm and caused pangs of agony, shooting knife-sharp pains up to my head. After the first minute or two I was in a daze and I must have passed out. The next thing I knew, I was on a stretcher-bed in Casualty, encircled by the family, guarding me tightly.

A doctor came and infiltrated my guard. He had a kindly expression, asking me questions. Malik glared at me not to answer so that he could say what he wanted, still in control.

The doctor seemed outwardly to accept Malik's explanation at first, but had a look of uncertainty. After I'd had the X-rays done, wearing a lead cape to protect the baby, I was wheeled back to Casualty and the same doctor came in about half an hour later with the results in his hand, which he held against a light-box on the wall.

'As you can see,' he began, pointing out what he was saying, 'this is a bad fracture of an unusual type. In fact,' he continued, wording his verdict carefully, 'the only times we usually see this type of complex radial fracture is as a result of non-accidental injury.'

His words passed over the women's heads as their English was too poor, but I noticed Malik and Eshrat exchanging glances.

'Well, on this occasion, you must be wrong, Doctor. I know she was fine when I left the room, but she is a very clumsy girl, always falling and hurting herself, as you can see from all her scars ...' Malik told him.

'Yes,' interrupted the doctor. 'I was going to ask her about that.'

He turned to face me but before he could say anything, the brothers stopped him.

'My brother's right. She's always falling down the stairs or cutting herself while she's cooking, or slipping over and knocking her head on the kitchen floor,' said Eshrat.

'And she bumps into things too,' added Malik, turning to me. 'Isn't that right, Yasmeen?'

I hesitated, desperately wanting to tell the truth – I knew this was my only chance. But they were both glaring at me, threatening me with their body language, their hands gripping the bed rails, jaws set in coercion. I knew the damage to me would be far worse if I dared to say anything. Then there was the baby to think of so I just had to agree.

'Yes,' I nodded my head at the doctor, 'that's right.'

At that moment, I'm sure the doctor knew I was unable to tell the truth and that I was aware of his disapproval and disbelief. I could tell that he wanted to help me. He looked daggers at Malik, but could make no further comment.

I had a plaster cast put on my arm and was given some strong painkillers to take back with me. And that was the end of my first and only opportunity to escape. Distraught, how I wished I had taken the chance and braved the risk. I could have got free if only I'd had the courage. Now I was in despair, and only the baby kept me sane.

* * *

Finally, two or three weeks later, Malik and all the family realised that I was pregnant – it couldn't be hidden any longer.

I had dreaded the worst when they found out, but it was quite the opposite: they seemed to rejoice at the news of Malik's first child.

Perhaps he will go easy on me now, I thought. But no, nothing changed, except that he avoided hitting or kicking my tummy. Otherwise, the abuse continued as before.

On many occasions since I'd been taken captive, I'd heard and seen the mother making trouble for all the women, not just me. I had recognised from the evidence – the bruises and black eyes, the limps and winces – that some of the other women were also being badly treated, especially Muneeza. Eshrat seemed to be the main culprit against both his wife Surayya and sad Muneeza. I suspected Bushra's husband also beat her sometimes. However, perhaps because I was pregnant and my senses were more acute, I now began to notice distant screams around the house, especially at night.

It seemed like some sort of torture camp that we all had to endure and survive but I think, being English, I suffered most. I shuddered to think what a terrible place this was to bring up a child – I hoped for the baby's sake that it was a boy. In this family, the men all got their own way, the women got nothing but strife.

Malik started taking me downstairs again sometimes. It was on one such day that I found out more about Muneeza. I could speak a few words of Punjabi now myself and we were therefore able at last to communicate. While helping her to scrub the kitchen floor, she told me in hushed whispers that she had been doomed when she gave birth to a 'damaged' baby.

'Hassan was born with a hole in his heart,' she told me, miming her words so that I could understand, 'so Khalid not want us.' So her husband, Kahlid, had thrown her out. That was how she ended up at this house, at the mercy of everyone. She was branded inferior and worthless, having borne a handicapped child.

'He will not live long,' she added. 'I must look after him.'

'You are kind to him,' I said in Punjabi.

'Yes,' she agreed with a nod and a sad smile. 'I try my best.'

Muneeza and her son had a strong bond and they were living on the family's charity, which clearly was far from charitable. The boy was now four, but he was not allowed out of his cot and had no toys of his own, only the cast-offs given him by the other children. He at least had a proper mattress, pillow and bedcover, but Muneeza had still only the one thin blanket, whatever the temperature, and had to sleep where she was told – on a hard settee in either Eshrat's or Malik's living room. I felt great sympathy for her, and I think she did for me as well.

What a cruel place this was.

* * *

I never knew when the baby was due as I hadn't seen a doctor about it. One night, while I was heavily pregnant, Malik attacked me as ferociously as he could manage, despite the baby slightly cramping his style. I had learnt more and more to try and separate myself from what he was doing, which helped me numb the pain and rise above the shame, but this only served to infuriate him. On this particular occasion, I could see his temper rising and I quaked at the thought of what he would do. Surely he wouldn't threaten the baby's safety?

He grabbed hold of my hair, as so often in the past, and dragged me to the top of the stairs. What was he going to do? I wanted to fight him off, but I couldn't – I had neither the energy nor the strength.

'What are you going to do?' I shrieked in my desperation to protect this baby.

'Ah, so now you understand,' he said, triumphantly. 'You have to remember who is boss here.'

'I *do*,' I protested.

'You must recognise me as your owner.'

'Yes, I do.'

I couldn't think of any other way to avoid his vengeance on my seeming lack of reaction to his violence – I suppose that was what had made him so cross.

'You don't deserve to be here with me,' he continued, eyes blazing. 'I work my fingers to the bone, driving my taxi at all hours, and you don't even thank me for it.' He paused. 'You don't deserve any kindness from me.'

'*Please*, Malik,' I begged, as he had me teetering on the edge of the top step, only held from falling by his hand grasping my hair. 'Please think of the baby, he'll be born soon. *Please* don't do it!'

How I hated having to plead, but that was all I could do. And he loved it. He let me teeter in fear for a few more moments before pulling me back.

'Only for the baby,' he said.

I could breathe again, for one more day at least. But would this hell ever end?

He pushed me back into the room and across the bed, then left without another word. As I fell asleep that night, I talked to my unborn child.

'Hello, little one,' I said, softly. 'I hope you are all right in there, safe and sound.'

I was so relieved when the baby kicked.

'Not long now.'

Then I hummed him a lullaby that I remember Nana singing to me when I was little and I was poorly. I didn't know many of the words, so I just hummed. It calmed him down, I felt, and it calmed me too.

'Hush-a-bye,' I whispered, and fell fast asleep.

CHAPTER 10

A GUN TO MY HEAD

That night I had terrible nightmares and woke in a sweat in the early hours, terrified and trying to back away from somebody. At first I thought it must be Malik, but he wasn't there. Alone in the room, I sat in darkness, trying desperately to remember what it was all about. So, was he in the nightmare? No, it couldn't have been. I felt as if I was a small child. Why was I in such a state? Something bad was about to happen, and I was trying to get away from it ... from somebody.

I was dead tired and I wanted to go back to sleep, but I just couldn't get it out of my head, so I sat up again, with only the streetlight's glow beyond the curtain for company. For a long time I puzzled about it, still sitting there as the sun began to rise and my baby started to kick inside me. That made me smile and I felt calmer.

Suddenly it came to me. It was an incident that I didn't remember because I was too young, but Nana had told me about it. I remember it started with me being curious and asking questions. I must have been about seven or eight at the time.

'Nana, why haven't I got a mum and a dad, like the other children in my school?'

I remember she stopped doing the washing-up, dried her hands and came and sat down with me at the scrubbed pine table.

'You do have a mum and a dad, Angel. Every child has to have a mum and a dad, but they don't always live with them.'

As I sat in my prison room, aged nearly 17, the conversation came back to me quite clearly now. I could almost remember it word for word, as Nana patiently explained it all to me.

'It was the only day your parents ever came to visit you,' she began.

'How old was I?'

'About 18 months, that's one and a half years old. You were a bonny toddler,' she said with a smile. 'You came to live with me on the day you were born because your mum and dad didn't feel able to have you with them, so they asked me and I was thrilled to have my own little great-granddaughter to live with me, my own little angel. I was the luckiest woman in Allerback.'

She gave me a cuddle.

'Why couldn't they look after me?' I asked.

'They had their reasons,' she replied, mysteriously. 'Perhaps they'll tell you themselves one day.'

'You mean I might see them?'

'Yes, maybe, when you're older.'

'But I don't even know what they look like.'

'They look like you,' said Nana, 'only grown up!'

She chuckled. Then she went on to tell me about the day they got in touch and asked if they could come to Nana's cottage and take me out.

'Of course I said yes,' she told me, 'but sadly it all went wrong.'

'What do you mean?' I asked.

'Well, your dad had a gun with him. They took you down

to the playground and he took the gun out. That's illegal, so the police arrested him and they took him to court.'

I was shocked. 'Did he have to go to prison?'

'No, they just made a court order that said he could never come and see you again, or come anywhere near my house.'

'What about my mum?'

'She never came back either.'

* * *

One day, when I was about 11, soon after the first time I ran away from my dad's house, Uncle Jack told me more about that incident.

'Your mum and dad tricked your Nana and took you out. When she realised you had gone, she came out to the garden and told me.'

'Why were you there?'

'Because Nan was my grandmother and I was on leave from the army, so I came to stay for a few days.'

Uncle Jack told me that Nana was worried because my parents didn't tell her they were going to take me out – they just disappeared with me that afternoon – so Uncle Jack went off to try and find me, while Nana phoned the police. They took me to the playground, but by the time Uncle Jack arrived, at the same time as the police, Dad had a gun out and pointed it at my forehead.

I gasped. 'Did he shoot me?'

'He tried to shoot you. He pulled the trigger, but it jammed because he hadn't undone the safety catch.'

'The policemen and I ran across the grass and got there just in time. One of the policemen took his gun, while the other one arrested him and your mum. Then I took you in my arms, safely back to Nana.'

'So you saved my life?'

'Well, yes, maybe,' he replied with a smile.

Good old Uncle Jack, I thought with a warm feeling. *He always came along at the right times.*

'When the police asked your dad why he tried to kill you, he said they had never wanted you so he thought it would be better for you to kill you.'

I was shocked. 'Neither of them have ever shown me any love. They made my life miserable, that's why I ran away.'

'Yes, I know.' He looked quite upset. 'I wish I could look after you. I would if I wasn't a soldier, but the army won't allow it. Even if you were my own child, I couldn't look after you in the army.'

That was the last time I saw Uncle Jack. I sat on that bed in my prison room and wished he would come looking for me. He always cared about me and brought me presents from his travels. If he knew I'd gone missing, I'm sure he would do everything he could to come and rescue me.

Maybe he will one day.

With that thought, I lay back, put my hand on my tummy and dozed off at last.

* * *

Throughout the next day, left alone in the room, my thoughts turned to that nightmare, to the conversations I had had with

Nana and Uncle Jack, and to my parents, who must have hated me so much that they wanted to kill me.

How could any mother hate her baby?

But of course my mother had left my dad and me soon after I arrived to live with them. She went off with her new man and I didn't see her again. So it was just Dad and me. It was not a good existence for any child. He was a very controlling man and took pleasure in making me do things I didn't want to do, and eating things I hated. It was like a game to him.

If he was in a good mood, he might give me beans on toast, which I loved. But that was rare. The one thing I could never eat was sweetcorn – I don't know why, but I hated it. One dinnertime, he called me down to eat. When I got to the table, there was a big plate piled high with sweetcorn, as much as he could cram on: nothing else.

'Your favourite dinner,' he announced with a grin. 'Come on, don't make a face, you know you love it. Eat up!'

I protested and begged him, but either way he wouldn't budge.

'Look, lovely sweetcorn – I bought it just for you. Now eat it all up.'

I sat there and looked at it, refusing to eat. That was when he brandished the cane he had laid across his lap, whacking it through the air for maximum effect. I picked up my knife and fork and took the first few kernels into my mouth, gagging at the taste of it.

'You'll have to do better than that,' he laughed, picking up a large spoon and forcing the whole spoonful into my mouth. 'Now get that eaten.'

I retched again as I tried my best to chew and swallow, the tears pouring down my cheeks. Finally, I managed to get through it all before I was violently sick all over the carpet.

Furious, he took his spoon and scooped up some of the sick onto my plate.

'Now eat that,' he said.

I vomited again, just looking at it. I had to clean up the carpet first and I got a caning twice across my bare buttocks for that.

Next, he demanded to see my fingernails and caned me five times across each hand.

'One for each nasty bitten nail,' he exclaimed. 'It's out in the coal shed for you tonight.'

He pushed me through the house and out of the kitchen door into the garden, where there was a low stone building in which he kept the coal. It had an ill-fitting wooden door, with a gap beneath, and a corrugated iron roof that made a thunderous roar when it rained. He pushed and kicked me inside to lie on top of the coal, with only a sack for covering until morning. I couldn't open the door from inside and there was no light, so it was a terrifying experience.

After that, he did it many more times and it was always scary, but I almost got used to it. I don't think he ever did it in winter, or I might have frozen to death. In the morning he would let me out and pretend nothing had happened, as if it was normal. Sometimes, as he let me out, he would say, 'I love you.' That really messed with my head.

The longer I lived there, the worse he controlled me, so that every night he would invent some reason for punishing me before bedtime, or after I went to bed. Some nights he beat me until I was black and blue all over, until I squealed and squealed. But we lived in a detached house and nobody seemed to hear. Eventually it came to the point where I didn't feel it any more, and he would stop. Later, if it was the right night, he made me sit and watch *Blake's 7* with him. Then he would turn to me with a smile and say, 'I do love you, you know.'

I always found this very confusing. If he really did love me, why did he get so much pleasure from beating me? Why did he shut me all night in the coal-hole? Was that what love is? No, surely it couldn't be. It all seemed like a mental game to him, but I was the one that suffered.

One night he really went wild with his beating, just because some of my school friends had called round for me with old wine bottles filled with water and joked that we were going to have a party. He hated me having friends, he just wanted me to himself. My having friends meant he lost control of me, so he sent them all away. Then he got out his belt and thrashed me all over until I screamed. He beat my back, my shoulders, the backs of my legs, and several stray whacks of the belt caught my arms and hands and even my face.

Maybe he didn't realise how badly he had marked me because he made me go to school the next morning. The teacher said, 'Come on, let's have you ready for PE.'

'No, I'm not doing PE today,' I said.

'Yes, you are,' she told me, looking rather oddly at the bruise across one side of my face.

'No, I'm not doing it,' I insisted.

'Right, straight to the head teacher's office,' she ordered me. '*Now!*'

So I went to his office and knocked on the door.

'Come in.' He looked me up and down as I gave him the note from the teacher. 'What's the reason for this behaviour?' he asked.

'Nothing,' I replied. 'I'm not doing PE.'

'You *will* do PE,' he insisted. 'You've got to do it.'

At that moment, I broke down. 'My dad's thrashed me, I don't want my friends to see my bruises.'

He changed his attitude completely and let me sit down in his office while he rang the police. Two of them arrived. They were very kind and just asked me some questions. One of them wrote down my answers. When they asked if there were any marks on me, I showed them the bruises on my legs and my back and down my arms. They noticed the one on my face too. Then they thanked me and left.

After they'd gone, the head teacher turned to me and asked gently: 'Why didn't you say anything?'

'Because I was scared.'

Later, I found out that they had gone straight to my father's work and arrested him in front of all his colleagues and bosses. Apparently, when they got him down to the police station, he told them I had been lying. He said I'd slipped down the stairs and hurt my arm and my leg on the banisters. So it was my word against his.

The police came back and took photos of my bruises. Then they took photos of the staircase at my dad's house, where he said I'd slipped. They asked me if I could see why it might have been possible for me to have these bruises if I'd slipped down the stairs. I was honest and said yes. They didn't seek a medical opinion and just discharged him with a warning.

Nobody bothered about me. Nobody followed it up. Where were social services? If my parents hated me so much, why wasn't I fostered or adopted?

For the next four weeks or so, he was fine, no violence at all. But then he turned Jekyll and Hyde again, and went back to beating me whenever he felt like it. If I was hoovering and happened to knock the skirting board, that led to a thrashing; if I was doing the washing-up and left a smear on a glass, that was a beating. It was any excuse.

One night, bruised and shaken, I'd had enough, so the next day I rebelled. It was the last day of the Christmas term in my first year at secondary school. I went round at lunchtime and told a lot of people to come round to my house that evening, when I knew Dad would be out.

'I'm having a party, we've got lots of drink.'

All these people turned up – I didn't even know some of them. My mother used to make wine, so there was still a lot of that in the house and we all started drinking it. Everybody got drunk and before too long, people were being sick. More people were still arriving and they pushed their way in, breaking the front door. They smashed the chandelier in the living room, put fish in the washing machine, broke the Christmas tree and completely ransacked the house. Everything was in a state. They broke a lock and found some jewellery my mother had left behind and stole that, then did a runner. So we were left with it, my best friend Donna and me.

Just then, my dad's car came round the corner. Somehow, I made him believe that I had been out and come home and that's how I'd found it when I got back. He rang the police and they came round. They started questioning us – Donna, my dad and me. They didn't seem to take any notice that we were giggly from the drink. Dad had picked up a tea towel from the floor and he was winding it up into some sort of noose.

'I need the toilet,' I said, making a face at Donna.

'Can I just go out and get some fresh air?' she asked.

The policemen nodded – they were finding out from Dad what was missing.

Donna and I met outside and did a runner. We ran as fast as we could to where there was a Water Board building and hid behind that. The police cars were going to and fro, looking for us. We were still quite drunk, so we hopped into the back of a white van and asked the driver to take us to a nearby town. Luckily, he didn't harm us but he was going somewhere else, so after a couple of miles, while he was stopped at a junction, we kicked the van doors open, climbed out and ran off. Donna went back home and got a roasting from her parents, who told her to have nothing more to do with me.

I didn't think it was safe to go back home so, at the age of 11, the only place I could think of to go was the house of a lady called Val, who had been a friend of my mother's. I walked there, knocked on her door and she let me in. I stayed there for a few nights. That's when I first got to know Val properly and she was very good to me. She lived with her husband, Ray, and their little boy. I remember we used to watch films together the first three nights and it was very cosy, but it didn't stay that way for long.

Why do good things always go wrong for me?

I wondered about this a few years later as I sat in the corner of my prison room, rocking to and fro, hands round my tummy, cradling my unborn baby. Yes, I'd had ten very good years, but after Nana died, my life had gone downhill. Was it me? Why did nobody love me? Why couldn't I be allowed to go on having a happy childhood? I was still a child, just 15, when I had been lured to this house and taken captive. Would I never be able to leave?

On my fourth night at Val's, I went to bed in their spare room, as usual. I closed the door and got into bed, said my Nana's prayers and went to sleep. In the middle of the night, I was woken by approaching footsteps that stopped outside my door. Bleary with sleep, I thought for a moment I was back at Dad's house and it was him with his belt, come to beat me.

The door opened very, very slowly and in came the dark silhouette of a man, who closed the door behind him and tiptoed towards my bed. Terrified, I opened my eyes wider and looked up. Before I had realised it, he got into bed. He didn't say a word – just got on top of me, squashing me. Just 11 years old at the time, I didn't know what was going on. Extremely frightened, I tried to push him off, but I couldn't budge him. I struggled, I kicked, but he was just too strong. He pinned me down and started to sexually assault me.

'Get off me!' I screamed. 'You're hurting me!'

But he had his hand over my mouth, so my screams were stifled and nobody heard me. He did what he wanted to do. I didn't know what it was, but I later learnt that it was called rape. He raped me, a little girl, in his own house, while his wife and son slept in their nearby rooms. Afterwards, he heaved himself off me and got out of my bed. Then he turned to warn me: 'If you tell anybody, I'll kill you.' He said it with such certainty that I believed him.

He went out the door and shut it behind him, leaving me bleeding in the dark. For the rest of that night I lay there, hurting, wide awake, sobbing my heart out.

I waited until I heard him leave for work the next morning then I went down to Val. I sat at the kitchen table with her and plucked up all my courage.

'I need to tell you something, Val …'

Then I wavered. How would she take it? After all, this was her husband.

Nobody is going to believe me, they'll probably think I'm making things up, I thought.

'Come on then,' she said. 'Tell me.'

'He sexed me.'

It was the only way I knew to explain it.

'Who did?' she asked. 'What do you mean?'

'Ray came into my room and got into bed with me.'

'*What?*' She was shocked.

'He got on top of me and sexed me. I tried to push him off, but I couldn't.'

By now I was sobbing uncontrollably. She started crying too, but she leant across and put her arm round me. That was when I knew she was taking it seriously, trying to believe me, awful as it must have been for her.

'You mean he raped you?' she asked gently. 'That's what it's called when the man goes inside you when you don't want him to.'

I nodded, bewildered and afraid.

She comforted me and asked me to tell her more details, which I did, then she dialled 999.

They were a different police force to the ones who came to my dad's a few days before, so they didn't know me. Val supported me to tell them my story of the night and they took me seriously. They took away my pants – in case some of his semen had dropped out, I suppose – and they took away the bedcovers too. Then they drove me straight down to Nailby police station. I had two medical examinations, 24 hours apart. They got a lady in to give me counselling, then Val came in and stayed with me as they took me to a Child Protection Unit.

Everyone was very kind and understanding. They realised that, at 11 years old, something precious had been taken from me.

At one point they turned to Val.

'I'm sorry to have to ask this,' one of them said, 'but we have to. Were you an accomplice to your husband?'

'No, certainly not.'

She was shocked by that.

'Where were you at the time this event occurred?'

'In bed, asleep.'

They asked her lots of questions. Did she and her husband share a bed? Was she aware that he got out of bed? Did she know where he was going? Why wasn't she watching me? Why was I at her house? Too many questions, and poor Val struggled to answer them all. I felt awful that I'd got her into all this trouble but of course, it wasn't me who caused it.

Val pulled herself up, looked straight at the policeman asking most of the questions and made it clear that she was not an accomplice. 'There's no way I knew anything about it,' she told them. 'I didn't even know he'd left our bed, and I didn't hear him come back either.'

I was so grateful to Val for believing and supporting me. She could have taken her husband's side and tried to defend him, but she didn't. That made it all a lot easier for me.

* * *

Back in my room, in my corner, remembering all this made me tremble. I didn't know why, but I supposed it was because it marked the end of my innocence – and also because Val cared enough about me to believe and support me. She left her husband straightaway after that.

We both had to go through a lot, helping the police and the lawyers to prepare for the court case. It was horrendous, having to explain it all over and over again to strangers, but Val was by my side whenever she could be. I had a lot of counselling and a lot of support from the Child Protection Unit. They were all very helpful, but it didn't stop me wondering: why me? I felt disgusted by it all; he violated me. The counselling did help, though.

When the court case started, two years later, I had to give evidence and answer questions, like I'd practised with the police lawyer, but I was allowed to do so through a video link, so I didn't have to see all the people's faces who were in the courtroom, only the judge and the lawyers. I think I was about 13 when the court case took place. I had to answer a lot of intrusive questions, and also things like: why didn't I scream or shout out, and why couldn't I push him off? But I could answer those quite easily.

Ray was found guilty and he got six years in prison for what he did to me. The judge also told him he would have to pay me £6,000 in compensation. But that never came, year after year. I supposed I wouldn't get it at all now – and all the money in the world couldn't get me out of this house of horrors.

I sat in my corner and the tears ran down my face as I realised the only hope I had in the world was this baby: I couldn't wait for him to be born. I wouldn't have minded whether it was a boy or a girl, but I naively believed that Malik would be kinder to me if I had a boy.

Life would surely be better then.

CHAPTER 11

FiRST BABY

The long, uncertain wait for this baby kept taking me back to my childhood memories. I seemed to be reliving the events of my past – all the things that might have been part of how I came to be in this degrading prison. I thought a lot about what being a mother would be like; what parents should be like with their children – loving, caring, encouraging, supportive – and how opposite to that my parents were to me.

After the rape by Val's husband, the police took me back to my dad's. I didn't want to go there – I tried to tell them, but they said I had no choice as I was underage and he was my parent. For the first few days he wasn't too bad, but he quickly reverted to his old ways and life was very bumpy from then on. I had nowhere else to go – my mother said a definite no – so I had to stick it out. My response to that was to rebel as much and as often as I could.

At the age of 12, on days when the weather was good, I would skive off school with my friends. We used to have lots of fun – anything to annoy my father, except that I hoped he would never find out.

At 13 or 14, I would go off to school in the morning, wearing a long skirt. Then on the way, I would hide behind a bush and change into the mini-skirt I had hidden in my bag. I wore it all day and only changed back again at the end of my road, into my long skirt to go home. I dread to think what my dad would have done if he'd found out, but thank God he never did!

Dad never approved of the things I wore when I was going out with my friends – short skirts, skimpy tops and too much flesh showing.

'You dress like a slag,' he used to say. 'You're asking for it.'

I was at the age when young girls want to wear make-up too, but he didn't approve of that either.

'You're a slut, you look like a prostitute,' he told me.

I had no idea what a prostitute was, but I guessed it wasn't anything good – I just wanted to be like my friends.

A day or two after my fifteenth birthday, things took an unexpected turn. I came downstairs in my nightshirt to use the bathroom before going to bed.

Dad gave me a look that made me feel uneasy.

'Come and get into bed with me,' he said, with a persuasive voice. 'Come and lie down in my bed.'

'No,' I replied. I had the feeling he wanted to sexually abuse me and I knew that wasn't the right way for a father to feel towards his teenaged daughter.

'OK, then.'

He shut his bedroom door and I went into the bathroom and locked it. As I brushed my teeth, I knew I couldn't stay there any longer, not after what had happened to me in Val's house. I wouldn't feel safe staying after my dad had said that; I could never have trusted him. It would only have been a matter of time, so best to go now, while I could.

I went upstairs, got dressed again, packed a change of clothes and my most precious things, then crept out of the front door, quietly closing it behind me. I'm never coming back, I thought, so I threw my front door key into a hedge as I walked up the road, away from the house.

When I got to the top of the road, I didn't know what to do. I didn't want to be found, so I crouched behind a bush with my little overnight case while I considered my options. It was a spring evening, not very cold, so I took time to think about it. I couldn't go back to Dad's and I knew Mum wouldn't want me so I didn't have much choice. Either I could go to a school friend's house and ask to sleep on their settee for the night, or go to Val's house in Nailby. Her husband was still in prison, so I thought she might put me up for a few days. I had virtually no money with me and I didn't have a mobile phone, so how could I get there?

I came out from behind my bush and turned into the main road. Then I did something stupid: I hitched a lift. Luckily it was a woman driver who stopped.

'Where are you going?' she asked.

'I want to get to Nailby,' I said, hopefully.

'I'm going that way,' she told me with a smile. 'Put your case in the back, then hop in and I'll take you.'

When we were nearly there, she asked me where I wanted to go, so I told her the address and she took me to the close where Val lived.

'Thanks very much,' I said.

Val's house was only three down from where I was dropped off, so I arrived on her doorstep and rang the bell. While I waited, it suddenly struck me that she might not be in. What would I do? I knew where she worked, at the taxi rank on the other side of town, but I would have to walk a couple of miles to get there.

But I was in luck again: Val answered the door and welcomed me in. When I explained my situation, she was very understanding.

'I've got a lodger now, to make ends meet, but you can stay for a few nights on the sofa,' she offered, 'until you get sorted.'

'Thanks.' I smiled. 'You're a star.'

'Just time for a cuppa,' she told me. 'Then I'm off to the taxi base. My boy is at his Grandma's over the weekend, so you might as well come with me and help me catch up on my mountain of paperwork, and we can talk in between, so you can tell me all about it.'

Val was a lovely, motherly lady – just the sort of mother I would have wanted. I was glad to be able to help her while she was helping me. I'd been to the taxi base with her before a couple of times, and the boss didn't seem to mind. So that's what we did. That night I went back home with her and stayed. When Monday came round, she gave me some bus money and I went back to school in the daytimes, then in the evenings I would go with Val to the taxi base. I liked it there – I helped Val with entering the jobs diary and telling her where the jobs were. The drivers were very friendly and often teased me, but most of them spent their time between customers playing pool in the back room. However, there was one man in particular paying me a lot of attention. He seemed genuinely interested in me. I craved that warm feeling he gave me with his friendly smile, so I gladly lapped up his attentiveness. That was my undoing – I should never have allowed myself to be taken in by his feigned interest and false smile. But I didn't suspect a thing. So was it my fault? I was only just 15, in many ways naive and, most of all, unloved. How could I possibly have recognised the trap I was walking into? And here I was, two years later, a tormented sex slave, a prisoner with no control over my own life and no future, but more of the same, or, God forbid, worse.

Doesn't anyone wonder where I am? I thought. *Why hasn't somebody come looking for me? What about Social Services – why haven't they tracked me down? Why haven't the police found me?*

Looking back, I can't understand how a 15-year-old girl could go missing yet nobody seemed to care. I'd love to go and ask Social Services: 'Where were you?' They go after the wrong people, while the real ones in danger are being missed. When a child dies, they say there's nothing we can do about it. And if it's an Asian person or an Asian family responsible, no one dares go after them. To me it's all wrong: nobody seems to have caught on yet to what goes on in some families. No matter who you are or where you come from, people who do awful things to children are still paedophiles, aren't they? That's what Malik was, a paedophile.

I don't suppose he'll ever be caught.

* * *

The compensation of £6,000 awarded by the court four years previously for the rape I suffered when I was 11 suddenly arrived at Malik's house. It had apparently done the rounds of both my parents, Val, my grandparents, my school and, finally, the NHS, who found they had records of a doctor attending me at this address.

Why didn't this cause any of them to come looking for me?

Although the envelope with the cheque inside was addressed to me, Malik opened it, of course. The only reason I found out about it was that the money could not be accessed without my going to a bank or a Post Office and cashing the cheque myself, then handing it over to him. Malik clearly thought the money was his, because he owned me.

I believe he gave the money to his mother and she spent it all on new gold bangles.

* * *

I was hoping the baby would be born any day now, though I didn't have a date. Malik had started to ease off in the past week or so, still with his needs to be met, but with less violence, thank God. 'Please do not hurt the baby,' I kept saying. I did what he wanted me to do, but I repeated, 'Please do not hurt the baby.'

The women were trying to make me eat well and they tried to make me drink milk too. I really didn't want to, but I did, for the baby. They kept pushing various fruit through the hole in the door as well.

I had never eaten much fruit, but whenever the baby kicked, I did eat some. I was a bit worried because the baby was now becoming less active, but Surayya told me it was because it didn't have enough space to move about.

'Baby soon,' she said with a smile, and gave my tummy a gentle pat. 'Baby will be boy?'

'I hope so,' I agreed, returning her smile.

I was really excited now. It was the first time in two years that I'd felt happy: there was a little person inside me who was mine. Nobody could take this baby away from me. When it moved around, it kept me sane.

Finally, the day arrived and I went into labour. Malik said it was a special day to have a baby because it was a Friday and coming up to Eid al-Fitr, the end of Ramadan. Soon after I arrived at the hospital, with Malik and most of the family in the room, much to the staff's consternation, they told me there were complications, but not to worry. After a few hours, I gave birth to a beautiful baby boy. The midwife gave him to me to hold.

'What is his name?' she asked.

'Purdil,' said Malik, before I could say a word. But I was too busy cuddling my tiny baby and gently stroking his soft skin and his thick black hair, so I didn't mind what he was called. He was mine, and I loved him immediately with a fierce love: he was perfect. How could any mother hate her baby like my mother hated me? How could my father have wanted to kill me? I found these things impossible to understand, gazing into my baby's eyes.

Malik took him from me and put him straight down in the cot next to my bed.

'Would you like to give him a little feed?' asked the nurse.

'No,' said Malik, stepping forward. 'Anna doesn't want to feed the baby herself.'

'Is that right?' asked the nurse, turning to face me.

I hesitated. I desperately wanted to feed my own child, but Malik glared at me and put his hand on my arm, gripping me tightly, with all the family giving me forceful looks, so I knew I had no choice.

'Yes,' I murmured. 'That's right.'

Malik loosened his grip.

'Take the baby away,' he told the nurse, so she did.

Some of the family stayed with me, to guard me and to stop me saying anything to the staff or trying to escape. Malik took the baby from the nurse and carried him out of the room with Eshrat and Surayya in tow. I could hear them singing to him outside.

'What are they doing?' I asked Bushra, the tears running down my cheeks. I yearned for him to be back in my arms.

'It's what must be done for all babies,' she explained. 'They whisper in his ears and put honey in his mouth. We give new babies sweet things to help them love the name of Allah.'

Later, I found out that a cleric from the mosque had come to give the baby a kind of blessing so that he became a Muslim.

* * *

The hospital wanted me and the baby to stay in for at least four days to have all our checks and make sure we were both fine after the complicated birth.

'No, no, *no!*' said Malik. 'It is Eid today. Anna must come home with the baby so that we all celebrate Eid together.'

But a doctor came to see us and insisted we stay, because I'd had a haemorrhage when giving birth. That was something

Malik couldn't control, although I feared I would suffer for it when we did eventually get home.

It was a few hours after the birth now, and I had not held or even seen my baby since those first few minutes, so I was delighted when the nurse brought him to me and put him in my arms.

'For a cuddle with Mum,' she said.

It was bliss, just the baby and me, even if there were a lot of people standing all around us, frowning.

* * *

We stayed in the hospital for two days and two nights, during which time the staff saw to it that I had baby Purdil with me as much as possible, despite the others coming up repeatedly with excuses to take him away from me. But finally, Malik could wait no longer: he ignored my protests and I was made to leave the ward, still bleeding and weak.

I walked out to the car, cradling the baby in my arms. It was only a short trip back to the house and he would be all mine.

Wrong again! As soon as we set off, Malik told Surayya to take the baby from me.

'Why can't I hold him myself?' I asked.

He glared back at me in the mirror. 'Because Surayya will look after the baby and feed him.'

This was a shock I had never anticipated.

'Why can't I feed the baby myself?' I wanted to know.

'Because it's dirty to feed a baby with milk from your breast,' Surayya explained, as if she really believed it.

'But it's the most natural way,' I protested.

She made a face, took out a bottle and started to feed Purdil, while all I was allowed to do was watch with a growing sense of unease. What other surprises were they planning to spring on me?

Back at the house, Surayya whisked my baby away and Malik pushed me upstairs and locked me in. I assumed Purdil would be brought back to me once he'd finished being fed and changed, so I waited and waited to hear Surayya's soft footsteps on the stairs. It was morning when we got home and as the day wore on I became increasingly anxious: my baby needed me and I needed him. I tried shouting for him to be brought back to me. Then I banged on the door and stamped my bare feet on the floorboards. Nobody came. It started to get dark and it was May, so I knew it must be mid-evening by now. Where was my baby? Why did nobody bring him to me? My heart ached; my body felt like it had a gaping hole in it. My head pounded with the stress of the enormous sense of loss I felt.

I could only imagine them all fussing round him, while I was distraught, alone and bereft. How could they do this to me? However much I banged for attention, shouting and wailing until I was hoarse, scratching and clawing at the door, there was no response … and no baby. Every instinct in my body was screaming for Purdil. It was worse than agony.

Late that night, I heard heavy footsteps, the turning of the lock, the grinding of teeth and I knew what that meant. He pulled off the eiderdown, pushed me roughly onto the bed, tore away the pad soaking up the last vestiges of my haemorrhage and thrust himself inside me with such force I nearly stopped breathing. Just three nights after the difficult birth of my baby, the monster subjected me to a vicious rape that almost killed me. As he tore into my insides, blood poured out, all over the sheets, over me and over him. His excitement rose as he wallowed in all this red blood and raped me again, then turned me over and thrust himself in and out of my anus, breaking open the old scar. It was strange how distant I felt during this onslaught – it was as if I wasn't really there, just an empty shell. Light-headed, I hardly felt the pain at all after a while. I knew that angered him, but I was by now beyond reasoning. That was when I passed out.

He must have tried to revive me, as I found the water glass empty on its side next to me on the bed when I came to, and my cheeks stung as if they had been slapped. But he was gone.

The next morning, early, he came stomping up the stairs. I pretended to be still unconscious, but he took no notice, pulling me off the bed and kicking me, presumably in an attempt to force me back to consciousness. I moaned when the kicking grew worse and he hauled me up by the hair.

'Get those bloody sheets off the bed!' he blasted at me. 'You're going to wash them until they're spotless. Come *on*!'

I felt very weak, with hardly enough energy to breathe, but somehow I managed to gather up the bright red sheets and take them to the bathroom, where I dropped them into the bath and started to run some water.

'Come on, you white slut!' goaded Malik as he stood in the doorway and watched me work. 'You're no better than trash. Get a f***ing move on! You're not coming out of there until those sheets are spotless.'

I had to find some strength from somewhere and set to. It took me two long hours to wash the blood out of those sheets, with Malik keeping guard and checking my work.

'Not good enough,' he barked at me when I thought I was done. 'Scrub this one harder, you whore!'

I don't think I've ever moved so slowly in my life, but I tried one last time to cleanse the sheet. Finally, he was satisfied and I slumped to the bathroom floor, unable to move. When he realised that I really was unable to get up and go back under my own steam, he picked me up, threw me over his shoulder and bundled me back into the bedroom.

All I remember having in my mind before I lost consciousness again was: *I think I've had a baby … but where is my baby?* I don't recall anything after that for a day or two. It was all a distant blur, with people looking over me and poking me, and voices and words I didn't have the strength to understand. Was I going mad?

* * *

They left me alone for another couple of days, only coming to moan loudly to each other outside my door that I had not eaten any of the food they had left me. What was the point of eating? I had no appetite. As the hours passed by I just lay there, remembering how my beautiful baby felt that first time I cuddled him in the hospital when he fixed his dark brown eyes on me alone. Would they ever let me hold him again?

Distraught and defeated, I fell into a restless sleep filled with nightmares of babies being killed.

CHAPTER 12

CIRCUMCISION

I think it was the fifth or sixth day after Purdil was born, when I was still very weak, but Bushra came to dress me and take me downstairs.

'The health visitor is coming to see you and the baby,' she explained. 'You must say nothing.'

'But what if she asks me questions?'

'Say nothing,' she repeated. 'Malik will answer for you.'

When the doorbell rang, Malik went to answer it, while Surayya came out of her room with baby Purdil and handed him to me. What a wonderful relief it was to have my baby back to hold and love at last. I stroked his cheek and adjusted his clothes like a true mum, and gave him a gentle kiss on his forehead. He seemed to relax in my arms – he knew who his real mum was.

'Hello, Anna,' said the young woman with a smile. 'My name is Sally, I'm your health visitor. If you have any queries or concerns, you can ring me. Here is my number.' She passed me a card.

'I'll take that,' said Malik abruptly.

The health visitor looked surprised.

'Just to keep it safe for Anna,' he explained, realising she might think him domineering. She would have been right, of course.

Sally and I sat down at a table while Malik stood behind me, his hands on my shoulders, exerting his pressure, as if he was my puppet-master.

'How well is the baby feeding?' asked Sally, looking straight at me.

'Very well,' replied Malik, gripping my shoulders more tightly.

'Are your breasts sore at all, Anna?'

I opened my mouth to answer.

'No,' said Malik, 'not sore at all.'

Of course, this was untrue. My breasts had been very swollen and painful, filling up with milk, leaking and throbbing. But clearly Malik didn't want me to have any relief.

'And has the bleeding stopped now?'

'Yes, it's all gone,' he assured her.

Again, this wasn't true.

'I hope you will all make sure Anna gets plenty of rest after losing so much blood in the hospital,' advised the health visitor, looking particularly at Malik and all the other adults standing with him.

'Yes, of course,' answered Malik and they all nodded.

'We will make sure,' added Bushra.

The health visitor gave baby Purdil a quick check over, and smiled.

'You're obviously doing very well, Anna, and the baby seems very contented in your arms.'

She stood up to go. I desperately wanted to catch her attention with a look or some sign to suggest I needed her help, but Malik made sure there was no chance of that, taking her swiftly to the front door and seeing her out.

Surayya bent over me to take back the baby.

'*No!*' I raised my voice as I clung to him, pressing him to my shoulder.

'Don't be so f**ing stupid!' scolded Malik. 'You didn't think you could keep him, did you? You're not fit to look after your own baby. He's going to have new parents, it's all arranged.'

He indicated the young Pakistani couple, standing across the room. I had noticed them earlier, and heard Malik talking about money with them. They smiled at me, but I was in no mood to smile back: they would be stealing *my* baby. I looked away, back to my baby's face, his long, thick eyelashes, the dimples in his cheeks. I traced the shape of his ears and kissed his little nose.

Malik turned to Surayya and spoke the words I dreaded: 'Take the baby.'

I tried to hold onto him for just a few moments longer, doing my best to make this a special memory before I lost him. But Surayya took the baby and Bushra immediately took me up the stairs and locked the door. Torn apart inside, I feared the worst. Malik had sold my baby, I was convinced of it – how could a father be so cruel? Was this child nothing more to Malik and his family than a commodity? Would I ever see my baby again? Waves of grief hit me, as if my baby had died – at least I would have known that he died in my arms, but now he was no longer *my* baby. He would live his life knowing nothing about me, and all I would have of him would be bittersweet memories of the day I held him in my arms, kissed him and said goodbye forever. Racked with anguish, I collapsed onto the bed, sobbing uncontrollably.

I don't remember anything more.

In the still of the night I was woken by heavy footsteps approaching up the stairs. After all that had just happened, I would yet again have to steel myself to that brute's demands. Still in pain and bleeding from the last attack, too soon after childbirth, I was appalled. My breasts were so tender and sore; my whole body and mind ached with grief and hopelessness. The lock turned and the door burst open as a stocky shape loomed in the doorway, gazing in my direction. But something was wrong. It didn't look like Malik's bulky body – it was a squatter, more muscled outline. Could it be somebody else?

'*Rrrrrow!*' he growled.

I recognised that voice, even without words.

He turned on the light. Eshrat stood, his feet astride, blocking the doorway – a predator leering at his prey. *This is terrible*, I thought. *It shouldn't be, he's married to Surayya ...* But there was no time for thinking. He made straight for me, pulling off his trousers as he leapt on top of me, a piece of thick black cloth in his hand and a wicked gleam in his eyes.

I tried to fend him off, but he was unstoppable. He attacked me voraciously that terrible night. Without pity for my weakened state, he rammed himself inside me, thrusting harder and harder, again and again, while holding the cloth across my nose and mouth, his hand clamping it down tightly to arrest my breath. Too weak to struggle as much as I needed, I resorted to hitting, biting and scratching him, but that only fired him up more. Repeatedly I reached the verge of unconsciousness when, at extreme intervals, Eshrat would realise and loosen his grip for just a few seconds, as I took in an enormous gulp of oxygen, then another, before I was smothered again.

Finally sated, he withdrew.

I turned over with relief.

He turned me back and forced me to sit at the edge of the bed.

'You English bitches are only good for blow jobs,' he jeered. 'Now, show me how good you are.'

I shook my head in exhaustion and shut my mouth as firmly as I could.

'Playing hard to get?' he laughed. 'Two can play that game!'

He made a fist and held it up for a few seconds, enjoying my discomfort.

I couldn't help betraying my fear. 'No, please don't hurt me. I can't take any more,' I cried out.

He laughed again and, opening his fist, struck me with the back of his hand across my mouth, cutting my lip and hurting my jaw.

This was his chance and he pushed himself inside my mouth, thrusting to the back of my throat, almost as if Malik had taught him. I retched repeatedly as he did his worst. When he finally finished, he saw my vomit on him and grabbed my hair.

'*I'll* teach you!' he yelled, and pulled me to the floor, then started to kick me repeatedly, on my head, my buttocks, my legs and my back. I curled up in a ball to try and protect myself, but it was too late: I felt a sharp stab of pain on one side of my back, which turned into a severe ache. I held it, in case that would help, but the damage had been done. This was the moment when my kidney was damaged so badly that it started to shrink.

In my feeble state, I lay whimpering on the floor. Thankfully, he stopped. Then, the strangest thing happened: he suddenly seemed to change.

'Do you need anything?' he asked me, almost kindly.

'No.'

There were all kinds of things I could have asked for, but I didn't want to ask him for anything. I didn't want him to come up to my room again.

Was this to be a new phase in my imprisonment? Did Malik know about it? Would he punish me for it?

Exhausted and strangely numb, with only the pain in my kidney piercing my consciousness, I took the last of the strong painkillers I'd been given when Malik broke my arm. All I could think of was my baby. Where was he now? Were they looking after him properly?

Nothing else mattered.

* * *

Seven days after Purdil's birth, Bushra came to dress me.

'What for?' I asked.

'Special day,' she answered in her simplistic English before reverting to Punjabi. 'Purdil returns today.'

My hopes rose to the ceiling, from depression to joy.

'He's coming back here?'

'Yes.'

'So he will be mine?'

'No.'

I was deflated. 'What do you mean?'

'He is coming here because he must be with his mother and father when he is circumcised.'

I didn't know that word in Punjabi – I don't think I knew it in English either – but I must have looked puzzled.

'He must be cut,' she explained. 'To be a Muslim, he must have his penis circumcised.'

'Oh no!' I said, horrified that a tiny baby had to be injured to become a Muslim. 'I thought he was already a Muslim,' I added. 'With that man coming to the hospital – the singing, the whispering in his ears and the honey on his tongue?'

'Well, yes. But this must be done too.'

I gulped. 'Well, at least I can see my baby again and hold him in my arms.'

She half-smiled. 'Yes.'

Whatever happened, I would have this time with him again, so I felt happy just for that day, as Bushra adjusted my clothes and scarf. Then we went downstairs to join the others. Malik and all his brothers were there, together with their wives and children and the old man with the satin hat. He was the one who came to 'convert' me to become a Muslim.

Muneeza and Surayya were in the kitchen, fishing scissors and tweezers out of a pan of boiling water.

What are they doing? I wondered.

The couple who took my baby away came across and passed Purdil to me. I felt a wonderful, warm glow inside to have him back in my arms again and I couldn't stop looking at him. But then I had to hand him over to the man in the satin hat, who promptly shaved my poor baby's head. I had to watch all his beautiful black hair fall to the floor to be swept up by Muneeza and thrown away in the bin. Deeply shocked, I had to bite my lip in an effort not to cry. *How dare they do that?* I asked if I could have a lock of his hair to keep, but they refused me. Then the old man took him and laid him down on a table in the sitting room.

The women brought through the instruments on a tray and I realised what they were for: the boiling must have been to sterilise them. But where was the doctor? Surely it should be a trained doctor doing that kind of thing?

It looked so barbaric – no doctor, no anaesthetic. I wanted to shout out, to stop them doing this, but I was afraid that if I protested, I might be sent back upstairs and I was desperate to stay.

At that moment, as he snipped Purdil and pulled off his foreskin, the baby screamed. It was his first real experience of pain – *unnecessary* pain. The shrill sound of his scream echoed in my head and I nearly fainted.

The old man picked up the still-screaming infant, blood splashed all over and oozing down his legs and with a ring on his penis. Surayya stepped forward with a big fluffy towel, which she wrapped around Purdil and handed him over to me. He was still screaming so loudly, I don't suppose anyone else wanted to hold him.

It was terribly distressing to see this seven-day-old baby in such a state. I knew he wasn't made out of love, but violent rape. However, he was *my* baby, the baby I'd been carrying inside me for nine months. Yet neither he nor I had any choice.

I tried all I could to calm him down, rocking him gently in my arms, attempting to sing to him to soothe the pain, and his crying eventually subsided to a pitiful whimper.

The old man was shown out and the moment I dreaded came far too quickly: the couple took him from me. But Purdil must have known: being passed from me to the other woman seemed to stir him anew and he took up his screaming again. It tore me in two to see this poor little waif, wailing in distress and holding his arms out in my direction, wanting me to take him back.

That was the last image of my baby, the image that would trouble my dreams every night and spear me to the core each day, whenever I thought of him.

CHAPTER 13

TRAFFICKED

Only ten days after I had to watch my baby being taken away, Surayya and Bushra came to help me get dressed in a new red Pakistani outfit and matching scarf, embroidered with thin gold thread. *This must be important*, I thought. I dreaded it might be Malik tricking me into marriage.

They made me up, with kohl around my eyes, and brushed my long, dyed-black hair, which now reached down past my waist.

'Why must I dress up?' I asked.

'Malik wants friends to meet you.'

Surayya arranged my scarf loosely over my hair, but with some wisps poking out. I wondered why they were taking so much care when it was only for Malik's friends.

'You no look at men,' instructed Bushra, as she led me downstairs and into the living room. 'Keep head down.'

Apprehensive, I nodded. I knew that the men often tended to get together separately from the women, but I was surprised that Malik wanted me there, in a room full of men, with no women other than me. It made me nervous.

Remembering that I had to keep my face partially hidden and not look directly at any man, except in private, I had my head bowed, with my scarf down over my forehead and partially covering my eyes. But it was such fine material that, even with my head down, I could see through it without anyone noticing.

Malik put his arm around me, which immediately surprised me. Even if it was affection, which I doubted, public displays of affection were frowned on. He led me to a space on one of the settees. I watched his sandalled feet as he went to sit down opposite me.

As I sat down, I briefly glimpsed from beneath my flimsy scarf eight old men sitting on the settees that made three sides of a square. Well, they looked old to me – the youngest must have been at least 40.

On the table in the centre were bowls of fruit and dishes of 'cakes' that looked like long biscuits, with the texture of rusks. I'd once eaten one and it made me feel sick. The men ate noisily and I could feel them all staring at me. Then they started talking about me. Although I didn't understand everything they were saying, I heard my Muslim name, Yasmeen. I recognised some words but others were new to me. In between I heard a lot of sniggers and I guessed they were perhaps making fun of me, or even worse. I kept quite still, surrounded by these men, as they finished eating.

As I sat, apprehensive and on the edge of my seat, they passed round some sort of fat clay bottle which they took turns to suck on, then blew out long streams of smoke into the already fetid air. It was like a big pot, with something burning on the top of it. I didn't know whether it was drugs or something, but I didn't like the weird smell.

By this time, as they continued to talk about me, their voices becoming increasingly excitable, laughing and joking, turning into giggling and sniggering, I was convinced I was on show but I had no idea why. I remember feeling threatened by the way they talked about me so I tried to concentrate on what they were saying. It sounded like they were making some sort of arrangement with Malik. I heard various numbers of pounds being mentioned, so I assumed it was about money. But what had that got to do with me?

Malik controlled the conversation, as usual, and he seemed to be leading the men to an agreement, with them all gradually saying yes. Nobody had talked to me and I wished I could just slink out of the room, but I knew I'd suffer for it later if I tried, so I just sat there meekly, as I'd been told.

Suddenly, the man to one side of me started to touch me. I went rigid with shock. Everybody seemed to be watching and goading him on as he touched first a stray lock of hair, then my cheek, my shoulder, my arm … straying to my breast, where he lingered, fondling me gently. Horrified, I could sense his excitement at my expense as I tried to keep still and detach myself from his pawing.

As he continued, an old man on the other side of me joined in with his heavier touch, tracing my figure, slowly down my body … *How could Malik allow this?* I sneaked a glance from the corner of my eye: he had a big grin across his face. The others looked expectant too, clearly waiting their turn.

'Enough!' called Malik sternly. I could sense the collective disappointment in the room as I breathed a silent sigh of relief.

I couldn't wait to get out, but I had to wait until Malik had shown them all out of the front door, then he took me upstairs to my inevitable fate. After he had raped me in a frenzy, he lay down beside me on the bed and fell into a deep, satisfied sleep, while I lay awake, anxiously turning over what he had subjected me to in that room full of strangers. I was puzzled by Malik's obvious pleasure in the way those men were touching me. Could it be that he had given them permission to do that, or even suggested it? If it was drugs they were taking, perhaps that was the reason. And why was he making them talk about money?

As I turned everything over, I shuddered at the gradual realisation of what might have been going on, and the dread of what could happen next. Would they be back again, and why the financial agreement? Malik wasn't selling anything ... Or was he?

Imagination multiplied my fears.

It must have been nearly dawn by the time I fell into a troubled sleep. For once, Malik must have got up, dressed and left for work without waking me. I was grateful for that small mercy, but wished I'd had the chance to ask him some questions, even though I would almost certainly have been beaten for my impudence.

* * *

A few days later, my suspicions were confirmed when I was dressed up and taken downstairs again. This time, I was made to sit alone on a settee in the living room. Two of the men from earlier came to the house. Both came into the room with Malik, who sat with the older man on the settee opposite me, while the other man, who must have been in his late fifties, came over and sat next to me, rather too close, so I sidled away.

'Don't be silly!' he said in good English. 'We are here to see you.'

What was happening to me? I glanced at Malik, hoping he would intervene, but he just smiled as the two of them watched intently. *Was this to be the situation I dreaded?*

Moments later, the man budged up closer and put one arm round my shoulders, while he touched and fondled my breast with the other. I pulled away and he pulled me back, his head closer to mine, the stench of his breath increasing. His smile was gone, his face expressionless.

I tried to push him off, but he pulled me closer and tilted my face up towards him. Then, without warning, he pushed his lips to mine and tried to kiss me. I felt physically sick and heaved, but it didn't seem to bother him. He kept forcing his kiss onto me. Then he pushed me down on the settee.

'Help, stop him!' I shouted to Malik, trembling with fear.

But he ignored me.

'Now I'll show you what a real man does,' said the old man. At this I trembled with fear. I didn't understand why this was happening to me. How could Malik allow it?

The man undid his trousers and pulled them down – the smell that suddenly emanated was horrific. Then he undid my sash, pulled down the trousers of my *salwar kameez* and pinned me down. He lifted up my legs and, without hesitation, suddenly thrust himself inside me. I tried to struggle, but it was too late: he was oblivious to me, other than as a vessel for his own sordid pleasure. It was so quick, it was job done in less than a minute or two – a very long minute. When it was over, without a glance at me, he left the room with Malik.

Appalled, degraded and deeply ashamed, I had no time even to rearrange my clothes. While the first man was laughing with Malik in the next-door room and passing over his money, the second moved across to my settee. Even older than the first, in his sixties, uglier too, he immediately pulled up the dress part of my *salwar kameez* to reveal my bra-less state. I turned my head away as far as I could, while he slid his penis between my breasts and squashed them against it to help him masturbate, shooting out his white semen all over my chest and neck.

I felt revulsed. But he didn't care – he just went straight off to hand over his money and tell Malik how wonderful he still was at sex.

After they had gone, Malik, having watched me being raped, couldn't wait to get me upstairs, where he subjected me to much longer and far worse abuse for his own pleasure.

* * *

Over the next few days and weeks, those two men came back several times, demanding a variety of positions, for which they paid extra. Malik usually came in and sat opposite, watching to make sure they didn't do more than they'd paid for. At least, that was what he made out to be his reason, but of course every time he would hurry me back upstairs afterwards and rush straight into his own voracious sexual acts, as if I was just a rag doll, with no feelings, physical or mental. In fact, that's how I had become, forcing myself to try not to feel, so often infuriating him further. It was a downward spiral, one I had no hope of climbing out of.

Every time those two men came, together or separately, I felt increasingly shamed and degraded. I had sunk to the bottom of the pit. *Was that what I was now*, I wondered, *a prostitute?* Money had changed hands, so I must surely be.

I shuddered to think about it.

* * *

Two other men from the original group also came on a regular basis for a while and they paid extra for oral sex because Pakistani women could not be expected to do that, only 'white whores'. They had obviously arranged in advance what they could do, but I wasn't told. I never knew what was to come, and they never usually spoke to me, or even paid any attention to me as a person, so, if it was full sex, the men would push me down along the settee. If it was oral sex they wanted, without even looking at me they used to stand in front of me, take down their trousers and push my head down. I never knew what to expect.

Unlike Malik, these two weren't aggressive with me. Probably in their sixties, they were quite gentle. It was all about the sex, at least as far as they were concerned.

A few days after those two first came, another pair – the two eldest of the original group – came for me. The one with a round hat came in first – he must have been about 70. He didn't seem to want full sex, thank God – he just kept pushing himself against me and covered me in stinking kisses. He smelt awful and he wouldn't leave me alone. I shuddered with disgust as he left the room to pay. Then Malik came back in.

The other man did want full sex, raping me without any thought of me. I was nothing to him, just a business transaction.

While this man and Malik sorted out their finances next door, I thought about what sort of carefree teenage life I would have had, had I not been lured here and kidnapped. Maybe I would still be at school or college, going to the prom, having parties with my friends and normal boyfriends – perhaps still Jamie, the boy in my photo.

* * *

As Malik took me back to my room that day, a big grin spread over his face, I thought about all of those men sexually assaulting a young girl against her will, without a care, then the next day going to pray at the Mosque. How hypocritical was that?

Malik was raking in the money now. It made me realise why I was such a good proposition – a sex slave for him to abuse and break at will, all for his own evil desires and satisfaction, though he could never have enough. But then to sell my baby (*his* baby), and finally to make as much money as he could out of hiring me out to anyone who wanted a lay, to do whatever they wanted, on demand … And not only was he receiving money from them, he was also enjoying the great excitement of watching what they did to me in order to fire himself up for what he would inflict on me afterwards.

Was there any greater shame than what he was putting me through, almost every day, sometimes several times a day? I was deeply disgusted with Malik for making me do it, with the family for condoning it all … But most of all I was disgusted with myself – I hated my body.

* * *

That night, after Malik had raped me again, then gone out to work at the taxi base, I was in despair, sitting in my corner, rocking. Having thought about Jamie earlier, I laid my hand on the loose floorboard, comforted to know that I still had his photo hidden safely there. I never usually dared to get it out to look at, for fear of Malik coming in and seeing it – I knew he would tear it to shreds and beat me mercilessly if he saw me with it. Or the creak of the board when I moved it might alert somebody to come up and see what I was up to. Just knowing Jamie's photo was there was usually enough, but that night I needed to see his friendly smile, not just in my mind but on the photo itself – a proof that somebody had cared about me, and that he was still there for me in the photo.

Carefully, I pressed on one end of the board and the other rose high enough for me to gently lever it out, desperately hoping it would still be there. Could fate be cruel enough to take it away from me? It might have slipped down into an inaccessible space, or a mouse could have nibbled it away. But as I moved aside to let some light into the corner, there it was, just where I had left it, intact. I picked his photo up as if it were treasure, which it was to me. It still had its dog-eared corner, from being in my pocket when he first gave it to me. I remembered that day, the day he told me he was joining the army, and I was disappointed so he gave me a long kiss – the best kiss I had ever had.

I started speaking to him, as if he were there, alive in the photo.

'Can you hear me, Jamie? Can you see me, like I can see you? I wish we were together. You were my first and only boyfriend and I really liked you – loved you, I suppose.' I paused. 'Do you remember the first time we met? It was in the park, when I was 13 and you were 15. You were a scooter-boy. I don't suppose you noticed me then, but sometimes after that we used to see each other in the arcade. You asked me out when I was 14, and we went out for a few weeks, but then we broke up because you were going into the army. Do you remember the letters you sent me from BFPO in Germany? You sent me that one with a copy of this photo in it, asking me to come and meet you at the station. Why didn't I go? I think it was because I would have had to come with your parents and I didn't really know them. That was the day I was lured into this house of hell.'

I sat and stroked his face in the photo.

'Where are you now, Jamie? Are you still in the army in Germany? Do you ever think of me?'

I felt the tears trickling down my cheeks and held the photo away, so that it didn't get wet.

'How did I come to this, Jamie? Did I really bring it all on myself? What did I do wrong? I should have come and seen you off at the station that day. If I had, none of this would have happened.'

That short, one-sided conversation with the boy in the photo gave me some sense of peace. I nearly rocked myself to sleep holding it, but I realised just in time and replaced it, managing again to avoid the creak.

That night I slept well, dreaming of what might have been.

CHAPTER 14

DOUBLE ACT

It was about three years into my captivity and by now I must have been raped hundreds of times by Malik, another few times by Eshrat and prostituted out to strangers, all against my will. Malik always called me 'white whore', but now that men paid to rape or abuse me, he was right – that's what he had made me. How much more would I have to endure? Disgusted with myself, I didn't want my body any more. And it wasn't just the degrading things I was forced to do: they were all judging me, laughing about me, ignoring the pain and shame they were causing me.

All these thoughts were constantly turning over in my mind. I wished I could erase them, but I couldn't; I had no control over anything. But there was one thing I could do. Already I had refused to eat most of the food they pushed through the door for me, and the women had told Malik, who sometimes beat me to make me eat. But I had eaten very little since they sold my baby. Now I decided not to eat at all, except maybe one chapatti a week. It seemed to me the only thing I could do, the only protest I could make. Already thin, now I lost even more weight.

Every day, when it was Surayya's turn and she found my food uneaten, she shouted down to the others.

'The white bitch hasn't eaten any of yesterday's food!' Or 'The white whore has refused her food again!'

Of course, Malik heard about this and came up to me, saying something that sounded like '*Me puddy Yum*', which roughly translates as 'mother-f***ker' or 'you had sex with your dad'. Then he ranted at me, smacked me in the mouth, pulled me around by my hair and whacked me or smashed my head against the wall.

Every now and then, Malik and Eshrat tried to force-feed me, literally pushing food down my throat, choking me. It nearly always made me sick, so very little went in. I drank water, but that was all. Now I know it's strange, but vomiting up any food they forced me to eat made me happy.

Malik didn't let up on my abusers either. I suppose he enjoyed the money side of it, as well as watching others have sex with me. Perhaps most of all, he enjoyed seeing my shame and despair – I think it gave him a feeling of power.

One morning, I was brought down in my special outfit and scarf, as usual when men came. This time it was two old men. They were about the same age, grey-haired and wrinkled. I wondered if they were brothers – they seemed to know each other well. I assumed they would follow the familiar pattern of taking turns with me, each watching the other, often with Malik there too, so I was caught by surprise.

Both smelt of an acrid mixture of garlic, curry, stale cigarette smoke and body odour. And they both attacked me at the same time: one sort of sitting across my face, his penis in my mouth, making me give him oral sex, at the same time as the other was beginning to rape me, pushing and thrusting inside me, whacking and scratching me with his filthy jagged nails to make me respond.

They talked to each other, with a running commentary and grunts, and they held hands or squeezed my breasts hard as things hotted up for them. I didn't know what they were saying because I couldn't concentrate on anything – I was just trying to cope with this double assault on my senses, trying to breathe and numb the pain of their forcefulness, as each goaded the other on. For them it seemed to be all part of the excitement, but for me it was devastating.

How I was able to cope, I don't know. And I wasn't allowed to be passive – they expected me to perform as well, so they constantly smacked me to be more responsive. The one with his penis in my mouth couldn't wait: he ejaculated in my mouth and down my throat. The one inside me took a lot longer. Pushing and thrusting, harder and harder, trying to come, he was making me terribly sore. He smacked my legs again, several times, and finally, he managed it and withdrew.

Without a word or a glance in my direction, they left the room. I was exhausted, sore and bruised, but worse still, I was disgusted with myself. Afterwards I could barely find the strength to climb back up the stairs, being pushed and shoved by Malik.

As ever, there was more to come.

* * *

It's strange how the men always seemed to arrive in pairs. A few weeks later, another two men from the first gathering also returned to have sex with me. They must have paid extra to take me out in their car several times and take turns to have sex with me on the back seat. As their car pulled away from outside the house the first time, they started to talk loudly in English, so they could be sure I would hear them, telling each other all the lewd details of what they wanted to do to me. Though I tried not to listen, I couldn't avoid it. I wanted to throw myself out of the moving car, but then I realised it was only a two-door model.

I can still remember my deep disappointment.

It was difficult and uncomfortable in the back seat, but they both raped me there, each watching the other, goading one another on, without a care for me. With every thrust my head hit the metal side of the car so my head throbbed and my insides were sore by the time the first one finished, and worse still after the second. But for me the most hurtful thing was that there was no modesty with all these men.

On one occasion, when one of them was fed up with the awkwardness of trying to rape me, squashed up in the car, he yanked me out through the front door with a firm grip on my arm. He pushed me across a field, until we came to a spiny bush at the far side. I'll never forget that bush – it was awful.

The man threw me down onto the hard ground beneath the bush and got on top of me, his full weight pinning me down, so that the sharp thorns that had fallen to the ground pierced my skin and dug into my back. Every time he pushed inside me, the thorns pierced further. I tried to tell him, yelling out with pain, but he didn't care.

He did what he had to do, then he got up, keeping his foot on my stomach to pin me down. But he needn't have bothered – I didn't have the strength to struggle. I remember he picked up a handful of soft green leaves to cleanse himself afterwards. He made me get up and pulled me by the arm, stumbling two or three times, back across the field to the car.

I remember thinking, on the way back to the house, I wanted to die: *Just kill me*, I thought. *Strangle me and leave me in a ditch. Kill me now. Put me in the boot of the car and let me suffocate. Freeze me … Just let me die.*

When I got back, Malik pushed me into the bathroom to have a 'bath'. What a luxury that might have been, to lie back gently in hot sudsy water and relax. But I wasn't allowed a proper bath. Instead I had to sit inside the bath with a bucket of hot water and a piece of fatty soap – no sponge or flannel of any kind – and no plug. In a moment when he was out of the room, I looked for a plug in the basin, but that didn't seem to have one either. Malik took the key out of the door, so that I couldn't lock it, and he took my clothes away, leaving me completely naked. He then came in at various moments and ogled me, washing myself – it made me shudder.

I sat there, naked in the bath, sobbing. I really thought I'd be better off dead than bear this sort of cruelty: I had no privacy at all, and nothing of my own. It struck me that if there had been any razor blades in this bathroom, I would have killed myself – bled to death. But I looked, and I couldn't find anything even to harm myself with. I couldn't stop crying and I couldn't get the spiny thorns out of my back for days, which increased the agony every time Malik raped me, which he did more ferociously whenever he'd watched me with other men, as if punishing me.

As always, he enjoyed hurting me and watching my reaction. One night he took hold of my arm, the one I had broken and was only recently healed, and pulled it up slowly behind my back, watching my tortured face as he twisted it again until he heard the snap. So it was another trip to A&E to have it set anew and a cast put on it. This time I didn't even try to respond to the doctor's questions, I just shook my head wearily. As ever, Malik made up some excuse for why it had been broken a second time. I didn't care any more.

Not a day went by without at least a couple of rapes, by Malik or one of the visiting men, or Eshrat – the most cruel and callous of all. In between, I still had occasional heavy bleeds of clotted blood, but I didn't want to tell anyone. Very occasionally, one of the other women would notice and tell Malik I needed to go to the hospital and he sometimes took me. Always it was a miscarriage and I had to have another D&C each time to stop the bleeding.

Throughout my captivity, and especially at this time, I suffered a lot from cystitis and had chronic thrush, for which I was prescribed pessaries when Malik took me to the GUM (sexual health) clinic. The thrush led to me developing pelvic inflammatory disease, which I will always have, and causes me a lot of pain.

This was the bleakest period of my life, with the various men coming and going, and having to comply with everything they wanted, as well as Malik's cruelties, and all the while still desperately longing for my stolen baby. And, with virtually no sustenance, I was getting weaker and weaker.

Once they realised how skeletal I had become, food became a daily battle, with Malik and Eshrat trying to force me to eat. But was it me they were trying to keep alive, or my cash-cow prospects? Malik certainly was raking in the money at the expense of my physical and mental health. All I had left was to wallow in my misery and grief. That was the worst and it never seemed to get any less raw. Where was my baby? I needed someone to love and to love me in return, but there was nothing except my cherished memories of Nana and my photo of Jamie. *Will I ever escape this purgatory? Will I ever see him again?* I wondered.

I found the shape of Nana on the rug and traced round it, which I hadn't done for a while. But I had thought of Nana a lot, almost every day. Now I needed to talk to her, as I used to do so often when I first arrived: I needed the reassurance that only she could give me, from beyond the grave.

'If you're there, Nana, stay with me, because I need you. Please come and hold my hand, like you used to do. I'm sure you know how to help me best.'

Talking with Nana had lost none of its power to ease and calm my troubled mind. I knew she was with me. It was as if she was in the room, keeping a watch over me that night, giving me a cuddle. I lay down and recited her prayers and I think I must have fallen asleep before the end.

CHAPTER 15

COLLAPSE

The rapes and abuses continued daily, ravaging my health and forming a frightening blur in my mind. Deeply depressed, I was almost certainly mentally ill – often catatonic when left on my own. I must have been in pain, but I barely noticed anything. They brought me a box of paracetamols, and I had the new box of extra-strength painkillers from the hospital, but I scarcely took any – I think I must have switched off.

Exactly when I realised I was pregnant I don't know, but I had a lot of sickness, which I put down to Malik's attempts to force-feed me, together with all the oral sex. But then the fluttery feelings began and just the tiniest swelling in my belly.

The family had been desperate for me to be pregnant again, ever since they took Purdil away from me, but there had been so many men, so much violent sex and so many beatings from both Malik and Eshrat that any conceptions ended in miscarriage. With all the damage they were doing, I didn't expect ever to conceive again.

I wasn't sure yet, so I wanted to keep it to myself. If true, I would keep it a secret for as long as possible, just as I did with Purdil. It would again be something of my own that nobody else could take control of, something only I could nurture and enjoy, for now at least, despite the terrible prospect that they

159

might want to sell this baby too. But I must try not to think about that.

Soon I realised I had a dilemma: if I kept it a secret, there was a real and daily danger that Malik or Eshrat would kick me in the stomach again. Could I protect my unborn child from that? If I told Malik, I knew he would be happy. It wouldn't stop him abusing and beating me, but perhaps he would confine his kicks and punches to other parts of my body if he knew. For some days I wrestled with this. The only 'people' I told were Nana, when I talked to her face on the carpet, or while trying to sleep, and Jamie, when I spoke to his photo, which I occasionally took out to hold ... when I dared.

Finally, one night when Malik was particularly aggressive, perhaps fuelled by drugs, I had to tell him. He was hell-bent on beating me black and blue for some reason or other – I can't remember what. He even had his proper shoes on so that his kicks would really hurt me. I curled myself up into a ball on the floor while he was kicking me, but he didn't like that, so he pulled me up by the hair and aimed a kick at my exposed tummy.

'*No!*' I screamed. 'I'm pregnant.'

He froze for a second before letting go of my hair, so that my whole body dropped back to the floor.

'Please don't kick my tummy,' I begged him.

I remember a slight smile curling his lips, but he said nothing to me, turned and walked out of the room, locking the door behind him. Utter relief! I was disappointed not to have the secret to myself any longer, but at least I'd saved the baby this time. Now Malik would probably be telling the whole family. Would it change anything?

I had my answer the next day, when Malik sent Surayya up to my room to bring me down. They had spread out lots of foods on the table in front of which Malik told me to sit.

'Now that you are pregnant,' he said, 'you must eat for the baby.'

All the women nodded their agreement, while Eshrat just looked on with an expressionless face.

'Yes,' I shrugged. 'I'll try.'

I picked up a samosa, filled with curried mince, which I had quite liked when I was first taken captive. I didn't feel like eating, but I knew I had to nourish this baby, so I would have to force myself now. Each little bite of samosa was difficult to chew and even harder to swallow. My body was unused to eating anything, so it was a chore. I felt every inch of its descent to my stomach and the churning inside me but somehow I managed to keep it down. I was proud of myself. After the samosa, I sucked the juice of an orange and drank the sweet 'tea' Muneeza put in front of me, returning her smile that no one else saw but me.

Over the next few days they brought me down for a few hours, just to sit with the family. I was apprehensive at first, but there were no more men – that was a huge relief. All the family watched me as if I were some sort of exhibit, especially when I picked up something to eat.

One day, I was very achy across my tummy and my lower back, which turned into an increasing pain. I told Bushra and she asked Muneeza to give me a massage. As I lay there on one of the sofas, she rubbed my tummy gently with some sort of oil that smelt of eucalyptus. Then I turned over and she rubbed my back too. It was quite soothing, but not for long: very quickly the pain became severe and I was writhing in agony.

'Please help me,' I pleaded with Bushra, whom I thought most likely to do something. 'I'm in terrible pain, I need help.'

Within seconds I was doubled up and trembling uncontrollably. I was in so much pain that I thought I would wet myself, so I struggled to the bathroom and sat on the toilet, with Bushra in the doorway to watch over me. As so often before, I haemorrhaged in the toilet and on the bathroom floor. My pale clothes were drenched red with my blood.

That was the last I remember.

On arrival at the hospital, they told me later, I was taken immediately up to Intensive Care. Only two of the family were allowed in, so Malik and Bushra came to stand at my side, while the doctor put up a blood transfusion for me. The rest of them peered through the window in the door. I was still unconscious at that point, so I only found out what was the matter with me afterwards.

They wanted to do an immediate operation and Malik told them he was my next of kin. He signed the agreement.

* * *

When I regained consciousness the next day, I was shocked to find myself in a hospital bed, a tube of blood going into one arm and a tube of transparent liquid going into the other. All around me were machines beeping and something like a television screen that had numbers and a graph on it – I couldn't make that out at all. I was scared stiff.

'What happened?' I asked, woozily.

'You collapsed at home and were brought in here. You've had an ectopic pregnancy,' answered the duty doctor, who was checking my chart. 'You've lost a great deal of blood, so we're giving you a transfusion. You've had nearly six pints now. And your fallopian tube ruptured, so you have had to have major surgery to get all that sorted out. Fortunately, the operation was successful. However, you will take some time to recover fully after losing so much blood and the shock to your body, and of course recuperation after the operation.'

'We can look after her at home,' interrupted Malik.

'No, I'm afraid she will need full nursing care for several weeks to ensure she is fully recovered,' the medic insisted. He had a kind face and was trying to break the news gently to me. 'You nearly died,' he added. 'You seemed so weak already and we weren't sure you would survive the operation.'

'Thank you for saving me,' I said in a wobbly voice.

Malik scowled and stepped forward to grip my arm, telling me in his own direct way that I was not to say another word.

'But sadly ...' continued the doctor, and I dreaded what he was going to say next. I had no idea what an ectopic pregnancy was and wanted to ask, but realised I couldn't. 'I'm afraid the baby had already died. He didn't have a chance, I'm afraid.'

I nodded heavily and mouthed a silent 'thank you'. So it was a boy. I hadn't seen him – hadn't even had a scan – but I immediately felt flooded with grief.

* * *

A couple of days later, when a nurse took my temperature in the middle of the night, I caught sight of my chart and was horrified to discover the name 'Malik Aziz' written in as my 'husband'.

Could that possibly be? I wondered to myself. *Surely not, I would remember. Wouldn't I have had to sign something to get married?*

I wanted to protest, but Bushra and Surayya were both in the room, guarding me – I was never allowed to be left alone, always at least one family member was awake in my room with me, so I could never get to speak to the staff or anyone else.

The next day, another doctor with a friendly smile came to see me. I recognised him from when I'd had Purdil in the maternity unit.

'I'm Doctor Stockwell,' he said. 'Do you remember me?'

I nodded, Malik's hand in place. 'Yes, when I had my baby,' I said with a weak smile. Malik's grip tightened and his face darkened with anger.

'It was a little boy, wasn't it?'

I nodded.

'How is he doing?' the doctor asked.

'He's fine,' answered Malik, while I kept my mouth firmly shut.

I noticed the doctor looking at Malik's grip, reddening my arm. Then he gave me a glance that I thought looked as if he understood but I wasn't sure and I didn't have the courage to dare say anything more.

'Why didn't you come to see me about your pain?' he asked. 'You could have come for an emergency appointment.'

I desperately wanted to tell him I couldn't, that I wasn't allowed out, that I was a prisoner with no rights at all, but I was too weak. I could only let things take their course, whatever that might be.

'Anna is always busy helping us out at home,' said Malik. His mother and sisters nodded their agreement. 'And she didn't tell us she was in pain. We didn't know there was anything wrong with her.' Nods all round.

The doctor bit his bottom lip in silence for a moment. 'I see,' he said a few seconds later. He glanced at me again. 'Well, it was touch and go, but you were very lucky this time, young lady,' he said in his soothing voice. 'Make sure you say if you ever feel poorly or in pain again.'

I nodded.

* * *

It was four days now that I had been under observation in the hospital, where they fed me intravenously and monitored my blood and made sure my operation wound was starting to heal. They wanted to keep me in much longer, but Malik insisted on taking me home as soon as I no longer needed tubes in my arms.

'Well, it is your risk, of course,' said Doctor Stockwell, looking straight at Malik. 'We would far prefer to monitor her closely, at least until her wound has fully healed …'

'No,' interrupted Malik firmly. 'She wants to come home.' He gave me a look. 'Don't you, Anna?'

I hesitated as long as I dared, then whispered, 'Yes.'

'Well, it is your choice,' the doctor said, looking straight at me. 'But if you are determined to go home with your family, then they must take very good care of you.' He turned to Malik. 'No going upstairs, no housework or lifting – she will need complete rest. She will need to have a bed downstairs, near a toilet and bathroom and where someone can keep a close eye on her. Can you do that?'

'Yes, of course,' he nodded. 'My sisters and my mother are at home all day. They will take great care of her.'

'And you must make sure she continues to eat.'

'Yes, of course.'

'And I will arrange for your GP and the district nurse to make regular visits to check on her progress and change the dressings.'

'That will be fine,' agreed Malik.

* * *

I was bundled away in the back of Malik's car, weak and vulnerable. The family did indeed put a bed up in the living room, which would be my bed when the district nurse or the family doctor came. But right from the start, Malik slept on that bed while I had to sleep on one of the hard settees.

I had just had a major operation, with six clips holding together my wound, not yet fully healed; I had lost six pints of blood and was grieving for my dead baby, but they put me to work straightaway – Malik made sure of that. I helped a bit in the kitchen the first day, but I was too weary to carry on – I thought I was going to pass out.

'I'm too tired to work,' I told him that evening.

'Get to f***ing bed then!' he snarled at me.

The next morning I was hobbling around in pain, but I still had to sweep the floors.

'I'm ill, I feel really ill,' I told Bushra. But Malik overheard me and came across to give me a backhander. I fell to the floor and he walked away.

Bushra and Muneeza helped me up and took me over to the settee, where I had slept. But Malik couldn't leave me alone, it seemed. He made me lie flat on my back, pulled up my clothes and took down my pants, then ripped off the dressing.

'What did you do that for?' I asked shakily, terrified and in pain. 'The doctor said I had to keep the dressing on all the time, and the district nurses would come to change it.'

'Shut the f*** up!' he growled, picking up a razor. 'They don't know what they're talking about.' He took one look at my groin. 'You look disgusting with all that hair, you dirty white slut!' he snapped as he started to shave my stubble, there on the settee, with various family members passing by, able to see.

I was horrified he was doing this to me. Not just that it was in front of everyone, but he was going dangerously near my wound. What if he nicked it, or disturbed any of the clips? And now that it was open to the air, and the razor wasn't sterilised, I worried it might get infected. But he carried on and finished the job, then left me to rearrange my clothes as he went off to join his brothers for a smoke of the clay pot in Eshrat's house.

At least that meant I could have a rest for a while.

I lay down and must have fallen into a fitful sleep full of mixed-up nightmares that haunted me again when I woke up later in the afternoon. I suppose that was because of the strong drugs the hospital had given me.

'Get up and help make us dinner,' ordered Malik, pulling the cover off me and kicking my leg to get me up.

For the next two hours, I had to chop up meat and vegetables, roll chapattis, wash up pots and serve curried lamb to the men, carrying dishes that I knew were too heavy for me – I was very anxious about my wound.

That night, I slept again on the hard sofa. I couldn't get comfortable for ages, while Malik snored happily across the room on the comfortable bed that was supposed to be for me.

The next day the district nurse was due to come. I wondered when I woke up what to tell her about the missing dressing.

Malik made me get up again, but as I stood up I had the urge to put my hand to my tummy. I was alarmed to feel a nasty bulge in the middle of my wound.

I said I needed to go to the toilet and Surayya came in with me. When I lifted my clothes to check the clips on my wound, I nearly fainted when I saw the blood and a pale liquid seeping out from where it bulged, stretching my skin against the clips. It looked as if the whole wound would burst open. Surayya saw it too.

'Help me!' I wailed, leaning against the wall.

She helped me to sit on the toilet seat, my hand on the basin to steady me, before running off to tell Malik.

Surayya and Bushra helped me to the car and Malik drove me straight to the hospital, with the family in the back.

'It's a haematoma,' said the young doctor in A&E. 'The best thing for that would be another operation, to make sure we can clean it all up properly.'

'No,' said Malik straightaway, 'no operation. She doesn't want an operation, do you?' He looked pointedly at me.

I couldn't say I agreed, so I just shook my head very slightly and hoped that would do.

'Can't you just sort it out and let her come home again?' he asked.

'Well …' the young doctor hesitated. 'Let me just go and ask my senior. I'll be right back in a couple of minutes.'

Malik paced the room as I lay on the trolley bed, with Bushra, Surayya and Farhat, the mother, standing round me.

The young doctor came back. 'Right, I've spoken with the registrar and he says we can treat it without another operation, provided it cleans up well, but I cannot guarantee that until we've done it.'

'What will you have to do?' asked Malik. 'Will it take long?'

'We will give Anna a local anaesthetic, undo a couple of the clips so that we can take away as much of the haematoma as we can reach, hopefully all of it, insert a tube to drain the rest and replace the clips and, if it's all OK, we'll put on a new dressing. But she will have to stay in until it's healed this time,' he warned. 'We can't risk it getting infected or opening up again.'

'But we can look after her,' protested Malik.

'It's this way, or the full operation, and she would have to stay in for even more nights after that.'

'All right,' he agreed, reluctantly. 'We'll take turns to stay here with her.'

'Oh, you don't need to do that,' said the doctor.

'We are a family,' insisted Malik, 'we cannot leave her alone.'

I wasn't fully with it as I lay there – I suppose that's why the doctor had spoken to Malik and hadn't even tried to talk to me. But I did register that statement: it's exactly what he meant, he couldn't leave me alone, but it meant something different to him than it did to other people, so the doctor didn't appear to notice.

* * *

As soon as they got me home a few days later, they made me go upstairs, which I found difficult. Every step was a huge effort and I tried to hold my stomach, as if that would stop it pulling apart, nervous they would at least leave me alone to rest, once I was there.

It would have been all right if I could have stayed there, but when it was time for the district nurse to come the next day, they let me out of the room and I had to inch my way downstairs again to lie on the bed in the living room, pretending I had been there all the time. I desperately hoped the clips would hold this time. Fortunately they did that first day, and I'd had a lot of time to rest in between, as Malik stayed away from me to begin with.

During my time in the room, that first full day, I couldn't stop thinking of the baby who had died. I craved for a baby to hold, but he was gone – died inside me. *What would he have looked like? Whose baby was he? What did they do with his body? Was he buried? Was there a funeral, or was he just an embryo, too small for that?*

I felt very alone again, back in the room, after being cared for by cheerful, friendly nurses in the hospital. In my sadness, my thoughts turned to Purdil. *Where was he now? How old was he?* I tried to work out his age. I knew he was born in May 1989, two years after I was kidnapped. Now it was winter and I had been captive for five and a half years, so he must be about three and a half. I imagined him running around, climbing, talking – Punjabi, I presumed. I remembered his thick black hair that had been shaved off on the day of his circumcision, the most awful day of my life, when my beautiful boy was taken from me by strangers as he screamed and wailed, his arms held out to me.

Did he know about me? Would I ever see him again?

CHAPTER 16

BABY MACHINE

The new project for this family seemed to be to make me pregnant again, as quickly as possible. They had taunted me in the past about not becoming pregnant.

The first I knew of this campaign was the tablets Malik made me swallow every morning. He came up with a glass of water and the tablet, placed it on my tongue and made me drink the whole glass. Then, just to make sure, he looked in my mouth to check the tablet had gone.

'What is this?' I asked him the first time.

'What does it f***ing matter to you?'

'I don't want to take tablets I don't need.'

'Well, we want you to take this every day because you need it to help you make new babies. Don't you want another baby?' He gave me a rare smile – the same friendly smile that had lured me in the first place. I was pleased to see him looking friendly again, but I knew it wasn't genuine, he just wanted me to swallow the pills.

I tried to refuse, locking my jaws together and keeping my mouth closed, but he was too strong for me. When I did that, he forced my mouth open, poked his fingers in to place the tablet right at the back of my tongue, then tipped up my head and poured water into my throat so that I was forced to swallow. That was a really nasty experience – like drowning, I suppose. I didn't refuse again.

One day, when Malik was out and couldn't get back home, he asked Bushra to give me the tablet. She came up with the glass of water, just the same. But she brought with her the whole packet of tablets. She put the packet down on the chest of drawers, slid out a foil strip and popped through a tablet. While she was doing this, I sneaked a look at the packet: it said 'Clomid'.

'What is Clomid?' I asked Bushra, when she handed me the tablet.

'It's to help you have another baby,' she explained in Punjabi. 'Don't I have a choice?' I asked.

She hesitated for a moment. 'No, women do not have choices.'

Did she really mean what she said? I looked her in the eye and she was unwavering in her gaze, so I think she really did believe that was right. I didn't want to get her in trouble, so I took it.

I was now seen as having a use there, as long as I became their baby machine. But what would that do for me? I realised the obvious: when they had known I was pregnant before, they had all been nicer to me, encouraging me to eat nourishing foods, giving me lighter jobs to do when I was downstairs, even helping me when I fell or was injured and in pain. Even more importantly, Malik was less cruel in his assaults and did me less damage when I'd been pregnant. I might even make him happier with me.

If I had to remain there, with no hope of anyone finding and setting me free, then I might as well be pregnant and make life easier for myself. The thought of more miscarriages or having my babies taken away was devastating, but perhaps the next pregnancy would be as easy as Purdil's was and there was always the possibility they might let me keep at least one child.

I took the tablets, one a day, for several weeks, which ran into many months. Nothing seemed to be happening, so, one day, Malik made me get dressed in my Pakistani clothes.

'Why?' I asked, dreading the answer.

Not those awful men again, I thought. *Please, God, save me from that.*

'I'm fed up with waiting for you to get pregnant, I'm taking you to the doctor's.'

He took me out to the car, along with Bushra and Surayya on each side of me in the back seat, and in the front sat Malik's brother Sayed, who was visiting that day. We all piled into the doctor's and logged in at the desk, then sat in the waiting room, with them all surrounding me, just in case I got it into my head to speak to someone, or to try to escape, I suppose.

My name was called and everyone got up and walked towards the door to the doctors' corridor.

'No, only two people maximum,' said the receptionist, with authority.

We all stopped and Malik told the others to wait while he took me into the surgery.

'What can I do for you today?' asked the doctor.

'We would very much like another child,' said Malik, 'but Anna has had trouble with this.'

'I see you have had one child already. How old is he now?'

I didn't dare speak.

'Go on,' said Malik, 'tell the doctor how old Purdil is.' He glared at me, for once needing me to answer the question.

'He's nearly five now,' I guessed.

'We haven't seen him here, have we?'

'No,' I said, looking at Malik.

'He's a fine, healthy boy,' he insisted.

The doctor looked again at my notes. 'I see here that you've also had some miscarriages and an ectopic pregnancy. I expect they explained to you at the hospital that the rupture of your fallopian tube, Anna, makes it more difficult for you to conceive another child.'

I shook my head in surprise – I didn't know that, no one had told me. But maybe they told Malik. Maybe that's why he was making me take the Clomid tablets.

'Are you sure?' asked Malik. 'We would like to have a big family.'

'Well, there is a procedure we can do to investigate whether there are any problems that prevent conception,' explained the doctor. 'It's called a laparoscopy.'

'Is it an operation?' asked Malik. 'Would she have to stay in the hospital? We don't really want her to do that.'

'It's what is sometimes called keyhole surgery. It's when a very thin fibre-optic camera is inserted through a small opening in the abdomen, usually in the navel, to look at internal organs and sometimes inside them. For example, we can check to see if your good fallopian tube is blocked and, if necessary, we can clear it. It can usually be done as a day surgery. We would have to monitor that you recover well from the general anaesthetic before letting you go home, but it's usually the same day.

'Shall I refer you for that?' the doctor asked me.

'Yes, please,' answered Malik.

Once I knew what he wanted, I could nod to confirm it. So that was arranged.

* * *

I came home from the laparoscopy with a few stitches just below my tummy button, but nothing major. When I went to bed that night I was fine and for once Malik left me alone to sleep. As I lay there, I remembered the doctor's words before I was allowed to leave.

'Your good fallopian tube is now all clear and we scraped out some debris from miscarriages, so you should have every chance in the future of having more children.'

Malik had smiled at me.

I felt happy with the verdict.

I might be able to get out of the house one day, I thought, *if somebody comes to rescue me. And I might want to have children of my own that I can keep forever.*

The anaesthetic must have still been in my system because I went straight to sleep and didn't wake up until mid-morning, when Muneeza opened the door to empty the barrel. While she was cleaning it out, I got dressed. Then she brought it back.

'Come down,' she said to me in Punjabi. 'Malik says to sit and rest in the living room.'

I followed her downstairs, slightly gingerly in case my stitches pulled, but they felt fine – it was my back that felt strange.

Malik gave me my tablet to swallow and I sat on the settee he pointed at, looking out at the washing in the back garden, while he sat on another settee, reading the Punjabi newspaper. The sun was shining and it was a lovely day. How I wished I could go and sit in the warmth of the sun, instead of inside in this stuffy room, but I knew it was no use asking. I sat and watched the birds, flying free, from one side of the garden to the other. If only I could be like them.

As I sat there, my back suddenly started twitching. It was only occasionally at first, which felt very odd. Perhaps it was a muscle or something, I thought, but then it became more regular, and faster too. I wondered whether it showed, so I said I wanted to go to the bathroom, which was downstairs, and Malik nodded.

There was a full-length mirror so I lifted up my clothing and twisted round to look. I could see some twitching, but it was what else I noticed that shocked me. What had happened to my feet? They didn't look right, turning in like that. My hands started to go out at a strange angle. What was going on? I don't know whether it was the shock of seeing, or part of whatever was causing it, but suddenly I felt hot and cold by turns, and I started having difficulty breathing.

Was this something to do with the laparoscopy? I tried to walk back to the settee, but by now I was twitching all over and gasping for air. Some of Surayya's and Bushra's children came through the living room to go into Eshrat's house. They stopped when they saw me, pointing at me and giggling. Malik put down his newspaper and told them off. They ran away, pretending to twitch and gasp for breath.

'Stop your stupid play-acting, you white whore!' shouted Malik. Then he called the other adults to come into the living room. '*Look at that f***king bitch, being stupid and pretending to be ill,*' he sneered, with a laugh.

Everyone laughed with him, but I noticed that it was mainly nervous laughter, as if they thought there might be something really wrong with me.

'Get up off that settee and go do some work!' he shouted. Then he came over and pulled me up by my arm, ignoring the weird angles of my hands, slapped me across the face and marched me, desperately trying to breathe, into the kitchen. 'Make me some lunch,' he ordered.

'But I can't breathe,' I protested, haltingly. '*Please* ... the doctor ... hospital ...' By now I was wheezing loudly as my lungs and throat burned with the effort of trying to keep breathing. I felt I was suffocating and dropped to the floor, still conscious and desperately trying to find a position that would help me breathe. That's how I ended up splayed on all fours, which gave my lungs more space, I suppose. But now I was fighting for air.

Malik's voice droned on in the background, shouting and jeering at me, as if I was some kind of stage show, but I was concentrating so hard on reaching for my next breath that I didn't hear the words, only the laughter. However, I did feel the heavy boot on his foot, kicking me right between the legs, and the pain that seared through my body.

'Get up, you stupid bitch!' he yelled, trying to pull me up by my hair, but someone must have stopped him and he dropped me flat on the floor. Winded and unable to catch a breath, I tried to lever myself back on all fours again.

'*Help!* ... Can't ... breathe ...' I screamed in terror.

Suddenly everything changed. Malik lifted me up gently and took me straight out to his car. Surayya and Bushra came too and I had to take up the all-fours position again in the back until I blacked out.

Apparently, when we got into A&E, they dealt with me straightaway and put me on a machine with an oxygen mask, while they ran some tests. My heart was racing so fast that they suspected I was having a heart attack. And I was in anaphylactic shock.

I was vaguely listening to all this in the background, surprised about it being a heart attack – I thought only old people had those. But I'd never heard of anaphylactic shock. I wanted to ask what it was, and what might have caused it, but the duty doctor started to explain to Malik and I listened in, over the noise of the machine next to me, and the interruption of a nurse injecting me in the hand with adrenalin.

'It could be a heart attack, and we are treating her for that,' he explained. 'But the racing heart could also be a symptom of anaphylactic shock. It could even be both. Does Anna have any allergies you know of?'

'No, I don't think so,' said Malik.

'Did she have any insect stings or bites in the last 24 hours?'

Malik looked at me, as if giving me permission to answer that. But I just shook my head – I didn't want to remove the oxygen mask.

'And has she eaten any nuts or anything usual?'

They both looked at me.

Again, I shook my head.

'So, the other most likely cause then is allergy to a medication. It's quite unusual with Metoclopramide, which I see from her notes Anna was given during a minor operation yesterday. The symptoms Anna has had today could be a rare set of side effects of this drug, especially if it is reacting to another drug that she is taking. Is there anything else?'

Always the master liar Malik hesitated, then said, 'No, not as far as I know.'

'Anna?' the doctor turned to me.

Malik fixed his stare on me. I knew I should have said something about the Clomid, and I wanted to, but I was still gasping for every breath so it was difficult to talk and I didn't feel up to braving Malik's anger. I shook my head.

'Well,' the doctor shrugged. 'It's a mystery for now.'

* * *

I had to stay in hospital for a couple of days to make sure my breathing and heart rate were both back to normal, and all that time the tribe were guarding me round my bed. The twitching and my odd feet and hand movements had stopped by then too.

From then on, they didn't give me any more Clomid and soon I was back to normal. But it wasn't the kind of normality I craved.

Alone and back in the room again, I went to check on Jamie's photo under the loose floorboard. Yes, it was still there. If only I could have gone to meet him and be his girlfriend, I might have had a very different life.

CHAPTER 17

TORTURE

On the morning after I came back from hospital, I was collected from the room by Muneeza with a sympathetic smile. She took me downstairs where, for the first time, I really did get to lie on the bed that had been put up for me. As I lay there resting, I listened to the children's happy voices as they played outside in the garden. After a while they became quite excited about something. I couldn't see them from where the bed was, but I heard them skipping across the paving stones and in through the door.

'Look at all the worms we found,' said the eldest boy, while they dangled them, wriggling.

But I shuddered and closed my eyes. I couldn't stand worms, or anything slimy that wriggled – I had a phobia. As I started to tremble, my throat went dry, my heart raced and I panicked. I had to suppress the urge to scream with fear. I kept my eyes closed and put my hands over my ears so I wouldn't hear them talking about the worms. But they shrieked with excitement right next to my bed. What were they doing? I had to take a quick peek to make sure I was safe, but I wished I hadn't; the children had about 15 worms, all squirming on the floor, close to my bed.

'Worm races!' squealed a little girl, dancing about with excitement. 'Do you want some worms too?' she asked, plonking two of the longest, fattest, slimiest ones right on the cover of my bed.

'Take them away!' I screamed.

The children looked surprised, and a bit afraid of me, but I just had to get away. For me it was a living nightmare. I leapt off the bed, nearly squishing one of the worms with my foot, and ran to the far side of the room.

Bushra came in from the kitchen. 'What's all the fuss about?' she asked.

'Worms!' I cried, hiding behind a settee. 'I need to get away, take me upstairs,' I pleaded. 'My heart!'

I felt as if I was going to have another heart attack.

'What's that stupid bitch doing now?' asked Malik with a scornful tone as he came in.

By this time other members of his family had also arrived to watch the 'fun'. They pointed and laughed at me, as I crouched down, averting my gaze. The children began to taunt me with the wriggling creatures, dangling them over my head. They didn't understand my morbid fear. Neither did the adults, who were standing round, jeering and ridiculing me.

I screamed and screamed. 'Take them away, I can't stand them, I'm *ill*! *Please* take them away!'

'Shall I take her upstairs?' Bushra asked Malik.

'Yes, take the f***ing c*** and lock her in upstairs, if that's what she wants. Get the bitch out of the way, it will give us some peace and quiet.'

Even after the door was locked and I was safe, I was still in a terrible state, trembling with fear. I knew it was foolish to be afraid of worms, but to me they were just like snakes and I often used to have nightmares about them when I was little. Once I woke Nana up with my screaming, so she held me close and stroked my hair, singing me a lullaby until I fell asleep. If only Nana was here now; she was the only one who could calm me.

Gradually my panic subsided and my heartbeat slowed to normal again. I felt so weary after all that, and from the after-effects of the previous day's anaesthetic, that I fell asleep, lying on the rug, next to the part of the pattern where I could see Nana's face.

* * *

I thought the incident with the worms would probably be the last time they would let me out of the room, but Muneeza came up again the next morning and beckoned me to follow her downstairs.

I dreaded what they wanted me for.

As if knowing what I might be thinking, she supplied me with the answer. 'You can watch the film,' she said in Punjabi.

When I sat down in the living room, a film was just starting and most of the little ones were sitting on the floor to watch it. Bushra and Surayya were sitting on the settees with the mother, Farhat. Muneeza went back to her huge pile of ironing, but was able to watch too, while she ironed, though when she slackened her pace at one point, Farhat shouted at her.

'You stupid bitch, get on with your work,' she spat, 'or I'll tell Eshrat to punish you.'

Muneeza looked down and said nothing as she picked up the next thing in the pile. I wished I had the strength to help her, but they wouldn't have let me.

I didn't know why they asked me to come and watch this film with the children but I didn't mind. It was all in Punjabi, of course, but I could understand a lot of the language now, so I was able to follow the story, which was about animals in a forest – I remember an elephant and a nasty crocodile.

Just before the end of the film, Malik came and took hold of my arm. 'Come on, white trash,' he said, 'time to go upstairs again. Come and see what we've put in your room to entertain you.'

He looked strangely excited.

'Can't I see the end of the film first?'

'No, it's only a kids' film,' he sneered and pulled me to the bottom of the stairs, then pushed me up faster than I felt confident to go, trying to keep my stitches intact.

When we reached the room, he stood in the doorway, waiting to see my reaction. At first I didn't notice anything, I just went and sat on the bed.

'Can't you see?' he asked, his face like a little boy with an ice cream.

He stepped forward and indicated the space behind the door, then looked back at me with his curled-up lips, waiting for my reaction. I had to move further along to see and that's when I saw something that looked like a large fish tank on a stand, with a cover and a lamp lighting it up inside. I wasn't close enough to tell if it had anything in it yet, other than some greenery, a small log and a couple of rocks on the sand.

'What is it?' I asked. 'It looks like a fish tank.'

Fish were never my favourite creatures, but at least they would be calming to watch, I thought, swimming in and out of the weeds.

'You got it half-right,' said Malik with a wicked smile. 'It's a tank, but it's not for fish.'

'What is it for then?' I asked innocently.

'What is your favourite animal?' said Malik, leading me on.

'Dogs,' I said. 'But you can't keep a dog in a tank.'

'That's right,' he laughed. 'It's something much better than that, something I know you're going to love. We can take it out sometimes and let it move around the room,' he added.

By now, I knew this was not going to be good and I had a feeling of dread.

Surely even he couldn't be that cruel?

'Eshrat helped me bring this tank up and install it with the infrared lamp to make it hotter for our friend, who likes the heat. There's a water bottle too, look. Have you guessed it yet?'

'No,' I said, shaking my head, trembling with fear.

'Come and look,' he beckoned, but I refused to budge.

'You *will* come and look,' he insisted, trying to seem nice, but I knew it was false.

I just sat there, shaking my head and rooted to the spot. I didn't dare move. I couldn't bear to look.

Malik came and grabbed me by the hair and dragged me closer to the tank.

'*No!*' I shrieked, my eyes shut tight.

'Open your f***ing eyes!' he yelled, backhanding my head and my face before punching my shoulder. 'Look, it's a beautiful, long, fat snake! A cobra.'

I screamed and screamed.

'See how it slithers around its tank,' he added, enjoying my terror.

He pushed me to the floor and kicked me several times, but somehow I managed to protect my tummy wound and keep the stitches in place.

'Well, you can look at him any time you want,' he sneered, as I lay in a bruised and battered heap. 'He's not leaving this room, so you'd better get used to him.'

He stormed out and slammed the door, locking it behind him.

For a long time I lay still, sobbing and trembling, racked with horror and fear. I don't know how long it was before I gathered myself and crawled to my corner, my safe haven. Not so safe now, as there was nowhere in this room where it was possible not to see the tank, except if I turned to face the corner, with my back to the room. So that's what I did, rocking to and fro, to and fro, desperately hoping it wasn't real.

* * *

He left me alone that evening, perhaps because of my stitches. I finally crawled across to bed without looking at the tank. It was dark now, apart from the lamp. Perhaps I could turn that off somehow, but it seemed to be plugged in just below the tank. I couldn't go near it. Would the lamp be on to taunt me all night? I felt in a permanent state of panic. How long could my system take this strain? I suddenly realised I had to go to the toilet, but the ghee barrel was just next to the tank. Had he moved it there on purpose?

Maybe I could steel myself. I closed my eyes and slid off the bed onto the floor, but there I froze, unable to move. Before I knew it, I had wet myself on the rug. My body ached all over with bruises and almost certainly some injuries, but I could numb myself to those. It was the snake that took over my mind and threatened my sanity.

I fell asleep there, on the rug. But I kept waking up, disturbed by horrific nightmares of snakes writhing all over me, fangs lashing out at my face, my eyes, their strong bodies constricting my neck …

Early the next morning, Malik reappeared to torment me anew. By now I was a quivering wreck, still lying on the carpet, unable to look up in case I caught a glimpse of the poisonous creature.

Malik stood by the tank. 'Do you like your new room-mate?' he gloated.

I shuddered and curled up in a ball, with my tummy to the floor and my arms and hands protecting my head, bracing myself for the assault that would surely come. But instead of kicking me, he pulled me up by the hair and tugged me over towards the tank. I tried to dig my heels in, but it was no good. He pushed my face against the glass front.

'Now, look!' he demanded.

Still I could not open my eyes. I was rigid with terror, so close to the creature of my nightmares. Desperate to lose consciousness, to die, but to no avail, I had to endure this fresh torture. My heart was on fire and I was shaking uncontrollably.

I heard Malik lift the lid.

'*No!*' I screamed.

'Shall I take him out so you can feel him?'

I couldn't say or do anything, I just heard myself mumbling high-pitched gibberish.

'If you don't look at him, I will take him out,' he threatened.

I had no choice. I opened my eyes and jerked back as I glimpsed the scaly green and yellow skin and the slow sliding movement before jamming my eyes shut again.

* * *

That morning's rape was a complete blur. I knew it had been violent because of the blood I saw afterwards on the bed, but I remembered nothing of it. My one abiding memory was of terror: I knew I would never get the horrific image of the snake out of my head.

Over the next few days, Malik used the threat of the cobra to make me do all sorts of disgusting things. Eshrat came up too and enjoyed tormenting me as much as his brother did. He even started to get the snake out of the tank, but I must have passed out – I don't remember what happened after that. But most often it was Malik: 'If you ever move from that bed, I will let the snake out,' he threatened. I knew I couldn't get off the bed all day, until he came back. I just sat there, rocking. It was a miserable, fear-filled existence.

'Poor snake, all cramped up in the tank,' he said one day. 'I think I'll let him out tonight, so that he can explore his surroundings and keep you company. Don't you think that's a good idea?'

I crouched on the floor, backing away and whimpering.

'No, no, no!' I moaned. 'Anything ... I'll do *anything* ...'

'That's better,' he smirked.

The depravity continued.

* * *

After a particularly violent beating, I had a heavy bleed following another early miscarriage. They took me back to the hospital for yet another D&C, but this time I wasn't allowed to stay in for even one night. Apparently the doctors were asking too many questions about my bruises and injuries. They did an X-ray and found I had a couple of fractured vertebrae and a broken rib. Malik told them I had fallen down the stairs, which seemed to explain everything. But just in case of any further questions, the family smuggled me out of the hospital and brought me back, coming in and out of consciousness from the anaesthetic, back to the room, back to the snake in my torture chamber.

I'm sure I must have become mentally ill during this time – relentless fear threatened my sanity.

The days and weeks blurred into a long stream of abuses and torments, with the snake ever present, never more than a few feet away from me. Constantly petrified that he might escape, I screamed at every sound he made. I shuddered at all the scenarios in my imagination. I found it hard to sleep and when I did, I was swiftly woken in cold sweats by snake-filled nightmares.

My days and nights were spent sobbing. Now I refused all food, although they still tried to force-feed me. I wanted only to die – but how? This slow starvation wasn't quick enough. In my more lucid moments, I began to focus on how I might end it all.

CHAPTER 18

HEARING THE CRACKS

I had been in captivity for so long now – more than seven years, I thought. It seemed like a lifetime. It *was* a lifetime: the end of my childhood and the whole of my adult life. I had no idea what was going on in the outside world, nor did I care very much any more. My whole experience was within these walls. No one had come to find me, so I'd got used to the idea that I would never be found. I would probably never be free again.

I was always covered in lumps and bumps, swellings, cuts and bruises, so I didn't notice my slight tummy until I felt the flutterings again. Most of my miscarriages had happened due to violent rapes or beatings, before I had any suspicion I might be pregnant so this time was special for me – a secret of my own again, something only I knew about, a new baby growing inside me. This was a reason to smile to myself at last. If only it could be a girl this time, I hoped. Boys were more important than girls to Malik and his family. Maybe if I had a girl, they wouldn't get as much money for her, so they might let me keep her.

As before, I kept my secret for as long as I could. I even started eating again, just a little, so they didn't suspect. I tried not to think so much about the snake. They always took me downstairs before they fed it, and I had become a bit more used to the tank and the scuffling, slithering movements that tormented me, particularly during the nights. But my tummy was growing, so one night Malik noticed, having pinioned me down on the bed to rape me.

'Is that …?' he asked, pausing as he held himself above me.

'Yes, I think so,' I replied. 'Please don't hurt the baby.'

He curled his lips into a weird smile. 'OK, we can't lose this one, can we? I'll be gentle.'

I didn't know what he was thinking; I didn't want to know. He wasn't gentle that night, I don't think he knew how to be gentle – it was forced, as always, but at least it was straight-forward sex that time. It was a huge relief not to have to struggle and fight to breathe.

For the next few weeks I was allowed downstairs more often, with various foods put on the table in front of me. I couldn't eat much, but I did have the occasional buttered chapatti or curried mince samosa, which I liked, and sometimes I'd try a bit of fruit.

I thought and hoped that Malik would take away the tank and the snake, to let me rest more easily while I was pregnant – but no.

'I can't sleep and I can't rest with that snake in here,' I told him one night, shuddering at the word. 'Please can you take it out, at least while I'm pregnant?' I was on my knees, thinking that might sway him.

'No, he f***ing loves it in here with you! And I want the baby to like snakes too.'

So that was that: no chance of a break.

My bump continued to grow and the baby began to kick more strongly. I convinced myself this would be a girl, and I loved every kick she made. This was a strong baby, so I hoped she would be a survivor. I tried to banish all thoughts of her being taken from me, but I was increasingly apprehensive about whose daughter she would be – probably Malik's, but possibly Eshrat's. They were both evil, so I hoped she wouldn't inherit that. Perhaps she would be quiet and shy like me. Surely that would be all the more reason for Malik to let me keep her? I don't know why I thought that, but it gave me some much-needed comfort. I imagined holding her in my arms, rocking her to sleep, whispering to her about Nana and the things we used to do when I was a little girl.

Alone in my room, I talked to the baby about my childhood to take my mind off the snake.

'Nana was my great-grandma,' I began, 'but she was my mother as well. She always looked after me and I slept in her bed. We used to put our arms round each other when we were falling asleep. That's what I want to do with you when you're born. And I want to teach you things, like Nana taught me. She taught me to love, she taught me to walk and talk. She showed me how to cook, like how to mix batter. Her Yorkshire pudding was always yummy.'

I hugged my tummy and hummed a nursery rhyme to the baby inside me.

'Then, when I was a little older,' I continued, 'Nana tried her best to teach me to knit, but I couldn't get the hang of it.' At this I smiled. 'I kept dropping stitches.'

It really helped to tell my unborn baby my stories about Nana. Lately I hadn't thought about her much, since the snake first arrived – I couldn't think of anything else while I was so terrified of that creature, it still dominated my thoughts. But talking to my baby was a welcome relief, and thinking of Nana took me back to my only happy times: the first ten years, when I was loved.

* * *

One freezing cold day, I went into labour and they took me to the hospital to have my baby. I was right – it was a girl. The birth was straightforward this time, so we only had to stay 24 hours. As before, I held her for a few minutes, just after her birth. She was beautiful, in a different way to Purdil: she had short, soft, downy hair and a dainty face.

'Her name is Durnaz,' said Malik to the nurse as he took her from my arms and gave my baby to her. 'Take her away,' he added.

I remember the nurse's alarmed expression as she turned towards me.

'Wouldn't you like to hold her a bit longer?' she asked me. 'It will help you to bond with each other.'

'No,' cut in Malik, before I could respond, 'they can bond at home.'

The nurse glanced at me again. I felt desperate not to lose hold of my baby so soon, but Malik gripped my hand under the cover and twisted my fingers painfully. All I could do was shake my head and wave the baby away. I wondered whether that nurse realised what might be going on, but I don't think she told anybody.

The next time I saw my baby was the following morning, when we were ready to leave the hospital, and the same nurse pointedly put her in my arms. She had a little hat on and a woollen shawl round her to protect her from the cold as Malik drove us home, with our usual family guards. It was only when I pulled her hat off when we got inside that I saw she had lost all that beautiful soft hair. Someone had shaved her head after they had taken her away from me. I shed tears to see her poor little bare head.

'It shows that Durnaz is the servant of Allah,' Bushra explained. 'It is good.'

'Surayya, you take the baby,' commanded Malik, 'so that Yasmeen can have her rest upstairs.'

'No, please, I don't want any rest. I want to feed her myself.'

'White people's milk is dirty,' snarled Malik. 'Durnaz needs good, healthy milk in a baby's bottle. Surayya will look after her very well. Now you go and *rest*.' He put the stress on the last word, as he roughly pushed me away towards the stairs.

My body, heart and mind were all crying out for my baby. I turned to see Surayya holding *my* baby while I had to go upstairs, alone and bereft. Was it all going to happen again?

Two or three days later, I was dressed up to come down for some sort of ceremony. I couldn't wait to see my baby again and I hoped they would let me hold her. I would have to remember every moment, how she felt in my arms, her smell, the sounds she made ... everything.

There were a lot of people there, quite a lot of them from Yorkshire, it seemed.

'Why couldn't I look after Durnaz myself?' I asked Malik as he stood next to me.

'Because you were too ill to look after her.'

'But I wasn't ill …'

He made a sign, waggling his finger on one side of his forehead. 'You were not capable. Surayya looked after Durnaz for you.'

'But she's *my* baby.'

'You gave birth to her, yes, but now she needs a proper mother.' He shot me a nasty look to shut me up.

'Can I hold her one last time?'

'If you want, I'm feeling kind today, but not for long. Her new parents have come to collect her.' He pointed to a middle-aged couple across the room.

'But they are too old to have children,' I said, horrified.

'They can't have their own, that's why they want to give Durnaz a good home.'

'But I'm her mother, nobody could be a better mother to her than me. I'm the one who gave birth to her.'

'Shut your f***ing mouth!' he snarled in a whisper, 'or you won't get to hold her at all.'

The couple were signing some papers, and Malik signed them too. Finally, he beckoned me over and I had to sign with my real name, Anna Ruston. They were all in the Punjabi script, so I couldn't read them. If I didn't sign, I wouldn't be able to hold Durnaz and say my last goodbye. I couldn't let her go without a hug and a kiss, without that memory of her.

As everyone was talking and getting ready to go, I became increasingly anxious. I thought maybe Malik would forget, or go back on his word, which he often did. I stood as near to the door as I could. I watched Surayya giving Durnaz a top-up with the bottle, then she put her little hat on her bare head and wrapped her in the same shawl she had come home from the hospital in. She handed the baby to Malik. He turned and took two or three steps towards the new parents. I was desperate. Surely he wouldn't let her go without my having a last hold? But I feared he might. My whole body locked in a silent scream. Suddenly Malik stopped, slowly turned and brought baby Durnaz to me. He laid the newborn in my arms.

'Quick,' he said, 'say goodbye to your daughter.'

Refusing to be stressed by him, I gently stroked her rosy cheek and her cute little earlobe, sticking out from under the hat. I tried to take a mental photo of her, put my cheek to hers and breathed in her scent to keep locked inside me.

'Hurry,' urged Malik, with everyone looking on.

I gave little Durnaz a kiss on the tip of her nose and another on her forehead, rocked her gently in my arms and hummed 'Rock-a-bye-baby', the same nursery rhyme I had hummed to her when she was inside me.

Malik snatched her from me before the end and took her across to the couple, who smiled sweetly and thanked him, completely ignoring me. They were gone in minutes. Gone with my new baby girl, my daughter whose sweet baby scent I would never forget.

* * *

It had been six years between the births of my first and second babies, but within weeks I was pregnant again. Of course, I didn't know it for a while. In recent years I had occasionally had periods, but they were never regular and didn't start up again after Durnaz's birth, so I had no clue to begin with.

Malik's rapes and assaults now returned to full strength. But I didn't care about anything any more: I had no future and any other babies I might have would be taken away, I knew that now. The snake was still resident, occasionally used as a threat or blackmail, and for traumatising me night and day. Once again I stopped eating and spiralled into a deep depression. I had no energy, and all I wanted to do was sleep.

When Malik attacked me, I just gave in limply, like a rag doll. He used to be so furious with my refusal or inability to struggle that he smashed me against the walls, kicked me to a miserable pulp and went to extremes with his assaults, often leaving me unconscious because he'd gone too far with smothering me, or with his beatings.

But somehow, I can't imagine how, this little embryo managed to hold on inside me and started to grow. This time, as soon as I realised, I did tell Malik straightaway. I had no hope now of being able to keep the baby, but I had enough mothering instinct left to feel a strong need to protect my unborn child. Malik backed off and left me alone for several days. For quite a while I had assumed he probably had other women – hopefully not 15-year-olds, as I had been.

Grateful for the few days' respite, I used this time to talk myself into eating again, for the baby's sake. It only had me to keep it going, and I could feel it moving now, so when the family pushed food through the hole in the door, I tried to eat a little of it. Buttered chapattis were my preference, though I probably only ate one or two a day, rarely anything else.

After Malik had been absent from the room for about a week, I heard the telltale footsteps pounding up the stairs, and the key in the lock. The door swung open and in walked Eshrat. I could see he was in a temper, though I had no idea why. He pulled me to the hard floor, right in front of the snake tank, tore off my clothes and pulled down his. His whole weight landed on me so heavily that I had no breath left and my lungs burnt with the effort to breathe – almost impossible with his weight compressing them.

That day, Eshrat tortured me as he raped me, causing me such pain that I could not numb it out, no matter how hard I tried to detach my mind from my body. I could hear myself screaming, again and again.

'Shut the f*** up!' he yelled, thrusting himself ever harder, everywhere he could, while smothering me tightly. When he had finally had enough, he started beating me, with the chapatti rolling pin he had brought in with him.

'*Please*,' I begged him, trying my best to protect my tummy, 'please don't hurt the baby.'

But I don't think he even heard me and I curled up as best I could. He was in such a frenzy, he was making loud sounds with every wallop he landed on me. I heard the cracks of my bones as he struck blow after blow, then I must have lost consciousness.

I found out later that Malik discovered me in a heap, still out cold. He took one look, picked me up and carried me out to his car. The women came too, but not Eshrat – he had gone out.

At the hospital, they were shocked by the number of injuries – I don't know what excuse Malik gave this time, I was still only semi-conscious. X-rays revealed I had fractured ribs and they were also concerned about some damage to my back. A scan showed one of my kidneys, the one injured in a previous beating, was now shrunken and inactive. I didn't hear about anything else.

I couldn't feel the baby moving so they checked its heartbeat and it was still alive. That was a miracle.

As before, though the consultant demanded that I stay in much longer, the family smuggled me out of the hospital after only 48 hours. I was allowed to sleep on the bed in the living room for the first few days, though my ribs caused me a lot of pain and my back ached badly. It looked as if there was a broken bone in my foot too. All the other damage appeared dramatic, but luckily it was mainly superficial. My face went from black and blue to red, green and yellow for about two weeks, but eventually returned to normal.

Those few days in the living room without the snake were a huge respite for me. I slept properly for the first time in years. Finally, I did go back to the room. The snake was still there, and soon Malik started his campaign of rapes and beatings again, but not as often or as bad as they could be. He just didn't seem able to derive full satisfaction without drawing blood and hurting me.

On one such occasion, as I was lying down on the bed to recover and he lay down next to me to go to sleep, he turned towards me.

'It's just because I love you,' he said. 'I do love you.'

Both pleased and horrified, I was completely confused. I didn't know what to feel. My father used to say that after he had beaten me or when he let me out following a night in the coal-hole. Now Malik was saying the same thing. *Is that what love is?* I wondered. I know that Nana's love was different and she would never have hurt me, but I was a child then and she was a mother to me, so I knew that sort of love was different. Even though my own mother told me she hated me.

Between the ages of 10 and 15 I lived with my dad, who beat me badly and often. He used to beat my mother too. Did all men need to hurt the one they loved? Was it only love if the man hurt the woman? The more the man hurts the woman, does that mean he loves her more? That would mean there had to be pain for it to be true love. So, did my dad love me after all? I was shocked when he tried to get me to go to bed with him, but maybe that was it. Did Malik really love me too? There was still a little part of me that shouted 'No' inside my head, but the evidence seemed to point to pain meaning love.

But then I thought about Jamie. Where would he be now? Did I love him? Had he loved me? He had never hurt me, so presumably that meant he didn't love me. Could that be right? I'd lost him now anyway – he would be about 27, probably married with kids. He must have forgotten all about me, after so many years.

CHAPTER 19

INTENSIVE CARE

It was just 11 months since Durnaz's birth, when I knew it must be time for my third baby to be born. I had tried to eat a little for it, but I couldn't rustle up any excitement for this baby, knowing for sure now that it would be taken away, just as Purdil and Durnaz had been.

I had started to feel unwell and became horribly ill, with a high fever. I kept being sick everywhere, so suddenly that it was all around the room – it was disgusting. Even worse was the constant diarrhoea. I worried about the baby, was I making him ill too?

The stench was indescribable. Poor Muneeza was sent up to clean and disinfect everywhere and she reeled as the smell hit her on entering the room. They'd given her a mask and rubber gloves to make sure she didn't infect the whole family, and I tried to keep away from her as she worked. I did feel sorry for her.

Surayya brought up a blue plastic baby bath for me to be sick in, so I sat next to it.

Malik rang the hospital maternity unit and they said to bring me in straightaway. He didn't want me being sick or having diarrhoea in his car, so he called an ambulance. I was becoming delirious, so I don't remember the journey, or the first few hours at the hospital. When I came to, I had a drip in my arm and the family were all sat around me.

'Ah, Mrs Aziz ...' said a doctor, who had apparently been talking to Malik about me when I woke up.

'No,' I corrected him quickly.

'Oh, I *am* sorry! I thought this man was your husband ...' He tailed off in embarrassment.

'No, I'm Anna Ruston,' I said.

'Oh, I see.' He seemed flustered. 'Well, that's probably why we couldn't find your medical notes. Could you just spell that for me?' Then he left us for a few minutes.

Malik stepped over to my bed and put his hand on my arm, then gripped it tightly so I knew I should say nothing more. I felt very light-headed and woozy. For a moment I wondered if perhaps he'd married me while I was unconscious, but then I realised I would have had to sign the certificate and I hadn't, so hopefully not. I wouldn't have put it past him to forge my signature, though.

When the doctor came back, he started to tell me what had happened. 'As soon as your family brought you in,' he began, 'we put you on a saline drip, as you were very dehydrated, because of the sickness and diarrhoea. We also gave you some medication to reduce those nasty symptoms. We seem to have it under control now. But when we did some tests, they confirmed what we thought: you are seriously ill and it's a very good thing your family called an ambulance when they did. You have septicaemia. It's a serious condition in which the blood is infected and this affects your whole body. If you hadn't come into the hospital today, it could have been very dangerous and started affecting your internal organs.'

'The baby?' I dared to ask, with Malik frowning at me and gripping my arm more tightly.

'Well, the baby's heart is beating, although it is rather fast, and we are monitoring him carefully, but in view of your illness we will need to do an emergency Caesarean within the hour.' He had a kind but worried expression as he put a form down in front of me on the wheeled table. 'Please could you sign this permission form.'

I looked at Malik, unsure if he would let me. He nodded, so I signed. Of course, I realised, he wouldn't want any harm to come to the baby, or he might not be able to sell it.

They sent for an orderly, who wheeled me straight down the corridor at quite a swift pace, pushing my drip stand alongside. I remember going into an ante-room and having a mask put on, then nothing else for a while.

I woke up when I was shaken in the operating theatre, with Malik wearing a gown and a mask to one side of me, a big green sheet pinned up in front of me. As I widened my eyes and looked to my other side, the theatre nurse held up a tiny, pale and puny baby for me to see. He had a screwed-up face, smeared with blood, and he made a soft whimpering sound.

'It's a boy,' she said, before whisking him hurriedly away.

'He is very poorly,' explained another nurse. 'So my colleague is putting him straight into an incubator and wheeling him down to the Neonatal Intensive Care Unit.'

'What's the matter with him?' I asked, in trepidation.

'It was difficult to get him breathing and he needs immediate attention to try and stabilise him,' she said with a sympathetic expression. 'It looks like you have passed on your septicaemia to the baby, as we expected,' she added. 'He is underweight and in a very serious condition, so he needs special care.'

As they wheeled me out and into a private room, surrounded by all the family, Malik looked daggers at me. I thought he would have felt anxious for the baby, like me, so it might have been a point of unity, but no – I could almost feel him telling me it was my fault the child was ill.

A doctor came in and connected me up to a monitor and checked my drip.

'Would you like to go to the unit to see the baby?' he asked Malik.

He nodded, and followed a nurse with his mother, Surayya and Muneeza, while Bushra and Talat, the wife of Malik's brother Sayed, stayed with me. As always, they had to make sure I did not say anything or give any clues about my situation, or try to escape.

'Can I see the baby too?' I asked the doctor.

Bushra glared, but I took no notice: this was not about me, it was about the baby needing his mother, and me needing to see that he was all right. Both she and Talat were mothers of several children – I felt sure they would understand.

'When we have your heart rate and blood pressure down a bit, we will wheel you along and down in the lift, with your drip on a wheeled stand, to visit your baby.'

I nodded, relieved they would let me visit him.

By the time I got there, the baby's naming ceremony had already taken place.

I peered into the hi-tech glass incubator and was horrified to see so many tubes and wires attached to him, with patches on his chest. He looked so scrawny and pitiful, stretched out flat on his back on the white sheet. I was desperate to pick him up and give him a hug, but I realised I couldn't. My heart ached for him. I knew I wouldn't be allowed to keep him, but he had been inside me for all those months. He needed to hear my voice to calm him and give him strength. I tried to speak to him through the glass, but I couldn't tell whether he heard me.

'What's his name?' I asked.

'Aalam,' said Malik.

One of the unit doctors came over to see me.

'Are you Aalam's mother?' she asked.

'Yes, how is he?'

'His condition is critical,' she began. 'He has septicaemia and there are also signs of meningitis, so we are trying to treat that in its early stages, but I'm afraid the two conditions together make this a very dangerous time for your baby.' She paused to give me a sympathetic smile, and put her hand gently on mine. 'But I can assure you that he will have the best possible care and we are doing all we can to stabilise him.'

'He may die,' added Malik, as if blaming me.

'That is a possibility, I'm afraid,' agreed the doctor. 'The odds are against him at the moment, but we believe he has a chance of pulling through.'

I don't know whether I fainted, or just lost my way mentally at that point, but I don't remember the rest of that day, or the days that followed. Apparently I was very ill myself, so they sedated me quite a lot to help me recover. On the odd occasion when I was awake and not too woozy, I saw at least two members of the family with me.

'Aalam?' I would ask them on waking. They usually nodded, which I assumed meant that he was still alive.

After a week or so, I began to be awake more often and I felt I was regaining strength. I had been fed intravenously, so I expect that helped.

'We have your septicaemia under control,' explained the consultant on his rounds. 'So you are now stable.'

'When can we take her home?' asked Malik.

It was the first time I'd seen him since Aalam's birth.

'Well, as you can see, she is still dependent on the drip and we have to monitor her vital signs on a regular basis, on this monitor. So it will be several days yet, I'm afraid.'

Malik showed his contempt for this answer: 'We need her at home now.'

'Well, I'm afraid she can't go home until we're happy she's over the worst and feeling well enough to leave. But she will be able to move onto a ward in the next day or two, so that will be like a halfway point.'

'If she can't come home, she must stay here,' grunted Malik.

'I'm afraid that's not possible, and it's not in the patient's best interests.'

I was relieved that this doctor had picked up on Malik's inappropriate anger and was assertive enough to protect me.

'How is Aalam?' I asked Bushra, after Malik and the doctor had left the room.

'Still alive and in his incubator. He had to have a full blood transfusion and he remains very ill. They say it's touch and go. The nurses are keeping a 24-hour watch.'

'Thank you,' I said, grateful for her detailed explanation, when I knew Malik would have ordered her not to tell me anything. At least he was still alive, but it was not very encouraging news. Hopefully he would improve.

I was on the ward now and still with my two 'guards', always two, but occasionally changing over during the daytimes, from early morning until the staff insisted they must leave the hospital at about ten o'clock at night, when they locked all the outside doors. Malik had stormed off to see a hospital manager to complain that there needed to be at least one family member with me, 24/7. But he didn't get his way.

It was always such a relief when they had gone and I was on my own – I could relax at last. I took to sleeping during the days, so that I didn't have to sit and watch the family's sour faces watching me. That meant I could be awake at night when they had gone. The nurses were all very good and didn't seem to mind – I think they may have realised I couldn't relax properly with my 'guards' there. One or two of them even came to chat with me sometimes, when the ward was quiet at night. I had the feeling one of them had sussed there was something not quite right about my situation, and she tried to get me talking about it one night, but I didn't dare in case Malik was trying to trick me. Later I found out that she had alluded to her suspicions in my hospital notes.

I know I should have taken that opportunity to tell the staff, to make a plea for them to help me escape. I did think about it, but I was afraid of Malik finding out, tracking me down and getting his revenge. I didn't even know where I could go, and I wasn't feeling well enough yet. Most of all, it was the thought of that little baby in the Neonatal Unit. I craved the chance to hold him in my arms, and if rescued from the hospital, I would never see him again. I would never see any of my babies. At least if I said nothing, I might have a chance, like Durnaz's recent six months check-up and Purdil's five-year check-up with the health visitor, when I had to pretend I was bringing up the children. But that was one thing I was happy to agree to, because it was the only chance to see my children.

That was such a wonderful day, Purdil's pre-school check-up, to see how he had grown and developed. I watched him run around, playing with the other children at the house. Of course, he was puzzled at having to sit on my lap for his hearing test. He had no idea who I was – just a stranger, I suppose.

No, I couldn't give anything away to the nurses, kind as they all were. It was too much of a risk in case I never saw any of my babies again.

* * *

After 14 days in the hospital, the doctor said I was well enough to go home, but first I asked to go and visit Aalam. I knew his condition was still critical, so I desperately wanted to hold him and give him some comfort. Because I had asked a nurse to take me, Malik couldn't stop me, but I felt his fury at my not having asked his permission first.

The poor little mite didn't look any better than the day he was born – very pale and thin. He was sleeping while I was there, and I didn't feel I should disturb him, so I couldn't hold him. That's when it hit me that he was 14 days old and I, his birth mother, had not touched him at all, yet. I said a silent prayer for him – Nana's favourite that we used to say together:

In my little bed I lie,
Heavenly Father hear my cry.
Lord protect me through the night,
And bring me safe to morning light.
Amen

As soon as Malik got me back to the house and upstairs in the room, he slammed and locked the door and beat me with all his fury because I had given Aalam septicaemia and made him so ill. It was my fault his plans for the baby had been thwarted, that the hospital had refused to release me sooner; it was my fault that I became ill in the first place. Everything was my fault. He shouted and swore the whole time he was punching and kicking me.

'You f**ing whore ... You white bitch ... Dirty c*** ... Father-f***er ...' Everything he'd ever called me, he shouted at me that afternoon. Though weak and in need of respite care, this assault was my welcome back to the hellhole.

Then, of course, having drawn blood with various cuts, he was too excited to leave me alone, so he had to rape me as well, to complete his revenge. It was a vicious rape, with no thought to my delicate state. To round it off, he tipped the lid off the tank, put a thick glove on and slowly, deliberately, picked up the cobra for me to see. Its head was poking out of the tank, its tongue out, hissing at me.

I screamed and buried my head under a pillow, my whole body shaking.

'That's what you'll get,' he threatened, 'if you don't do exactly what I tell you.'

Unable to look up, I heard him replace the lid so I opened my eyes a little to make sure he hadn't let the snake loose in the room. I breathed a sigh of relief that I could glimpse it slithering inside the tank, though I couldn't stop shuddering for hours until, desperately tired and hurting all over, I eventually fell asleep.

* * *

Aalam was in his incubator in the Neonatal Unit for 28 days. He'd had his circumcision as soon as the nurses allowed, but I wasn't well enough to attend. I didn't even know about it until weeks later. Several of the family visited him and sat with him there every day. I was desperate to be with him too, but Malik wouldn't let me. Finally, his condition started to improve and everyone, especially Malik, was happy that he would soon be discharged.

The following week, Aalam was brought to the house and I was only allowed downstairs to see him once before he left with his new parents. I felt distraught for myself and for the baby, as always. At least, this time, I had known for sure I would not be allowed to keep him, so I had no false hopes. But there was one thing I needed to do. Fortunately, Malik went out of the room and Surayya brought Aalam over to me to hold.

I was filled with joy to have him in my arms at last: it was a release from all the tension, the desperate longing to hold my own baby. He was such a tiny scrap. Smiling at him, I put my little finger in his hand, which he clutched and held onto. I stroked his cheek and his downy hair, now growing back, having been shaved off the day he was born.

I didn't have long holding him, but it was enough to make a memory that I would keep forever. Finally, I had to let him go and watch as his new thirty-something parents walked out with him, to start his new life without me.

But that wasn't all. Because Aalam had been so ill, the health visitor rang to speak to me. Malik told her I couldn't come to the phone and he would speak for me, but she stood her ground and insisted. So Malik sent Muneeza up to get me. He handed me the receiver and stood right next to me to listen in.

'How is Aalam doing?' she asked.

What could I say? I knew I mustn't let on that he didn't live with me.

'I think he's fine,' I told her nervously, with Malik's black eyes glaring at me.

'Because he was so ill to start with, I have been asked to come and give him a three months check-up,' she paused. 'Will it be all right with you if I come tomorrow at 2pm?'

Malik nodded.

'Yes, that's fine,' I said.

Surayya took me back upstairs again, while Malik rang Aalam's new parents to make sure they brought him back in time for the visit.

Aalam's parents arrived at 1pm and I was brought downstairs so that Aalam and I could get used to each other a bit, and his parents could fill me in on his progress, in order to convince the heath visitor that he always lived with me.

At 2pm, the doorbell went and Malik let in Sally, the health visitor, together with a young man. I could see Malik didn't like it at all, having another man in the house.

'Who is this?' he asked Sally rather abruptly.

'This is Ben, a trainee psychologist who is accompanying me on my visits, so he will be with me each time I come.'

I gave them both a slight smile, which was more than I was allowed to do, but Malik wasn't looking at me just at that moment. He was staring at Ben, as if trying to stare him out. But Ben didn't play Malik's game.

'This is Aalam,' I said, holding him half-asleep against my shoulder.

Sally asked the questions, while Ben took notes. I saw the way he was looking from Malik to me and back again, as if trying to work us out. I wondered what he was writing down about us.

The health check went well.

'He's low-height and weight for his age,' Sally observed, 'but considering his perilous start in life, I think he's doing quite well.'

'Good,' I smiled.

'Are your older two, Purdil and Durnaz, here?' she asked. 'I could give them a quick check-over too.'

'No,' said Malik a bit too quickly. Then he paused: 'Purdil is at school.'

'Oh yes, of course,' said Sally. 'I did his pre-school check a while ago, didn't I?'

'And my sister-in-law has taken Durnaz out for a walk in her pram this afternoon. They've only just gone, and then I think she was going to stay at their house for tea.'

'Oh, I see,' nodded Sally. 'Perhaps I could come back tomorrow to see her?'

She got her diary out.

'No, I'm afraid we will all be out for the day tomorrow – it's a busy week. But if you want to make an appointment ...'

'I'll maybe call you next week,' she said to me. 'I expect she is doing well?'

'Yes,' I nodded.

She wrote something in her diary without giving any hint of disbelief, or even concern. But the young trainee gave me a puzzled look, as if asking a silent question, followed by a fleeting smile of sympathy.

As soon as they were gone, Malik tore the baby from my arms, making him cry. He took him into another room and sent me upstairs again.

It was wonderful to have had that hour and a half of holding Aalam, my youngest child, but somehow that made it even worse when we were parted.

Alone again, back in my room, my mood plummeted into a deep chasm. I wondered whether the health visitor and the young psychologist had talked about us after they left. Could they have suspected anything? I thought there had been some signs there, if they had noticed them. Perhaps they would alert the authorities.

Much as I loved to see my own children on those rare occasions, could I really face a lifetime in captivity, just in case I might see one of them again? It would be extremely unlikely after the age of five anyway, when the health checks stopped, so Purdil was forever out of my reach.

CHAPTER 20

A WAY OUT?

After one horrendous night, Malik got me up early and dragged me downstairs.

'Sit there,' he said. 'And don't move.'

The television was on in the corner, but nobody was watching it – they all seemed to be busy with different things, in different parts of the two houses. Nobody had asked me to do anything, so I just sat there, on the hardest settee, gazing out of the window. It was a fine, sunny day in early summer. I watched the washing drying on the line, dancing in the breeze. Every now and then a butterfly fluttered by and there were birds soaring in the sky. How I wished I could go and sit in the garden and feel the sun on my pale skin. I never had the chance to enjoy fresh air and sunshine. The curtains had been closed in my prison room for nine years now, so even daylight sometimes hurt my eyes.

Sitting and looking at the white clouds scudding across the blue sky that day, my eyes began to accustom themselves to a wider and brighter view. I wish I knew the names of the different birds and butterflies, but what use would it be anyway, if I could never be free? As I sat and watched, I envied them their freedom.

I suppose I had been sitting there for the best part of an hour when my attention was caught by the sound of a door opening. It was the living-room door of Eshrat's adjoining house, through the hole in the wall. The glass door swung open and out stepped Muneeza. I watched her walking down the scrubby lawn to the end of the garden, where she sat down, so I had to stand up to see what she was doing. It looked like she was picking weeds and pulling them apart.

I knew that Muneeza got very depressed, like me, because everybody ill-treated her. Her husband had abandoned her for his three younger wives, each in their own houses, so she was left with one blanket, no bed and her constantly ill and handicapped son. Eshrat beat her almost daily and perhaps abused her in other ways too. She was the butt of everyone's insults and ridicule, again like me, but at least I didn't have to do all the never-ending housework that everyone forced on her.

As I watched her mindlessly tearing the weeds apart, I suddenly realised that she had left the door to the garden open. It was only the other side of the ill-fitting door in the wall, which was ajar. There was nobody else outside and no one near me in the house. Perhaps they were all in the prayer room.

I thought Muneeza wouldn't notice me going outside and she probably wouldn't tell on me if she did. Without thinking, I just went straight through the two doors, to the patio, barefoot as always.

I turned and ran to the big arched tunnel that passed between us and the neighbours on the other side – I think it was an Englishwoman who lived there. I expected to be able to run through, but there was a locked wrought-iron gate in the way; I could see the street beyond, but I couldn't reach it. I turned and scanned the garden. There was high fencing all round and another building across the end, but over by the swing I noticed a loose fence panel hanging down. I ran straight for that and scrambled through the gap to next-door's garden.

Phew! I thought I was free.

I spotted a wide alleyway down the far side of the woman's house and went for that. But Muneeza must have seen me and alerted the family. As I reached the alleyway, so close to freedom, that's where it all went wrong.

I crept a couple of paces down the alleyway, then ran for it, just as Eshrat, Sayed and Khalid, Malik's brothers – blocked the front end. The three men strode towards me, gloating that they had caught me red-handed, and full of repressed anger that they couldn't show until they got me out of public view.

I had nowhere to go. From the elation of thinking I'd reached freedom, to fear of the consequences that I hadn't, I was petrified. They caught me and two of them took hold of my arms, while the third pushed my back, taking care not to look aggressive or suspicious. Together, without alerting any neighbours or passers-by, they propelled me swiftly round the front of the houses and in through Malik's front door, slamming it shut and double-locking it behind them, removing the key as always. Filled with dread, I thought my life had ended. They would probably kill me now, especially when Malik came back to join them.

By then Muneeza was back in the house. When she saw them bringing me in, she put her head down and went through to Eshrat's living room. I'll never know if she was the one who told on me, but I couldn't blame her – she would have been in serious trouble if she hadn't alerted them.

I was thrown on the settee and they all stood round me.

'How *dare* you disrespect our family like that!' yelled Eshrat, backhanding my face with his hand full of rings. 'You're a disrespectful white slut and you're never going out again!' he ranted.

'Yes, you've done a very bad thing,' grunted Khalid. 'You've put shame on our family.'

'You've got to be watched all the time from now on,' added Sayed, the eldest brother.

Then their mother, Farhat, came in and started swearing, poking me with her stubby fingers.

Eshrat went to phone Malik and by the time he arrived, I was shaking with fear. I could hear Eshrat telling him in Punjabi how wicked I'd been and all the exaggerated details of my attempted escape and how they had thwarted me.

Malik came into the living room and headed straight for me. He slapped me about the face several times and pulled me about by my hair, so hard he tugged some of it out. He shouted and ranted at me, even more than Eshrat had done, every swear word he knew. Then he hit me, punching me with his fist.

'Hit her again,' his mother goaded him on.

Malik punched and kicked me a few more times, then took me by the arm and dragged me upstairs. He threw me sprawling into the room, slammed the door shut and locked it, before stomping down the stairs, shouting back further obscenities at me.

* * *

I didn't get the chance to go downstairs for a long time after that. When I eventually did, I could only stay there if somebody else sat with me, to watch me and make sure I didn't try to escape again. But I didn't care – I preferred to sit peacefully on my own.

For several weeks, Malik was deliberately rougher when he attacked or raped me.

'You bitch! Why did you try to escape?' he barked in anger. 'You needn't think you can get wise to me. I'm your boss, I control you.' He paused for breath and stood up, presumably to make himself even more intimidating. 'If you *ever* try to escape again, I will break both your legs!'

He then made his right hand into a fist.

'That's for what you did!' he shouted, punching my face repeatedly before delivering the winning blow: 'I have to go back to the shop now, but next time I come up here, I will let out your friend the snake and see how you like that!' He cackled as he pulled the door shut behind him and locked it.

I sat and trembled with fear. My whole face hurt; both my eyes swelled up so that I could hardly see. I could feel the blood from my nose and the cuts on my chin, my cheeks and my forehead, made by the rings on his fingers. My jaw felt strange and it was getting stiff on one side. But the pains were nothing compared to the dread of that writhing snake being let out.

I couldn't stop shaking with terror; I wanted to die.

In the weeks that followed, I was so depressed that soon the thought of dying filled my days, so that I didn't have to think about my stolen babies or that terrifying snake any more.

I must have been mentally ill – it seemed like a positive thing to me, a way I could take control.

If I die, I will be joining Nana, I thought. *Maybe they could bury me in her grave.*

I talked to Nana a lot. Later, I started thinking I had her coffin under the bed and she could hear me when I talked to her; I could hear her voice too. I ran my ideas past her.

'I just want to die,' I told her. 'I can't take this life any longer. I want to come and join you, but how can I kill myself?'

I sat and thought about it. I had nothing sharp to cut my wrists, and no rope to make a noose with; I didn't even have any painkillers left, I'd used them up long ago. I could ask for more, but that still wouldn't be enough to kill myself with. I couldn't go near the window to jump out. Even if I could, Malik had told me it was locked and only he had the key. It seemed I couldn't even find a way to kill myself, to finally leave all this behind.

Then, one morning, Muneeza forgot to lock the door after she had emptied the ghee barrel and brought it back into the room. I didn't notice at first, but a few minutes later, in a lucid moment, I suddenly realised that I had not heard the key turning in the lock.

This was my chance. I went over to the door and quietly turned the handle: it opened. I poked my head out to see if anyone was on the landing, but there was no one there so I stepped out to stand at the top of the stairs. I must have stood there for several minutes, counting the stairs, thinking how best to do it. I had to jump up and outwards to have the maximum impact; I needed to make sure.

I took a breath in, stood ready to spring, and leapt out as high and as far as I could. It was weird: it felt like slow motion as I flew through the air, then hurtled downwards, clattering and bumping myself against the walls, tumbling down the stairs at odd angles, until I finally came to rest at the bottom.

There I lay. It felt like I was inside my head, looking out at myself: my body and legs lying crumpled across the last two steps, head bleeding on the floor.

How come I could see this? How did I know? Shouldn't I be dead, or was this what death was like?

Time seemed suspended, but I think it was only a minute or two until the whole household gathered to see what all the noise was. Somebody picked up my arm before someone else shouted out: 'Don't touch her! Call the ambulance.'

I remember nothing else until the next day, when I woke up in a hospital bed. This time, of course, it wasn't the familiar maternity unit. I opened my eyes and saw the people round my bed: Malik, Eshrat, Bushra, Surayya and Farhat, with a middle-aged doctor and a nurse writing something on my chart.

'What happened?' I murmured weakly. 'Am I dead now?'

'No, Anna,' said the doctor, with a kindly voice. 'You are in the orthopaedic ward in the hospital. You fell down the stairs and sustained a number of injuries, so we are looking after you here, to keep you immobilised.'

'What injuries?'

'Stop asking the doctor questions,' said Malik, furious.

'It's all right,' the doctor assured me. 'Ask any questions you like.'

But Malik glared at me and I knew what that meant.

'You had a particularly nasty fall,' the doctor continued. 'The X-rays show you have some cracked ribs and vertebrae, and a small bone broken in your wrist, so that's why you're wearing a brace on that arm. Two of your vertebrae have hairline fractures, so it's very important that you lie flat on your back and keep as still as you can, to keep them stable while they start to mend.'

* * *

That night, in the gloom of the ward, surrounded by snoring patients, I started to weep. It was like opening a sluice, I couldn't help myself – this wasn't meant to happen, I was supposed to be dead.

I can't even kill myself properly.

There was nobody with me, thank God. They weren't allowed to stay overnight.

I sobbed and sobbed as quietly as I could, trying to muffle the sound by stuffing the sheet half into my mouth. But one of the nurses heard and brought a chair over to sit with me. She took my hand and held it in hers, sitting in silence for a minute or two.

'Did you do it on purpose?' she asked.

I just nodded, trying to slow my sobbing.

'Did you really mean to kill yourself?'

I nodded again.

'You don't have to tell me anything, but is it something to do with family troubles, with the people you had visiting you all day?'

I nodded again.

She sat silently, holding my hand and stroking my hair. It was quite calming. Then somebody needed her and she stood up to go.

'Thank you,' I whispered, trying to give her a tear-stained smile.

'Try to get some sleep,' she said. 'Sleep is the best healer. It won't solve all your problems, but it can give you the strength to cope better and try to sort them out yourself.'

I nodded and off she went, into the shadows, as I wondered how much she guessed.

I didn't see her again.

* * *

Back to the house, a few days later, and everyone seemed to ignore the doctor's advice that I was supposed to lie on my back and rest.

Malik left me alone the first night, but the second evening he strode into the room with a long, thin truncheon. I thought he was going to beat me with it, but no, he had another plan. He swung it about for a bit, taunting me with what he was going to do to me. Then he tore my pants off and pushed this thin truncheon straight into my vagina. I was in agony. I hadn't been expecting it, so I hadn't had time to steel myself against the excruciating pain. He hung his head over mine, staring to see what effect it had on me, as he rammed it in as far as he could, then tried to whack it about inside me.

I closed my eyes to hide my fear of the damage he was doing to me – I knew that was what he wanted to see, and my pain.

The more pain he could cause me the better, and he wanted to see it in my eyes. He slapped my face a few times to make me open my eyes again. He pushed the truncheon in and out and around a bit more.

'Are you enjoying that, you white bitch?' he asked with a demonic grin. 'There.' He rammed it again and I couldn't help but take in a frightened breath. 'Are you enjoying that?'

I shook my head, but I could see that he was. Then he suddenly jerked it right out, causing me to wail with the pain. I stayed lying on my back, desperately hoping he hadn't worsened my injured vertebrae, and assuming he wouldn't do anything else to me when my back was still so fragile. But I was wrong.

Malik was so excited at what he had just done that he couldn't contain himself. He raped me so hard, I feared anew for my back. I could almost feel his thrusts pushing against my spine; he was so sadistic. I don't know how I coped. The mental anguish was almost worse than the physical pain, though at least I had developed a way of making my body feel paralysed to numb the pain when things got really bad.

I was too weak for it to be effective that night.

* * *

As I recovered from my injuries, I decided the only way to kill myself now was not to eat at all. I had once found a big bag of cotton wool on the wardrobe floor so now I started to eat it to trick my body into thinking I had eaten, then I forced myself to be sick. That was the only way to do it. The only way I could live without any food and just a few drops of water. It made me happy every time I made myself sick.

Malik got Eshrat to help him again to force-feed me when I became skeletal. But I resisted as much as possible and when they had gone, I just ate some more cotton wool and made myself sick everything up.

CHAPTER 21

DRUGS RAIDS

Everyone was angry. Muneeza, the saddest, most neglected, overworked and abused family member, had escaped.

I had been a prisoner in this house for ten years now, and I knew that all the women were physically abused, and possibly sexually too. Not as often or as badly as me, but it happened. I'd heard the screams from all over the house. But Muneeza was the butt of everyone's cruelty.

She had always seemed so weak and submissive, with no friends in the house apart from me, and nobody to help or comfort her in looking after her ill and disabled son. I couldn't imagine how she had summoned up the strength to run away, especially leaving her son behind. How could she bear to do that?

I was downstairs, sitting in the living room, biting off the skin round my fingernails; I don't remember thinking about anything. I was being guarded by one of the brothers, who was reading a newspaper. Suddenly Eshrat came storming through the hole in the wall between the two living rooms, ranting and raving, looking for Muneeza to punish her for some misdeed or other. He was speaking so fast, scattered with so many swear words, that I didn't catch it all.

They searched both houses and the garden; they checked the archway gate was locked and it was. And the fence had been mended.

'How could she have run away?' asked Sayed, the eldest and most reasonable of the brothers, trying to calm everyone down.

'She must be here somewhere,' agreed Asif, the youngest, who had once come to my aid when I was badly injured after a beating.

But Muneeza wasn't anywhere. The family gathered in the living room, ignoring me, and discussed what might have happened.

My first thought was that Eshrat had killed her. If it hadn't been that he was looking for her, I would have suspected him of perhaps having beaten her fragile body so badly, as he often did, that she had died. Perhaps his shouting was a charade? But all the family seemed convinced that Muneeza had escaped.

The brothers went off to ask the neighbours if anyone had seen her go.

'The Englishwoman next door saw a strange car pulling up outside and opening a rear door,' said Sayed. 'She said she saw Muneeza creeping out of the house and getting in. Then the car drove off.'

Everyone was furious at that explanation.

'How dare she leave, after all we've done for her?'

'She's a disgrace!'

'Yes, she's put shame on this family.'

'Who's going to do her work now?'

* * *

In the days that followed her disappearance, nobody in the house seemed bothered about Muneeza herself, other than losing their skivvy, who always did the worst jobs. They never mentioned her name again. Her sickly son Hassan, in his second-hand wheelchair, disappeared the day after she left – I never found out what happened to him. Perhaps his father, Khalid, took him to one of his other wives, though he'd never paid the boy any attention before.

My mind was in a bad state at that time, but I do remember feeling a mixture of surprise, disbelief and sadness. Above all else, I was glad for her. Whether she had escaped or died, she was out of this hell-house.

Later, I heard the family saying they found out that Muneeza had somehow made a phone call to her family in London and they had driven up to the Midlands to fetch her. I hoped this was true. If it was, she must have remained free and I liked to think of her having an easier, happier life with her birth relatives.

I think it gave me a tiny grain of hope that I myself might also be able to run away some day. But she had her family to help her – who would help me?

* * *

'Police!' yelled a deep voice, followed by a lot of noise and what sounded like several booted people rushing up the stairs. They tried my door, but it was locked. I heard Malik's voice.

'There's nothing in there, it's just a bedroom.'

'Unlock it or I'll batter the door down,' came the gruff reply.

I drew myself down, under the bedcovers, as the key turned and the door was flung open.

In walked a tall, broad white man in navy or black police uniform and a hi-vis tabard with 'Police' written on it in big letters. Behind him were several others, coming and going, all wearing the same. They ran around, searching all the rooms, shouting to each other and at all the occupants of the house.

'She's been ill,' Malik explained as the policeman gazed at me while I pretended I'd just woken up. He seemed to pre-empt the policeman's next question. 'We locked the door to keep the children out, so that she could have a sleep.' The officer paused for a moment, then shrugged. It was a plausible explanation as there were lots of children downstairs – Malik was always very devious and quick in his thinking. I remember feeling disappointed that the policeman didn't seem to suspect anything.

The policeman searched every nook and cranny of the room, including the ghee barrel, the stench of which sent him reeling – I wondered what he was thinking. He gave Malik a look, but said nothing. I had to move for him to search the bed and its surrounds, but he left the snake tank until last.

'What kind of snake is this, sir?' he asked Malik.

'A cobra.'

'Would you mind taking it out of the tank safely so that we can search it?'

Malik put on his thick leather gauntlet gloves, lifted the lid and that's when I had to hide back under the bedcovers. I imagined he held the cobra's neck and head in a special grip to lift it out safely, without it getting free, or at least, that was what I hoped, and of course that he put it back safely too. I shuddered, and tried my best not to look up too soon.

Finally, I heard the officer and Malik walking out, so I dared to take a peek. The lid was back down and I could see slow movement in the tank, so at last I began to breathe normally again.

There was a lot of noise and upheaval as the policemen searched the whole house from top to bottom. Two or three of them were going up the pull-down ladder to the loft outside my room. I wondered what they were looking for. Being so naive, I didn't know about drugs, where they came from or how they were used. I didn't even know you could grow them.

The police rummaged through every room, looking in every possible hiding place. They spent a lot of time in Eshrat's house too. I don't know whether they found anything that day, but apparently they took both Malik and Eshrat down to the station for questioning. However, they came back that evening. Malik stomped upstairs, fuming, and stormed into the room without even looking at me, eyes glazed and grinding his teeth.

I was so frightened that I rolled up into a ball on the bed. He grabbed my thinning hair and yanked my head back so that he could backhand my face on each side. Then he pulled me down and forced my legs apart, as wide as he could, to ram himself inside me and start his vicious rape, taking his fury out on me, instead of the police. I tried to clear my mind, to numb body and soul. I don't know how long his assault was that night, but I do know he drew blood and he then pulled me onto the floor and started kicking me all over, with his shoes still on, again and again. I must have passed out.

I don't know when, probably only moments later, I felt cold water on my head. When I came to, he carried me back onto the bed, my head still reeling. Then he sat down next to me and put his arm round me.

'I do love you,' he said, and smiled at me.

Confused, I felt like I had when my father used to beat me with his belt before telling me he did it because he loved me. But there was still a part of me that yearned for love. Did Malik really love me, or was it simply a ploy, a trick of some kind, deliberately messing with my emotions?

Then he raped me again, this time more gently.

What was I to think? I tried not to think about it at all. When he had left the room to go to his work at the taxi base, though cut and bruised all over, I crawled across the carpet to the picture of Nana. As always I traced round her head and kissed where I thought her cheek was. I suppose I was still suffering some kind of mental illness, but I really thought that night that Nana was in the room with me. I heard her voice – in my head, I suppose.

'I love you, Angel,' she said. 'I am with you. Let's say our prayers together.'

So I would recite the three prayers we used to say. As I said the words, I could hear her voice saying them with me. First was *'In my little bed I lie ...'*. This was the prayer I said most often. Then I heard her voice starting the next prayer, and so I joined in:

> *May the grace of our Lord Jesus Christ,*
> *The love of God and the sweet fellowship of the Holy*
>   *Spirit,*

Be with us, now and evermore.
Amen

Finally, we said the Lord's Prayer, but I don't remember getting to the end. When I woke up again in the morning, I was still curled around Nana's face on the carpet.

* * *

There were frequent police raids in the following weeks. I think there must have been some violence with rival gangs too.

One day they arrested Malik and charged him with stabbing a man. The police came round and told Malik's mother, Farhat, we all had to appear in court. Surayya came up to fetch me and as we went downstairs, I could hear Farhat giving the police a bitter tirade, all in Punjabi, which none of them understood. Malik and Eshrat were both down at the police station, so they asked if anybody could translate for her.

'No talk English good,' said Surayya, shaking her head.

'And I not good English,' added Bushra.

None of the other brothers were at the house, so it was one of the children or me. They must have realised it wasn't suitable to ask the children, so the officers turned to me.

'Yasmeen no speak,' said Bushra.

I had to keep my head down, as usual, and say nothing.

I don't know why I didn't speak up and tell them about my captivity. With Malik and Eshrat both in police custody, it was the ideal opportunity, but I suppose I must have been brainwashed over so many years. With the three women looking daggers at me, I couldn't say a word, for fear of the consequences – the cobra was always on my mind. I shuddered anew just to think of it. By then, I had somehow taught myself to shut down my mind when I needed to, so that's what I did at that moment. It was as if I was some sort of automaton, just doing as I was told.

The police phoned their station and had a conversation before beckoning us to go with them.

'Hospital,' the officer said. I suppose they didn't bother to explain, assuming none of us would understand.

'Malik?' asked Farhat.

'Malik OK,' replied the officer, realising she was worried about her son.

It was all too confusing to take in, so I didn't trouble myself to wonder what was going on. But when we got there, I realised the man Malik stabbed was his cousin. Malik himself had also been stabbed by his uncle, during a fight between the two branches of his family, outside the house. He was in hospital having his wounds treated, and when the police started to ask him questions, he had asked them to bring us in as eyewitnesses.

When we walked into his side-room, he was handcuffed to the heavy iron bed. Of course, I knew nothing about what had gone on, apart from the noise, as I was locked away when it happened. But the police didn't know that, and I couldn't tell them, with Malik staring darkly at me. He spoke to us in Punjabi, telling us what he wanted us to say.

When the police asked us what we'd seen, we each said what Malik had told us, including me, even though I hadn't seen anything at all.

'So you see,' he said to the police in English. 'It was just a family feud. We'll all be friends again tomorrow.'

Both families agreed not to press charges against each other and the police dropped the case. They just took us all home again and, as Surayya escorted me upstairs to lock me back in the room, I heard Malik and Eshrat triumphantly celebrating. Malik always got his own way in the end.

Just as he did that night.

* * *

I was not surprised to hear heavy footsteps approaching up the stairs, but when he turned round to lock the door, my heart sank. In his hand, behind his back but now visible, he had a cucumber. I was filled with dread.

He came straight over, laid me out on the bed, forced my legs apart and with no lubricant or any preparation, rammed the cucumber into my vagina as hard as he could. It must have touched the top of my cervix, wounding it so that it immediately started to bleed profusely. Even though I tried my best to numb the pain, it was excruciating. He could see the pain in my face and hear it in my screams. Lapping it up, he pushed the cucumber in and out repeatedly to increase both my torment and the blood-flow. As ever, the blood racked up his excitement. Then he suddenly pulled it out, with a sharp tug so agonising it took my breath away.

Next, he made me stand up, pulled my head back and pushed the cucumber inside my anus, in and out, causing a searing pain and once again splitting it open to add to the blood already running down my legs.

'Your turn,' he said, giving me the same bloodied cucumber and turning his back to me. 'Go on, push it in ... *hard* ...' he urged me, almost shrieking with pain. '*Harder!*'

To me that was detestable. He loved the pain almost as much as his pleasure at causing me pain.

Inevitably, he had to smother and rape me after that, with all the enthusiasm my blood provoked in him. But now it didn't hurt any more because my body switched off – I no longer felt the pain. Yet, I couldn't avoid the terrible shame, the degradation and despair. I was exhausted long before he had finally had enough. Within minutes he fell into a loud, snoring sleep. I lay awake, sobbing, numb and wretched, silently talking to my great-grandma.

Nana, I know you're with me. Please help me to find a way out, a way to kill myself, the only way to end it all. I just want to come and be with you, to be held in your arms.

CHAPTER 22

A SECOND CHANCE

It was Thursday, which was slaughtering day, as always. But this Thursday was also a special day for the family as it was Feeding the Dead, in memory of Malik's late father. They closed the shop, and all the brothers, their wives and their pre-school children came to the house to join in this ancient ritual together.

Surayya came for me early in the morning and I had to go downstairs to the kitchen to help prepare the foods, while the men were in the garage, killing chickens. I had never got used to hearing the last, desperate shrieks of those birds as they had their necks wrung. Like knives cutting through my brain, the sound continued long after they were plucked and trussed. But, like almost everything else in this house, I had gradually learnt to try and detach myself, so that the sounds became distant echoes, as long as I was concentrating. I also tried hard to block the images of the killing from my mind. It was easier to block them out when I had a job to do, so on this Thursday I focused on rolling the chapatti dough. I imagined that I was rolling out Malik, squashing him flat, so they were the thinnest chapattis I ever made.

That morning, everyone gathered for prayers. I did not have to join them, if someone was willing to guard me, so two of Khalid's wives sat with me in the living room, watching over the little ones as they played with their toys. The television in the corner was on, but nobody seemed to be watching it. The women couldn't talk English, so I just sat and watched the children.

It made me think of my own three children, all stolen from me. I could never stop grieving for them. How old would they be now? I worked it out – Purdil would be nine, Durnaz would be three and Aalam two. Where were they now? Were they well looked after? Happy? Loved? They couldn't possibly be as loved as they would have been with me. I would have showered them with affection, encouragement and shown my love for them every day. If only I could see them again and give them all hugs. They were the one and only reason I hadn't tried to escape earlier, to keep the chance, the hope of seeing them again. Not that I had many opportunities to escape, always guarded, in person or by threat. Besides, I was just too frightened of Malik: it was as if he had complete control over me, pulling my puppet strings. In my saner moments, I resented that, and mourned for my lost self – the carefree teenager I used to be. Now I was just an empty shell, a broken toy – would I ever be free again?

I helped to put out all the foodstuffs for the Feeding the Dead feast – a variety of savouries and tropical fruits. Everyone helped themselves. I was allowed to choose as well, but I couldn't eat.

'Eat something,' said Malik with a frown. 'It is disrespectful to the family if you do not eat today.'

I nodded and picked up an orange quarter. I sucked the juice out of it, until long after it was dry, so that it looked like I was eating.

* * *

After lunch I helped with the washing-up, then had to sit on the hard settee in the living room. The brothers were all out in the garage, killing animals again, with various men coming and going, delivering live birds for slaughter, or taking away oven-ready chickens. All the wives were doing the plucking and trussing work, while I sat doing nothing. The television high up on its wall bracket in the corner of the room was showing a Punjabi film, so I vaguely watched that for a while, though I had no idea what was going on; my mind was blank. Looking back, I could have entertained myself better gazing at the patterns on the curtains upstairs, making up stories in my head. But I was so depressed by this stage that I had even stopped doing that – I think I passed whole days without thinking.

There was supposed to be somebody guarding me, but it was such a busy day, with the many comings and goings, they must have forgotten. I sat on the settee, chewing the skin off my thumb, and gazing out the window. I don't think I was looking at anything in particular, but it was a bright day and there were sheets billowing on the washing line, so I must have looked at those for a bit.

I heard distant voices, laughing and joking in Punjabi. But I didn't bother to listen to what they were saying: I was in a world of my own, an empty world.

I don't know what it was – a voice in my head? Something made me wake up from my dazed state. It was as if I was being told to look in the kitchen. I could hear no sounds from there, so I leant back far enough to see through the arch but I couldn't see anyone. Where had the women gone?

I tiptoed over to the kitchen, thinking I'd ask for a glass of water if anyone was there. But the room was empty and the back door wide open to the garden.

Run, said the voice in my head. *Run for it!*

So I did. But I had no plan, no idea of where to go. I just walked out the door, looking furtively towards the garage, but it had no windows overlooking the garden. I went straight to the arched tunnel between the houses, where the iron gate had been locked the first time I tried to escape. This time it was open and I ran through it, out onto the street and down the road, as fast as I could.

My bare feet had walked on nothing but floorboards or carpet, so the hard pavements scraped my soft skin, but I kept on running, in my Pakistani clothes and scarf, until I ran out of breath. I had not run for the past 11 years; I had not even walked further than a few yards in all that time. Painfully thin, my lack of nourishment meant I had no energy. I was only about a couple of hundred yards down the street, but I knew I had to stop and catch my breath, so I turned into a driveway that led to some sort of builders' yard.

It was early evening so all the workers had left. The ground was gravelled, which hurt my feet, so I was wincing with every step. I had a quick look round to find a hiding place. There were lorries, piles of rubble, stacks of bricks and stone slabs, huge bags of goodness knows what. I tried the lorry doors to see if any of them would open, but they were all locked so I went to the far corner and sat down behind some large bags of straw. I'm not sure why I chose that spot, but perhaps I had it in my mind that I could sleep on one of them if I had to.

Now, for the first time, I realised what I'd done: I had escaped. I took in a deep breath of fresh air, which tasted and felt like heaven.

I was alive; I was free!

They can't get me now, I thought. *I'm me at last.*

My breathing gradually slowed to normal as I rested. I don't remember thinking about what to do next. I realised I was too weak to run far, so I thought I would just stay there that night and run away further in the early morning, before the builders came to work.

Just as I was settling down, trying to make myself more comfortable, I heard voices. At first I thought they must be in my head, but they grew louder and louder, calling the name they had given me.

Yasmeen, Yasmeen, where are you?

I froze. I shrank myself down into the smallest ball I could, on the ground, behind the full sacks in the corner. Would they find me here? Maybe not if I could be silent and still – but what if they did?

'Yasmeen, come out!' shouted Malik's voice. I would have recognised that voice anywhere – the voice that struck fear like a knife in my heart.

I started trembling; they were coming closer. I could hear all their voices, even the youngest brother, Asif. He was the kindest one, yet even he was part of the pack, hounding me down.

'Yasmeen, Yasmeen, come home! It will be cold and dark soon. Come home with us and have something to eat, We'll make you some samosas.'

They were my favourites, but I wasn't hungry now. I wasn't even cold. I was just petrified of what Malik would do if he found me.

I held my breath as I heard the crunching of feet on gravel, drawing closer.

Suddenly, I was being pulled up by my hair, like the poor, cornered creature I was.

'I've got her!' Malik shouted to the others. Then he lowered his voice to snarl at me. 'You will *never* forget this night; you will *never* forget I'm the boss. What made you think you could run away from me? You will *never* escape! Do you hear that?' He bared his teeth at me and widened his eyes to a demonic stare. 'You are in for the worst beating of your life!' he growled. 'Just you wait and see.'

In a way, I felt I deserved it, though I was shaking at the prospect. I know that seems strange now, looking back, but it's what I felt then.

Malik and Eshrat dragged me, my feet gashed and bleeding, across the gravel yard and down to the road, where the others had gathered like a lynch-mob. Eyes ablaze, they were ready to make me suffer – all except Asif, who almost looked sorry for me.

All five brothers were there, plus Bushra's husband and three other men I didn't know. They dragged me onto the pavement and surrounded me to march me back to the house: nine hulking Pakistani men surrounding one thin English girl with bleeding feet, walking along the pavement. There were cars and vans going by, people walking their dogs or going home from work. What were they thinking? Surely they might have noticed and questioned what was going on – maybe even phoned the police, raised the alarm … but no.

The men manhandled me in through the front door and locked and bolted it behind them. Malik seized my arm in a vice-like grip and propelled me through to the living room, where he threw me down onto a settee. Then he and Eshrat gave me a double beating, taking turns to slap, punch and kick me, shouting out insults, with all the others looking on, baying for blood. I must have screamed out a few times, when particularly heavy blows landed on me, but I don't recall much other than the desperate need to try and protect my head.

About five minutes after the beating started, there was a loud and insistent knock on the door. The family ignored it to start with, but it was repeated almost immediately, with a shout through the letterbox.

'Open up – Police!'

Sayed went to open it. Meanwhile, Malik and Eshrat stopped their assault of me and straightened themselves up.

'Sit up,' Malik ordered me in a harsh whisper. 'Wipe the blood off your face.' He handed me a grubby handkerchief, so I did as he asked. 'Now, put your scarf on properly and bow your head. Act normally and don't say a word, or you know what you will get.'

The police asked Sayed to gather the whole family together, so he called them in and it was like a flood of people pouring into the living room. Most of the brothers were there, plus Surayya and four of her children standing in the doorway with Bushra, and of course Farhat, the mother. There were 13 family members altogether, with the men stood around the settees, while the two policemen came in and sat on the settee opposite mine. One of them got out his notebook to write everything down, while the other with stripes on his sleeve – a sergeant, I assumed – did most of the talking.

I could feel Malik's stare piercing through my scarf, ensuring I didn't look up or reveal my face.

'Can you please tell us what is the reason for your visit?' Malik asked the policemen, as if there couldn't possibly be anything wrong.

'There has been a complaint from one of your neighbours that she heard a lot of screaming and shouting going on in this house this evening. We have come to investigate the complaint.'

Malik realised that the garden door and windows were still wide open. That was obviously a mistake, as they were usually careful to close every double-glazed unit in the house.

'Are you OK?' they asked. I sensed they were looking at me.

But I wasn't allowed to speak, so I just nodded. What else could I do? I had 13 of the family watching me closely for any giveaway signs or body language, listening in closely to everything.

'Do you want to put a report in?'

This time I shook my head. If only I'd been braver, but Malik had stripped my courage away from me long ago. All I could do was endure and survive; I had no alternative.

Of course with my head bowed and my scarf concealing most of my face, the policemen didn't see my black eye, or the cuts and bruises across my cheeks and forehead.

'What was going on here?' asked the sergeant. 'What was all the screaming about?'

Surayya stepped forward and glanced at Eshrat. He nodded, so she spoke, in Punjabi.

'That must have been my younger children,' she said. 'They were having a playfight in the bath, but they're in bed now, probably asleep.' She paused. 'Do you want me to go and wake them up?'

Then her husband stepped forward to translate her words.

'No, no, don't worry about that,' the sergeant reassured her. The other policeman wrote it all down. 'But what about the shouting?'

'That was me, sir,' answered Eshrat. 'I had to go in and tell my children off for making so much noise.'

'I see,' said the sergeant with a nod.

'Will that be all?' asked Malik.

'Is there anything else going on here we should know about?'

Again, I felt the sergeant looking at me, but I didn't dare say or do anything. I kept absolutely still, yet I couldn't stop the tears slowly running down my cheeks, tears of utter frustration that I couldn't ... I didn't dare ask for help. How I wished the policemen could have seen my tears through my scarf.

'Oh no, no, no!' answered Malik. 'There's nothing going on here.'

'It must definitely have been the kids making the noise,' added Eshrat.

I got the impression that the sergeant looked round at the rest of the family and they would all have nodded their agreement.

'Well, if we do have any more complaints, we will come and investigate,' said the sergeant, getting up to go. 'Sorry to have bothered you, but I'm sure you understand that we have to follow up any concerns of this kind.'

'Yes, of course,' agreed Malik, showing them to the door.

Eshrat and his brothers went round shutting all the doors and windows, while Farhat led me through to Eshrat and Surayya's living room, further away from the English neighbour, whom they must have suspected as the police informant. Then Malik and Eshrat came through and started a terrible tirade at me, calling me every swear word they could and smacking my head or face with each one.

'We can't trust you any more, you white bitch!' snarled Malik.

'Yes,' agreed Eshrat. 'The only thing we can do now is tie you up and bind you to the bed upstairs.'

'You brought disrespect on our family,' said Surayya.

'So you cannot sit with us any more,' added Bushra.

Farhat nodded and smiled her cruel smile.

'You don't ever try to run away again,' commanded Malik. 'If you even think of it, I'll get my Jamaican friend to come and kneecap you to ensure you'll never walk again.'

Then they started the real beating I had dreaded. They took out all their fury on me, for daring to escape, for screaming, for raising the police suspicions ... for *everything*. It started with pulling out clumps of my hair, already weak and brittle from lack of nourishment, and taking turns to punch me in the face. Then came the body blows, kicking and hitting me until I finally lost consciousness.

CHAPTER 23

PASSPORT TO PAKISTAN

It seemed unbelievable, 12 years into my captivity and after all my recent beatings and assaults, but I was pregnant again. I didn't show at all yet, but I did feel different: I felt pregnant. I couldn't really describe it, but I knew. It was bliss knowing and not having to tell anyone ... yet. After all my miscarriages, I had to do my best to avoid angering Malik, to do everything he said, no matter what, so that I could avoid major violence and keep my tiny baby growing inside me. But it was a dangerous situation, with him beating me almost daily for not being pregnant. Part of me realised I should just tell him and I hung onto the tiniest scrap of hope that he might let me keep this one.

Although they had threatened to tie me up and bind me to the bed, they must have forgotten because they never did it, so that was something to be grateful for. But the snake was still there, still tormenting me as he hissed and slithered about the tank. I desperately tried not to look at him, and mostly I didn't, but sometimes I couldn't help it. If I was using the ghee barrel, or going to my corner, I had to cross the room. And often he kept me awake at night, when he became more active. They fed him with bits of chicken and other small animals they had slaughtered when I was out of the room. I knew he had grown bigger in the years since he'd been placed in my room: what if he was strong enough to push the lid off the top of his tank? Night and day, this was my worst fear. And when I finally got to sleep, I had nightmares about it.

The sickness started to kick in, as it always did, so I pretended that I wasn't well. Soon the tiny bump became bigger and I had to tell Malik.

'Good,' he said with a smile, and put his arm round me. But I was confused, part of me lost. It reminded me of my father all over again. Were love and violence inseparable? But I craved affection of any kind so I was glad of it, though disgusted with myself for my weakness.

Of course, it all changed once he forced himself on me again. I think he did try to be less rough in his rapes and assaults when I was pregnant, and he beat me less often and usually only on my back and legs, unless he went out of control. But he couldn't ever leave me alone for more than a day or two: he needed to let out his aggression, so the baby and I just had to take it.

This has to be a strong baby, I thought. I did start eating again. Not much – I was never hungry – but I drank lots of their milky tea to make stronger bones. The baby grew and fluttered, then kicked inside me through the summer. I hoped it would be a boy; Malik would be pleased with me. Part of me didn't know why I cared what he thought, but I couldn't help it. I was convinced now that I would never escape so it seemed to change my attitude. Life here was easier if I pleased him, so that was what I had to do.

My fourth full-term baby was born in October 1999. This time it was an easy birth, with no complications.

'It's a little girl,' said the nurse, passing me a healthy baby, with her little fists and black downy hair. I held her in my arms, her skin against mine. Her dark eyes gazed up at me with a puzzled look, as if trying to work out who I was. It made me laugh. She was just perfect and I loved her straightaway.

'Her name is Rafeeqa,' said Malik, unable to resist a smile before whisking her away, as usual.

Like all my babies before her, she was already promised to a couple, quite young this time, who had come to the hospital to see her on the day she was born. A few days later they came back for her, to the house this time, and returned at the end of the month for the health visitor's check-up. As always, it was Sally who came. Again she came with the young man whom she had previously introduced as a trainee psychologist.

I had almost given up on them seeing what was really happening, but again I could see the trainee looking carefully at me and at the family on this particular visit, as if he might have some suspicions. I wondered whether he would raise it with Sally after they left.

'Well, she's a very healthy little girl,' said Sally with a smile, passing her back to me. 'You say she's being bottle-fed?'

I nodded.

'What formula are you giving her?'

I had no idea how to answer that question, so I might have looked a bit flustered. But Malik knew and answered straightaway, as he'd bought it for Surayya to feed Rafeeqa on when she was looking after my baby.

'I bring back the baby food milk powder from our shop,' he explained. 'That's why Anna doesn't know its name.' He looked pointedly at me.

I nodded to Sally to agree with Malik's answer.

They got up to go.

'I'll be back for Rafeeqa's six months check-up,' said Sally. 'I'm sure you'll enjoy this baby,' she added, 'she's such a sweetie.'

I nodded, trying to look more than half-hearted, when I knew I would not see Rafeeqa at all from this day until Sally's next visit.

* * *

As happened every time when my babies were taken away and sold, I fell into a deep depression, refusing to eat anything, sitting in my room and thinking of nothing most of the time other than my beautiful Rafeeqa – longing for her touch against my skin, deeply grieving for her. I lost track of time while in this state, all the days seemed the same. Malik resumed his ferocity, raping and assaulting me every night, and sometimes in the mornings too, plus frequent beatings for whatever story he'd made up to convince himself I deserved it... or for no reason at all.

Eshrat came back to raping me too around this time, when Malik was out. Each as cruel as the other, I was too weak to care.

I grew frailer by the day so I suppose it was no surprise that I became ill. But I was almost glad of it: I wanted to die. I had a deep, chesty cough, always coughing up green or yellow phlegm, and a high fever that rose to dangerous levels. Within days I was delirious. Malik had to bring his mother into the room to see me – I was only vaguely aware that they were talking about me.

The doctor was called out to the house and I had to be downstairs for him to examine me, as they knew he wouldn't approve of the dark, airless bedroom, not to mention the ghee barrel and the cobra in the tank. They brought down a single bed and made it up for me before Malik carried me gently down. In and out of consciousness, I heard the word TB being whispered by someone as they waited for the doctor to arrive.

'No, it's just a chest infection,' insisted Malik.

Bushra used a wet flannel to cool my forehead, which I remember being very soothing. I think I was surprised at the mention of TB, as I knew it was a serious illness that used to kill people. How had I got that? I wondered… before welcoming it.

Let it do its work, I thought. *It's my only way out.*

The doctor came and Malik showed him into the living room, where I was lying on the bed. I don't remember, but I suppose he took my temperature and my pulse and probably asked some questions, like how long I had been ill like this. Malik answered all his questions, but I was too woozy to take in any of the conversation, until near the end.

'So, should we call an ambulance, or take her into hospital ourselves?' asked Malik. 'If it's TB …'

'No,' interrupted the doctor. 'It's not TB, I'm sure of that. But I think Anna has pneumonia, which needs to be got under control using strong antibiotics and she may need an oxygen mask to help her breathe. So I will call the hospital and tell her you are bringing her in straightaway.' He scribbled something down on a sheet of paper and handed it to Malik. 'Give them this note and they will take her straight through without waiting.'

The next thing I remember was waking up in a hospital bed, surrounded by a haze of soft lighting.

Was I still alive, or had I died and this was a sort of waiting room before I joined Nana in heaven?

I must have been sedated because I remember nothing more until some time the next day, when most of the family had formed a guard around my bed.

After the antibiotics had kicked in and my fever lowered sufficiently, the hospital doctor told Malik he could take me home to rest as I would be very tired for the next three months. Spotting his scowl, I knew he would take no notice – I was right, of course. As soon as he got me upstairs and into the room, Malik locked the door and forced himself on me. Like a limp rag, I could do nothing, which infuriated him so he was all the rougher with me. At this point I was past caring: if he killed me, so be it. I had nothing to live for.

The next time I was allowed to go downstairs, when Malik was there, I quickly became aware of the flurry of excitement pervading the house. Usually, if they were happy, it was bad news for me.

What was happening?

I let it all pass over me for a couple of days, and then I asked Malik.

'Asif is getting married,' he explained. 'And we're all going over to Pakistan to attend his wedding. It will be a wonderful celebration, lasting several days.'

'What about me?' I asked, daring to hope they might leave me behind and set me free. But no, they had plans for me.

'You're coming with us,' said Bushra in Punjabi as she came to sit with me for a while, to watch the film showing on TV. 'Isn't that exciting?'

Horrified, I tried my best not to show it yet, until I knew more.

'When is Asif's wedding?' I asked.

'In June 2000 – this year. We've bought the tickets already. We're all going together and I'm sure you will love Pakistan. We have had a mansion built for us all to live in when we go there, and we want to show it to you.'

The conversation that March afternoon was about nothing else – just Pakistan this and Pakistan that. With every revelation, my heart sank. They seemed to be trying to persuade me how much I should like it there, so that I would want to go.

But I didn't; I definitely didn't.

* * *

As I was taken back to my room that evening, too weak to stay downstairs any longer, I turned it all over in my mind. I had a feeling of dread, a premonition this would not go well for me. Why would they want to take me to Pakistan? What could happen to me there? Would I be sold as a sex slave and suffer a lifetime of drudgery in some faraway village, never to be seen again? Or would they throw me down a well at the slightest misdemeanour? When I was a child, before I was kidnapped, I'd heard of women being thrown down wells, but I couldn't remember if that was Pakistan or India, or somewhere else.

After Malik raped me that night, all the more fired up because I was on my period – he always loved the blood – I asked him about Pakistan.

'It will be a wonderful trip,' he said with a persuasive smile, putting his arm round me again. I didn't know whether to flinch, suspecting coercive tactics, or just to take what little affection was offered.

'How long are we going for?'

'Oh, I can't remember. About three months, I think – maybe more.'

Suddenly I thought of something.

'I can't go, I don't have a passport.'

Phew, this could be my way out! I wouldn't be allowed through security without a passport.

'No, that's why we've booked an appointment for you to have your passport photo done at the Post Office tomorrow. I will take you there myself, I want you to look your best.'

So, the following morning, Malik made me put on my best Pakistani clothes and took me downstairs. Farhat herself sat me down and used her finger to spread black kohl all round both of my eyes, concealing the black eye I had at the time.

The postmaster had a little room upstairs where he took passport photos, so we trooped up his narrow stairs. Malik wouldn't let me go up on my own, so he and Bushra stuck close to ensure I said nothing.

I sat down on the little stool, in front of the camera, with my scarf draped round my head and neck, as they had insisted, but the postmaster didn't like that.

'Remove your scarf, please,' he said quite abruptly.

'No, she must keep her scarf on, it is our custom,' explained Malik.

'I'm afraid it's a rule of the British Government: no headwear allowed for passport photos,' replied the postmaster, almost standing to attention.

Malik looked as though he was going to argue with the man, but after two or three seconds, he bit his bottom lip and turned to me.

'OK, if that's the rule, take your scarf off your head and keep it round your neck.'

I signed the form that Malik had filled in, without even being allowed to read it. I did notice that he had had to do it in my own name – Anna Ruston – rather than Yasmeen, which they always called me in the house.

Three weeks later, my new passport arrived. Malik showed it to me very briefly, but long enough to see the sadness in my eyes. Then he whisked it away somewhere.

By now it was early April and I was distraught. Everything I knew about Malik and his family told me not to believe their assurances of happiness in Pakistan. How could I ever be happy with them? All the signs warned me otherwise – all the scars on my body and my mind, the few cherished memories of my stolen babies, the miscarriages I had suffered in between as a result of violent rapes and beatings. Hugely threatened by the prospect of being taken to Pakistan, I had a great sense of foreboding. But I knew it was out of my control. I had no choice except the two almost impossible options: kill myself, or escape. I'd tried both before, ending in miserable failure. What could I do now, with only two months left?

'*Please*, Nana,' I whispered. '*Please* can you come to me. Please hold my hand. I need your love, your help, the warmth of your arms around me.'

For that brief moment, all my fears melted away in the warm surge that healed my body and calmed my mind. And I heard a voice, whether in my head or in the room I did not know.

'*I am with you, Angel. Our prayers will come true.*'

CHAPTER 24

DESPERATE MEASURES

For almost exactly 13 years now I had been a prisoner. An unlucky number – but could it be any unluckier than the preceding years? I had three months before the flight to Pakistan, so less than three months to find a way out. Either I had to succeed in killing myself or find a more successful way to escape.

I started to make a mental list of all the ways I could kill myself. Already I'd tried jumping down the stairs, and that had failed. What else was there?

I knew I couldn't hang myself, because there wasn't anywhere high enough to hang from, except the bare light bulb hanging from the high bedroom ceiling that I couldn't reach. It probably wouldn't have been strong enough anyway. I looked around the room. All the furniture was too heavy to move so that was no good. Maybe I could find a way to strangle myself. After rummaging through the wardrobe and the chest of drawers, I found only Pakistani clothing, the white handbag, sheets and blankets. I had hoped to find shoes (for their laces), but they were all kept downstairs. I looked for English pyjamas (for their cords) but the only pyjamas were loose, buttoned, Pakistani ones; for ties or sashes, but there were none.

I tried twisting a sheet and putting that round my neck, then tied a knot at the front and twisted it to tighten it more and more. It did make it harder to breathe, but that was all. Maybe it was too much thickness of material. Next, I took one of my Pakistani scarves and did the same with that, but when I started to pull it tighter, it tore, so that was no good either. I tried other items of clothing but they were all no use. Finally, I put my hands round my neck, squeezing as hard as I could, pushing in at the front with my thumbs. It made my throat sore and my breathing went wheezy, but as soon as I started to feel faint, I must have loosened my grip.

So, hanging and strangling were out.

The next possibility was a heavy fall on my head, but there was no way to climb onto the top of the wardrobe, which probably wouldn't have been high enough to kill me anyway. If I could find something sharp, I could cut my wrist and bleed to death. But I couldn't find anything with buckles, or sharp edges. I searched the corners of drawers in case there might be one of Malik's razor blades there, but he always took them away with him after he'd had his fun, shaving me as roughly as he could. There wasn't a belt or shoe with a buckle and even the handbag didn't have a strap to it.

Could I smuggle up a knife from the kitchen one day? That seemed very unlikely indeed, as they all watched me so carefully and nowhere in my Pakistani clothing could I have hidden one, which meant I couldn't kill myself that way.

I had my suspicions about Malik and Eshrat and their drug dealing, convinced they would have illegal guns somewhere, but they weren't in that bedroom. I supposed Malik might use a gun to enforce his will against rival dealers, but he hardly needed one to make me do what he wanted. So I couldn't shoot myself.

Could I fatally injure myself with any of the furniture? Perhaps make the wardrobe fall and crush me? But I couldn't move it, and even if I could, it would need somebody to push it from behind to make it fall forward on me, so that wasn't possible. I glanced at the big, old-fashioned double bed, with its heavy wooden frame. I remembered once, when I was terribly depressed, after they'd taken my first baby, Purdil, away from me, I did try to kill myself. Somehow I managed to lift up the end of the bed and tried to get my body underneath it while holding it up, then dropped it, but all that resulted in was a broken arm.

I went and sat in my corner to seek inspiration. I picked up the loose floorboard and took out my dog-eared, wept-on photo of Jamie. Gently, I touched his face, and gazed into his eyes. 'Where are you now?' I whispered. I must have sat there for hours in a kind of trance, just looking at Jamie's boyish grin and wondering what might have been. Finally, I tucked the photo back out of sight and gingerly replaced the floorboard to avoid making it creak. The tears rolled down my cheeks with the realisation that he must by now have moved on – married, had kids, been promoted, travelled the world – while I had just sat in this corner and chipped away the wallpaper.

My back was feeling stiff from crouching all afternoon, so I stood up and walked back to the bed, closing my eyes as I passed the snake in his tank. As I did so, I thought of another way I could kill myself. Why hadn't I thought of it before?

Malik had told me it was a cobra. I wished I knew more about snakes, but with my phobia I could never have even picked up a book about them in primary school. I had a vague idea that a cobra might be poisonous enough to kill. What if I opened the lid and put my hand in? He could bite me with his fangs – I shuddered – and nobody would know for hours, or even a day or two, by which time I could be dead. That sounded so simple. I steeled myself to take the few paces over there; I needn't even look. By now I knew that room so well, I would be sure to get to the tank all right: I could feel for the lid, lift it, and that would be that.

I slid myself off the bed, closed my eyes and took two nervous steps forward ... But then I froze. It was as if my feet were glued to the floor, I couldn't move an inch forward. My heart raced and my whole body was in panic mode, shaking violently. I tried to will myself – just go one tiny step at a time – but I was rigid with fear. I knew then it was impossible.

What else could I poison myself with? There was no alcohol in the Muslim household and I had no access to drugs, other than painkillers. What about the paracetamols? Weren't they supposed to be dangerous, if you took too many of them? I had quite a lot stashed away in one of the drawers.

All the years I had been in the house, any time I was ill or injured somebody would bring me a packet of paracetamols. For the last few years I usually took a few of them and hid the rest. I had no idea how many I had in the drawer – perhaps enough to take an overdose? Delving in, under the sheets, I took out all the half-empty boxes. Then I slipped the silver strips from their boxes and laid them all out on the bed to count: there were about 40 tablets. I was amazed to find so many of them.

I had no idea what quantity I would need to take to kill myself, but perhaps I needed a few more, just to make sure. I tucked them all away again, back beneath the sheets in the drawer. Over the next few days I managed to persuade Surayya that I was in great pain and had run out of painkillers, so she gave me another box of 32.

That should do it, I thought.

Next, I would need a lot of water. I pretended to be very thirsty and they brought me a whole big jug of water and a glass. The one thing I didn't want was to be interrupted, so I had to wait for the right time, after Malik had gone off to the taxi rank. He would be away for at least four hours then, before his break.

The time came and I took the pills out of their foil strips and laid them in a line, counting as I went. Yes, that should be just right. I started to swallow them, one at a time. That was very slow, so I then tried taking two at once a few times, but one caught at the back of my throat and the taste was horrible, so I went back to taking them singly. It went OK for a while, but the more I took, the more my throat hurt. I began to feel each one as it passed like a hard lump down my gullet. It was hard going but soon I became quite woolly, which made it easier to take quite a few more. I think I took most of them before I began to feel sleepy. That made me smile … then I must have drifted off.

My next moment was not in heaven, but a hospital bed. Apparently Malik had come home early for some reason, found me unconscious and rushed me to A&E, where they pumped my stomach. When I woke up, I had tubes in my arms, a monitor bleeping and an angry-faced family round my bed.

'Yes, she has caused some damage to her liver,' a young doctor was telling Malik, 'but we don't think it's life-threatening.'

I'm here, I wanted to shout, *speak to me!* But everyone continued to ignore me as I wallowed in my misery.

I couldn't even kill myself properly.

* * *

A couple of days later, Malik discharged me from the hospital and took me back up to the room. I was relieved when he locked me in and left me in peace – but it didn't last long. That evening, he stormed back upstairs.

'You white bitch, how *dare* you cause such a f***ing fuss!' he yelled, pulling me off the bed and kicking me furiously. 'You disgraced our family and wasted all our time. You're nothing but a white whore who must be punished.'

He pulled me up and smashed my head against the wall, then let me drop again, sliding down and folding onto the rug. I focused on numbing out the worst of the pain. More kicking and punching followed, and finally he raped me on the floor, so brutally I lost consciousness.

When I came to, it was dark, my head was pounding and my whole body ached and throbbed, outside and in.

How could he do that to me when I was supposed to have stayed in the hospital and I needed to rest?

I crawled back to the bed and pulled myself up, but every move was agony. I felt sure I must have some cracked ribs, possibly a broken shoulder too, but I knew they wouldn't do anything about that. They probably wouldn't give me any more painkillers now after my overdose. As I lay on my back in the darkness, distressed and in dreadful pain, I was talking to Nana. I said the prayers we used to say, which calmed me down.

'*Deliver me from evil,*' I repeated, over and over.

* * *

For the next few days, Malik stayed away and I tried to cope with the pain of my injuries, which prevented me from moving much. I had to be careful of my bad shoulder and held my other arm across my chest to try and help my ribs to heal. I did the only thing I could do – I slept a lot, when I could. I don't remember whether they brought me any food, but I didn't eat anything: I just drank water, it was all I wanted.

Surayya usually came up to empty the ghee barrel, but on the second day it was Bushra. She saw me lying awkwardly on the bed and asked if I was all right.

'No,' I said in Punjabi, 'I'm in a lot of pain.' I pointed to my ribs, my shoulder and my back. 'I need to go back to the hospital.'

'Malik?' she asked.

I wasn't sure whether she was asking whether Malik had been responsible for my injuries, but I nodded anyway.

'I come back.' She left and locked the door.

I assumed she would be asking Malik to take me to hospital, but I think he must have been out – he would have refused anyway. Within minutes Bushra came back up, with some cushions, a length of cloth and a mug of their milky tea.

'Drink,' she said, holding it out to me with one hand, while she helped me to get into a better position with the other, placing the cushions to bolster me up. 'You drink tea. Good for pain,' she added. 'Good for bones.'

I didn't want to drink it, but as she was trying to be kind for once, I took a few sips. She had obviously put a lot of sugar in it, perhaps thinking I needed it for shock. I drank about half the mug and it did make me feel less shaky.

'Thank you,' I said, trying to smile.

Then she unfolded the cloth and used it to make a simple sling. Instead of pinning it, she tied a knot. It did help and I was grateful for that.

Over the next couple of weeks I began to heal. I think Bushra must have said something to Malik because when he did finally come up, he treated me more gently than usual. As always, he raped me, but I was able to block out the pain, becoming numb for the duration, and there was no beating this time.

'You must get better to come to Pakistan,' he said when he'd finished. 'No more stupid behaviour, you be a good girl now.'

After he'd gone, I realised there was only a little time left. I was desperate to find a way out of going with them. I'd tried suicide and it hadn't worked so the only alternative was to escape – but how could I do that? Even if it was possible, could I do it in time?

It was early April and Eid was coming up, when the family would celebrate the end of fasting. I suddenly realised that it was now six months since Rafeeqa had been born. Surely the health visitor wouldn't forget to come and do her six months check-up? My one chance to hold my baby again, I longed for that special moment. Whatever happened, it would be the last time.

The thought of the health visitor's visit and the fate of my stolen babies made me all the more determined not to go to Pakistan, where I would be on the other side of the world from them.

That's when the idea started to form – a last, desperate plan.

CHAPTER 25
THE LAST HOPE

Escape was my only option, and it had to be soon. But as I started to formulate a plan in my head, I realised that it was going to be extraordinarily difficult. In all my 13 years in captivity I had never planned anything, and my brain had reduced to a grey fog. Now I had to make it work again – it was a huge challenge.

Whatever the rest of the plan would be, and I had the germ of an idea, it came to me in a flash that I would have to turn into an actress and do everything I could to persuade all the family that I wanted to go to Pakistan, that I was excited about visiting Lahore to see their mansion, that I was keen to attend Asif's wedding. The more positive and enthusiastic I became, I thought, the more Malik and the rest of the family would accept me joining them downstairs. I was still recovering from my injuries, but they were beginning to heal and Bushra even gave me a few paracetamols to ease the pain.

'What is a Pakistani wedding like?' I asked her in Punjabi.

'It is very happy and lively, with bright colours everywhere, especially red for the bride. The women wear their best gold bangles, all up their arms sometimes, showing them off. There are many delicious foods and a lot of loud music and dancing.'

'That sounds much more exciting than English weddings,' I said with a smile.

'Do you like to dance?'

'Yes, I used to,' I nodded.

'I will teach you.'

'Thank you.'

This was just the relaxed relationship that I needed to build, if I was to sufficiently gain their trust.

'Asif is the youngest son,' Bushra continued. 'He will have the most lavish wedding of all. Everyone will be there.'

'Who is he marrying?' I asked, genuinely curious.

'A cousin in Lahore.'

Through these conversations my hope was that they would come to accept me a bit more and allow me to win their trust, in small ways at least. I needed to make them feel I was at last becoming part of their family. Gradually, Bushra, Surayya and even Farhat seemed to feel at ease with me being downstairs and they would talk with me. Sometimes I offered to help with the cooking or serving of food.

* * *

'My mother and my sister tell me that you have been helping and talking with them more,' said Malik with a look of approval one evening. 'Are you glad we are taking you to Pakistan?' he asked, putting his arm round my shoulders, making me wince with the pain on one side. Noticing, he lightened his touch.

'Yes,' I said with a smile, as natural as I could make it. 'I want to come and see your mansion. And I am looking forward to Asif's wedding. Bushra told me what Pakistani weddings are like.'

'Yes, a lot of food and music!' Malik laughed. But then his expression saddened as he looked at me, silhouetted against the curtains.

'You are too thin,' he noticed. 'You must eat.'

'Yes, I will eat.'

As much as I tried to keep him talking, I couldn't avoid the forceful rape that took place that evening, but I felt he was at least trying to be more considerate of me.

* * *

The first part of my plan was going quite well, though I did have to push myself hard to pretend so much. Inside I flinched every time I had to feign enthusiasm or lie that I wanted to go to Pakistan – I just hoped desperately that it would help me with the next stages of my plan.

It was now just over six months since Rafeeqa's birth and Sally, the health visitor, hadn't arranged her six-monthly check-up. As well as the desperate longing I had to see and hold my baby again, this visit was to be another important step. So, after a lot of puzzling about how to make it happen, I finally worked out a way to remind her.

Every fortnight, the family made me accompany them to the Post Office, a few doors down the road, to collect my family allowance and child benefits for the four children who were supposed to be living with me. Apparently, for them to have the money, they needed me to go to the counter for it.

That morning, as usual, I walked down the road, surrounded by the posse of Malik gripping one arm, Bushra gripping the other, plus Farhat, Surayya and her pre-school children. Sometimes, Eshrat came too, but not this time. On arrival, Malik and Farhat escorted me firmly inside, while the others guarded the door.

Malik always wanted to come to keep hold of me, but the postmaster wouldn't allow that. 'Only Anna at the counter,' he said. 'And two others waiting for her in the shop.'

My two guards in the shop, about ten paces away, watched me like spies. Always I had to be under Malik's full control. As I had discovered early on, the only exit from the Post Office was through the shop door, so I couldn't have escaped anyway.

Over the 11 years since Purdil's birth, I had been a regular visitor to claim the allowances, so the postmaster knew my name and who accompanied me, but he seemed particularly unobservant. He never appeared to notice my minders' close vigilance and control, nor my anxiety and discomfort. To begin with, Malik would wait until we got outside before making me hand over the money. These days he didn't bother to wait. As soon as I'd finished at the counter, I had to walk over and give it straight to him, yet no one seemed to question this. I had never dared speak to the postmaster, or anyone else, except for a whispered 'hello' – any attempt at conversation would lead to a terrible beating, I knew.

I was quaking as I approached the counter. This time, I would need all my courage. I had prepared carefully in my mind what I was going to do, and now I had only this one chance to make it happen.

With the family coming to accept me more in the past couple of weeks, I had been able to pick up a pen and a very small notebook that the children had left on the settee without anyone noticing. Now, as the postmaster counted out the money for me, I took a slip of paper from up my sleeve and passed it to him.

'Please could you call the health centre,' I whispered, my back to my guards and keeping my head still, 'and ask for the health visitor to ring me and arrange to visit my youngest child. Tell them it's urgent.' I passed the slip of paper across the counter with my sleeve. 'Here is the phone number. *Please* do it today, it is *very* urgent.'

Luckily, he was a man of few words and even fewer expressions, so he didn't say a thing. As he handed over the money, he just gave the slightest nod. That was enough for me. Now all I could do was go back to the house and wait. I had to trust he would do it. If not, I was almost certainly doomed to my fate in Pakistan.

* * *

Later that day, while I was still downstairs, the phone rang. It could have been anybody, of course. I watched as Malik went to pick up the receiver and saw him nod as he said a few words. He looked annoyed.

Malik strode over to me. They didn't have a cordless phone, so he couldn't bring the receiver.

'It's the health visitor,' he mumbled. 'I tried to put her off, told her we don't have time for a visit now, but she said it was already late and she had to come.' He looked at me. 'She said she couldn't arrange it with me, she has to speak to you. Tell her we can't see her.'

I nodded, sadly, as I stood up.

'Or if she must come, tell her to come this week.'

I expect he hoped she wouldn't be able to fit us in, but I was sure she would if I could somehow get across to her the urgency.

'Hello?'

'Hi Anna. It's Sally here, your health visitor.' She paused. 'I've just had a phone call from your local Post Office. He said you needed me to call you urgently about Rafeeqa …' She paused. 'Has something happened to her?'

'Not that I know of,' I said, aware that Malik was standing only a few feet away, listening to my every word.

There was a moment's silence at the other end. I hoped she was thinking about my answer. 'Shall I come for my six-month visit?'

'Yes, please. But Malik says you can only come if you can fit us in this week.'

'OK, I'll juggle a couple of appointments around. What about tomorrow afternoon, at two? Will that be soon enough?'

'Let me just check with Malik,' I said, again hoping she might interpret my brief comments.

'Tomorrow afternoon at two?' I asked, turning to him.

He nodded, with a scowl.

'Yes, that's fine,' I replied. 'Thanks …' I paused, not daring to give anything away. 'See you tomorrow.'

My heart soared to think I would be holding my adorable baby Rafeeqa just 24 hours away. That would be a precious new memory to make, to last me forever.

But Malik wasn't satisfied. 'What did you mean when you said, "Not that you knew of"?'

'Oh,' I thought quickly, 'that was when she asked me if the health centre had been in touch to arrange a visit. I said that because I didn't know.'

'Mmm,' growled Malik. 'Well, you'd better watch what you say tomorrow,' he added. 'Remember, leave all the talking to me.'

'Yes.' I nodded – I was OK with that because if my plan worked, I wouldn't need to say anything.

* * *

The following day, at lunchtime, Rafeeqa's new mother brought her to the house, ready for the health visitor's appointment at 2pm. I had the chance to sit with her for a few minutes and she told me her husband couldn't leave work that day, so she had brought Rafeeqa on her own. She told me her husband was a relation of the family – she wasn't sure what.

'Is she a good baby?' I asked her in Punjabi.

'Yes, very good,' she replied with a smile before handing her to me. 'You hold,' she said in English.

I took a gentle hold of little Rafeeqa, still sleeping, and held her up against my shoulder, stroking her black hair, now down to her shoulders. She was so light and so comfortable, I could have held her there for hours.

'Does she sit up now?' I asked.

'Yes,' she nodded. 'She has a lovely smile and she hardly ever cries.'

I was happy to think that she was such a contented baby. I knew she would have been so with me, but I was glad it was part of her nature. She didn't get that from Malik, for sure.

The woman told me the toys they had for Rafeeqa to play with and what her cot was like, and the mobile above it. She seemed a really kind person, so I was relieved my baby had a good home, but there was a pain in my heart, knowing this would almost certainly be the last time I could ever see her or hold her.

A tear fell down my cheek and I wiped it away.

At two on the dot, Sally arrived and brought in her bag with all the paperwork in it, together with her portable weighing machine and tape measure. I had Rafeeqa back in my arms for this visit, ready for Sally's questions. Malik was standing beside me, keen to take over if I looked like hesitating, but because her friendly adoptive mother had told me quite a lot about Rafeeqa, I was able to answer everything myself.

Once Sally had checked her weight and height and looked over her body, she seemed happy with the baby's progress.

'Well done, Anna,' she said. 'You've looked after your baby very well.'

At first, I was disappointed maybe she hadn't picked up on any of the clues. But then I saw her give a pointed look first at Malik then across the room at the mother, ignoring the rest of the family surrounding us. Then she looked back at me. Was it just an idle glance, or was there something more? She had a slightly puzzled expression, I thought.

'Right,' said Sally, getting some forms and a pen out of her bag. 'Let's fill this visit record form in now.' She filled in the measurements and added a couple of lines, then turned again to me. 'Perhaps you could just check I've spelt Rafeeqa's name right and read it through to make sure I haven't made any errors?' she asked.

We sat facing each other across the corner of the table. As I looked down, I let my sleeve fall loose, pushed down the bangle Malik had given me to wear when people came, and shook my arm slightly, so that a piece of folded paper fell out of it to the floor.

Sally carried on writing something, so I nudged her knee with mine, under the table, and looked down to the floor. She followed my gaze. As soon as she noticed the piece of paper by her foot, she dropped her pen, as if accidentally, then leant down to pick it up, together with my note, which she stuffed in her pocket as she brought up her hand.

I deliberately didn't make eye contact. Whether or not they were looking at us, I knew Malik and the others were close by and I didn't want them to have a reason to suspect anything.

At the bottom of the form Sally wrote a long number, then used the palm of her hand to tear it away from the rest, while I put my hand on the table, as if ready to get up, and gathered up the torn-off scrap. I guessed it might be her phone number – I would have to keep it hidden until later.

Once Sally had left, I asked to go to the bathroom. Malik nodded, so I went to use the toilet and tucked the precious number into the waist of my long skirt. I had no idea how I would be able to use it, as I was not allowed to touch any of the phones in the house. I'd be in terrible trouble if I tried, and that might undo all my good work in winning a small degree of the family's trust.

I got back to the living room just in time to have one final hug with little Rafeeqa, who gave me a big smile. Then off she went, out of my life, with her new mother.

That night, after Malik had been angry with me and given me a thorough kicking for holding Rafeeqa so much, then raped me furiously, he fell asleep. He snored loudly and I had to lie next to him, with empty arms and nothing but my thoughts.

I knew I might be wrong, but I had a good feeling about Sally. I had seen her stuff my unread note in her pocket, and imagined her, once she was in her car, getting it out, unfolding it and reading my brief message: 'Help me!' and underneath the date, 21st April, which was the end of the following week.

I had chosen that date deliberately because it was their sacred month of Muharram and 21st April would be a Friday, which was always a Muslim holy day. It was to be a special day because all the family would come and join in the prayers that morning, and it was especially holy the following week because it was a day of fasting.

If ever there was a chance for me to escape, this would be the day, though I wasn't sure how ... as long as they let me downstairs.

As I lay in the darkness, I desperately hoped that Sally would take my note seriously. She was the only one who could help me now, so I said the Lord's Prayer, like I used to say it with Nana. Only this time, it was an urgent plea to God. I used to believe in Him when I was a child, but since I'd been a prisoner, I wasn't so sure.

Tonight I needed to believe again, to help make things right.

* * *

The following day, around lunchtime, the phone went. As usual, Malik was home from the shop and he answered it. I kept my eyes down, not wanting him to see any hint of the hope I felt. He had a quiet conversation, which I could tell was quite prickly, but I couldn't hear most of it, until his voice rose.

'I can tell you all of that information better than Anna can,' he snapped. 'So ask me your questions.'

Finally, he shrugged and called me to the phone. 'The white bitch won't talk to me,' he snarled, then lowered his voice, realising she might have heard him.

'Who is it?' I asked.

'The health visitor. She says she can only speak to you.'

He almost threw the receiver at me and stormed off across the room to sit on a settee and look at the newspaper. I breathed a sigh of relief that he wouldn't be standing beside me, but I knew he had excellent hearing and would almost certainly be listening and watching me, so I couldn't give anything away.

'Hello?' I said, tentatively.

'I've told Malik that I need you to check the details of all your children's births and the spelling of their names,' said Sally. 'Is that OK?'

'Yes.'

'Good, now I want you to answer my real questions. Are you in trouble?'

'Yes.'

'Do you need help?'

'Yes.'

'Are you able to get out?'

'No.'

'Have you still got my mobile phone number?'

'Yes, that's right.' I thought I'd better vary my answers a bit.

'Well, that's in case you need to get in touch with me. Are you able to use the phone when you want to?'

'No, I'm afraid that's not correct.'

'But you will, if ever you get the chance?'

'Yes, that's better.'

'Now this date you've given me, 21st April. Is that the date you need me to help you?'

'Yes.'

'Do you need me to come and collect you?'

'Yes.'

'I realise you can't say much, and you won't be able to answer the phone, but I will give two rings on the landline number at your house when I arrive in your street. Will that be all right?'

'Yes, that's fine.'

'Good. I will rearrange all my appointments and take the day off, so I will be sitting in a black car, near the cakes factory down your road, all day until you can get free. OK?'

'Yes, thank you.' I wanted to say so much more, but Malik glanced in my direction. 'Goodbye,' I said, and put the receiver down.

'Did you help her get it all sorted out?' asked Malik as I sat down next to him.

'Yes, she'd got most of it right already.'
Fortunately, he seemed satisfied.

* * *

From now on all the days were special days for me. No matter what happened, no matter how fiercely Malik abused me, I had a new secret, a gleaming diamond of hope in my heart. For the first time in 13 long and terrible years, I had the possibility of something I could look forward to. I had never received a single gift since I had arrived there, apart from the children. Now, at last, I might be able to give a gift to myself with Sally's help: the gift of freedom.

It was that or Pakistan and disaster.

But I chose not to dwell on failure: I had to be positive now to stand any chance of making my plan happen. I have no idea where I drew the mental strength. Physically, I was a wreck, always covered in bruises, thin and weak.

I think my strength must have grown from Sally picking up that note. From then on, even the awareness that I now had someone on the outside knowing I wasn't free was an enormous boost. I don't recall much about those days in between, except they seemed long and I could hardly stop smiling to myself. All the family noticed, especially Malik.

'You look happy,' he said to me one day. 'I like to see you happy.'

'Yes, it's all the talk of Pakistan,' I lied.

I think he believed me.

* * *

On the morning of Friday, 21st April, I waited in the desperate hope that somebody would come to collect me and take me downstairs.

What if no one came?

I started to panic and fantasise about tying sheets together and finding some way of breaking the window, but finally I heard light footsteps on the stairs. It was Asif who unlocked the door that day.

'Malik said I could come and get you. I thought he'd forgotten about you and I wanted you to share this special day with the family.'

'Thank you,' I said with a smile.

Asif was the one person in this house since Muneeza had disappeared who I felt had any sympathy for me. He once saved me when I had been badly injured and could have died if he hadn't gone for help.

'Do you remember when I first came here?' I ventured.

'Yes, you were only a child, like me,' he said.

I could see in his soft brown eyes that he would have liked to say more, but thought better of it. I said nothing either, as I didn't want to get him in trouble.

I was just so relieved to be going downstairs. If nobody had come for me, my future – if I had one at all – would have been both black and short.

* * *

It was mid-morning and people had been arriving every 10 or 15 minutes – mostly brothers and their families, and other relatives. The front door kept being opened and shut.

At one point, the phone started to ring, just twice, then stopped. Asif was standing near it, about to lift up the receiver. He looked puzzled, then turned towards where I was sitting. I'm not certain, but I think he suspected something. However, nobody else seemed to have noticed and he said nothing – just gave me a smile before joining his older brothers.

As I sat in the living room, watching yet more arrivals, I imagined Sally sitting in her black car down the road, near the cakes factory. But there was nothing I could do now so I rehearsed in my mind the ways I might be able to escape.

A few minutes later, Eshrat announced prayers would be said in his adjoining living room, through the hole in the wall. All the men filed in first, then the women. I had hoped to hang back, thinking they probably wouldn't notice I was missing, with so many people there. But Malik spotted me.

'Come and pray with us,' he beckoned through the hole in the wall, so I had no choice. I pulled my scarf down over my face as he led me to a space next to Bushra. He obviously wanted her to keep an eye on me.

The prayer leader stood at the front and spoke to everyone first, probably about the sacred day, but I wasn't listening. My mind was racing.

How could I get out of this room?

Then he started off the prayers.

After about half an hour, I was getting impatient, though I couldn't show it. When there was a pause, I turned to Bushra and whispered: 'I need to go to the toilet.'

For a few seconds she hesitated before nodding.

I didn't wait to check that she was giving me permission; I believed she was.

'I won't be long,' I added.

She nodded again.

Until recently, I wouldn't have been trusted to go anywhere in the house on my own, but my acting seemed to have had a good effect. We were at the back of the room, so I tiptoed out, through the doorway to the other living room and to the door to the bathroom. Here, I paused and looked around me. I had thought of creeping out through the back door, if it was unlocked, and along to the left, crouching below the windows in case there was anyone in that part of the house, then down through the archway, if it was open, or across the garden. Somehow I would get over the fence and down the alleyway, as before, then away. But all that depended on the door from the kitchen being unlocked. The only other exit was the front door, but that didn't have a latch and was always double-locked with a key.

As I turned to look at it ... a miracle. The key was in the lock! I had never seen that before, they were always so careful. With all the morning's comings and goings, somebody had slipped up.

I went into the bathroom and flushed the toilet, thinking that would create enough noise to mask any sound the door might make. Then I crossed the hall to the front door, making sure there was no one looking. I took hold of the key and turned it... The door opened.

With the fresh air on my face, I ran as fast as I could.

Can it be true, I wondered, *am I free at last?*

CHAPTER 26
AFTERMATH

I picked up my long Pakistani skirt and ran, barefoot, as fast as I could down the street. I could see a parked black car in the distance… I ran towards it, panting and gasping for breath from being so weak and unfit, but I didn't hear any footsteps behind me and I somehow kept going until I reached the car. Sally opened the door for me to step in.

'Well done,' she said with a tense face, breaking into an anxious smile. 'You made it!'

She passed me a big hat with a floppy brim, a thick scarf and some large sunglasses.

'Put these on, in case they chase after us,' she explained. 'And keep your head down. Now I've got to get you right away from here.'

As she drove off at speed to the far end of the road and turned into the traffic, my only thought was to get away, as far as we could, to make sure they couldn't come after us. I wanted to turn and look behind, to make sure we weren't being followed, but I didn't dare.

It wasn't until we were through the town and out the other side that I could begin to breathe properly. That's when it finally hit me: I was free.

Could it be true? After 13 years of hell, was I really free at last?

'Are you all right?' asked Sally. 'How do you feel?'

'I feel great! Free at last. Thanks to your help.'

In fact, I felt euphoric, yet weighed down by fear that this freedom was unreal and any moment they would track me down and punish me worse than ever before. How could I ever be completely free? I had come away with nothing but the scars of my physical and mental traumas. The 13-year-long nightmare would always haunt me, I feared.

And of course I had no possessions bar the Pakistani clothes I was wearing when I ran out of that front door ... and the precious photo I had tucked into my waistband.

* * *

'Where do you want me to take you?'

'I don't know, I've nowhere to go.'

'OK, you can stay at my place tonight if you want.'

'Yes, please.'

'We can talk properly later, but do you mind if I ask you a couple of things that puzzled me about your help note and our phone conversation the other day?'

'Go ahead.'

'Were you a prisoner?'

'Yes, Malik kidnapped me when I was a few days past my fifteenth birthday, and I've never had a birthday since,' I paused. 'So he was a paedophile. He held me captive for 13 horrendous years.'

Sally turned to face me briefly, long enough for me to see the shock on her face.

'And where is Rafeeqa, and the other children? Could you not have brought them with you?'

'No, they weren't mine to bring.'

This time Sally looked astonished.

'But you had Rafeeqa with you when I came last week.'

'It was all a charade.'

I told her about Malik taking my babies from me, selling them, then getting them back just for Sally's visits. Though I tried to wipe my tears with my sleeve, it was no use.

'As long as I live, I don't expect I'll ever see them again.'

'That's appalling,' said Sally. 'So cruel, I had no idea.'

We sat in silence as she drove, each occupied with our own thoughts. My emotions were in turmoil – unbelievable relief and triumphant happiness mixed with immense sadness at the loss of my children, fear that Malik might find and punish me and take me back into captivity, and self-loathing at how he and all those men had used and abused my body, reducing me to worse than a whore.

'I can't tell you most of what happened,' I said, sobbing.

'You've had an appalling life with them by the sound of it, but none of it was your fault ... and you're free now,' she told me.

I knew she was trying to be kind, but no words could take away my shame.

* * *

Sally's home was a one-bedroom flat.

'Will you be all right sleeping on the sofa tonight?' she asked.

'Yes, it looks a really comfortable one,' I replied. 'Not like the hard settees at the house.'

She got out some bedding for me. Then she made us a cup of tea and we sat down at her small kitchen table.

'Thank you for helping me to escape,' I began. 'I couldn't have done it without you.'

'I only wish I'd realised earlier,' she said. 'What puzzles me is, didn't anyone come looking for you? What about your family – didn't they report you as missing?'

'I don't think anyone realised,' I explained. 'None of them wanted me, and I had to run away.'

We talked for a while, with me filling in some of the answers to her questions. She was very kind and understanding, but for me the most important thing was that she didn't seem to judge me – she just accepted what I told her and sympathised with me. I'd had no one for 13 long years, and now I felt I had a friend who was not only my saviour, but also someone I could talk to, truthfully, though I daren't go too deeply.

Sally asked what I'd most like to eat and I said I wasn't hungry.

'Is that why you're so thin?'

'Partly.' I nodded. 'But mostly I think I was very depressed. I didn't want to eat, I didn't want to stay alive.'

'Depression can be very harmful to physical health as well as the mind. But you are extremely skinny, almost like a skeleton. I've got some scales in the bathroom, do you mind if we check how much you weigh?'

So I stood on the scales and the dial showed just under six stone.

* * *

We talked a lot that evening and over breakfast the next morning. As it was a Saturday, Sally didn't have to go to work. I did enjoy having a small amount of English breakfast – the first cereal and proper toast I'd eaten since childhood. I told Sally about my family, especially Nana, and how neither of my parents seemed to love me so I had to run away. I told her about my grandparents too, and Uncle Jack.

'I know you didn't want to phone any of your family last night,' she said, 'but I think you should maybe just get in touch today, if only to tell them you were kidnapped, but now you are free again. They have a right to know.'

'I don't think so,' I said, quite indignant. But then I thought about it. 'Well, maybe later,' I agreed.

'OK, so let's decide what you want to do today. First, we will go to see the doctor about your weight. Then how about getting you out of your Pakistani clothing and buying you some English clothes to wear?'

'Yes, please.'

'OK. I don't have much money, but we could go to the Saturday market and see if we can buy you some things you like.' She smiled. 'Come on, let's go.'

'No, not to the market!' I said, horrified. 'A market would be too crowded, somebody might see me there.' I shook with fear. 'Please can you go and choose some things for me?'

At first Sally looked surprised, but her expression soon changed.

'I'm sorry, I should have realised. You've been on your own so much as a prisoner.'

I nodded. But I didn't want to tell her the real reason, about all the men – any of them could live in the area.

'OK, I'll go, but I'd better measure you first.'

Sally took me to the doctor's as a visitor and he prescribed some tablets to restore my appetite and an iron tonic to help me feel better. He told me to go to my own doctor's as soon as I could. Then she dropped me off, saw me in and went off to the market.

Alone in the flat, it did feel strange. It could have felt like another prison, I suppose, but I opened all the windows and breathed in the fresh air. I could even taste that fresh-air smell: this was freedom.

I sat down and put the TV on – at last British TV! But I don't remember watching anything; I must have nodded off. The next sound I heard was Sally turning her key in the lock. I panicked. For a moment I thought I was back in the room. I picked up a cushion to hold in front of me, as some sort of protection. But then I realised where I was, and breathed a huge sigh of relief.

* * *

Sally came in, carrying an assortment of carrier bags. 'I hope I've bought you all the things you need to start with,' she said.

I had been a girl, just turned 15, when I'd gone into the house and now I was a 28-year-old woman. For almost half my lifetime I had not had any new clothes, other than the hated Pakistani ones.

'I had to guess your shoe size,' said Sally as she got out a pair of mules. 'That's why I bought you these.'

I tried them on and they were fine. But it felt very strange – I hadn't worn anything at all on my feet for 13 years.

Sally then unpacked all the other things she had bought me and I changed into them. She had bought me some English underwear, which felt wonderful, a pretty T-shirt, blue jeans and a gilet – all on the market stalls.

'When I gave them your measurements,' she said, 'the stallholders told me that would be a regular child's size, apart from your height.'

I looked at the labels and sure enough, the gilet and T-shirt said 'Age 12–13'.

'But I had to get adult jeans. I know they'll be much too loose at the waist, but I've got an old belt I never wear, so you can have that to keep them up!'

She emptied out her last bag.

'I've got you a toothbrush and toothpaste too, a flannel and a box of tampons. I'm afraid I ran out of money then, so I couldn't buy you any make-up.'

'Thank you so much, Sally. I don't know how I'm ever going to be able to repay you for all you've done for me.'

'You'd have done it for me, if it was the other way round.'

* * *

That afternoon we had to decide what to do next.

'We ought to go to the police,' she suggested.

'I suppose so,' I nodded. 'But, please, not today.'

'Ok, but we must go soon.'

We discussed which of my family to contact so that at least they would know I was still alive.

'My mother hates me,' I explained. 'And my father is violent and abusive, so I don't want anything to do with him.'

'No, I can understand that. Thank goodness you had your Nana,' said Sally softly.

'Yes, but she died when I was ten, that was when we were staying with Grandma Kathleen and Grandad.'

'What about phoning them?'

'Maybe. They did love me once but I last saw them on the day after Nana's funeral.'

'How old do you think your grandparents would be now?'

'Oh, I'm no good at maths!' I sighed. 'I expect they were about late sixties or seventy-ish when I was kidnapped, so I guess they would be in their eighties now. Is that right?'

I had missed out on my last year and a half of school before GCSEs and I was never an academic student. Since then I had never had anything to read, so I really lacked confidence.

Sally nodded. 'I hope they're still alive,' she said. 'I can only keep you here over the weekend. After that you'll have to find somewhere else to live. Perhaps you could go there. What do you think?'

'Can't I stay here a bit longer?' I asked. 'I'll do your housework and cooking, everything.'

'No, I'm afraid that would get me in trouble. You see, I was already breaking the rules when I helped you to escape – I should have referred you to the police or social services. We're not allowed to have any kind of personal relationship with any of our patients, so I could lose my job if anyone at work finds out that you've stayed here in my flat, even over the weekend.'

'Oh, I'm sorry. You should have said – I don't want to make trouble for you.'

'Don't worry, I expect it will be all right, as long as we find you a place to stay from tomorrow.'

'Well then, I suppose my grandparents would be the only people who might have me, or possibly Val. But she was only in a rented house before I was kidnapped, so she's probably moved by now.'

'Do you remember your grandparents' address?'

'No, but I would recognise their house in Allerback – I lived there for two years.'

'Oh, I know Allerback,' said Sally. 'I have a patient who lives there. Let's go over there and find the house.'

So that's what we did.

* * *

'That's where I tied up Grandad's dog,' I said, as we passed the village shop. 'But when I came back to untie him, he was gone.'

'Oh dear!'

'Go up that road and turn right,' I directed Sally. Then, as we turned into the road, 'That's the house. Look, it's still got a green front door.'

I didn't have the courage to go up the path on my own, so Sally came with me. I rapped the knocker and rang the bell, then waited. I could hear someone shuffling up the hallway towards the door, then it opened.

'Hello, Grandad,' I said with a smile, hoping he would recognise me.

Old and bent, he looked stunned for a few seconds before the realisation dawned.

'Anna, is that really you? Where've you been?'

'I was kidnapped, Grandad, when I was 13.'

'Kidnapped? That's terrible. How did that happen?'

'It was after I ran away from Dad. I've only just escaped.'

'That man never was any good – a bad penny, like your mother. We haven't had any contact with either of them since your Nana died.'

'How is Grandma Kathleen?' I asked. 'Is she here?'

'No, I sent you a letter to tell you she was ill. Didn't you get it? She had breast cancer. She was very ill – she died the day before yesterday.'

'Oh no, I'm sorry, Grandad! I didn't get the letter and I didn't know anything that happened while I was away.'

'Oh dear, oh dear!' he said, looking confused and wringing his hands. 'Well, if you want to see your Grandma, you'll have to go to the Chapel of Rest, that's where she is now. They'll tell you when the funeral is.'

Sally asked him where the Chapel of Rest was and we got in the car. Then I waved him goodbye as he shut his front door and off we went.

'How tragic that you just missed seeing your Grandma alive,' Sally sympathised.

'Yes, I would have loved to have seen her, to tell her I cared. Now she'll never know.' A tear trickled slowly down my cheek.

* * *

When we got to the Chapel of Rest at Dunsford, we went in. The lady on the desk took us through.

'Some of your relatives are already here,' she told us.

As she opened the door for us and we went in, I recognised Uncle Steve, my mother's brother. Despite having last seen me as a ten-year-old, he knew who I was. His face reddened and he scowled.

'Oh, you've turned up now, have you? Where were you when she needed you? You were her only granddaughter – all the rest were boys. She wanted to see you before she died – but oh, no, you couldn't even do that for her.'

I wanted to interrupt him and try to explain but I could see he didn't want to know, and probably wouldn't believe me anyway – who would?

'Look at that body now – that was your grandmother, the woman who doted on you and Nana in her house for two years. She never saw or heard from you again. You've been in here and you've seen her body now,' he continued. 'I want her to haunt you for the rest of your days. It's your fault she's lying there, after all she did for you.'

He pointed a finger at me. 'You killed her because of your neglect.' He paused. 'So you needn't think you can come to the funeral. We don't want you there, understood?'

He turned and strode out of the room.

At this I burst into tears.

How was it my fault? What did I do?

I was indignant, but I knew it must have looked as if I didn't care. Even though I couldn't have done anything, that did make me feel guilty.

I stood by Grandma Kathleen's open coffin and took one last look.

'I'm really sorry, Grandma,' I whispered shakily. 'I wish I could have come.'

As we left, the lady at the desk told me the date and time of the funeral and I thanked her – I could hardly tell her the family didn't want me there. She asked if I'd like to order some flowers. Of course, I would have loved to, but I had no money. I didn't even glance in Sally's direction because she had already spent more than enough.

Driving back to the flat, she suggested we go to the police station first to report that I had been kidnapped but had now escaped.

'No, not yet, *please*,' I begged her. 'They might want me to tell them all the details and I don't feel ready yet.'

'OK then, we'll go straight back to my place. But you'll have to talk to them soon,' she insisted.

* * *

Sally's answerphone was beeping.

'I'd better check it,' she said, switching it on.

I overheard it all.

Hi Sally

It's Mike here, I was hoping to catch you in. I'm sorry to disturb your weekend, but I've had an urgent call from the police. They've put out an alert, looking for one of your patients, who's gone AWOL, so I thought I'd better ring to

*see if you might know anything. Her name is Anna Ruston
and apparently she's been reported as a missing person. She
went out yesterday and didn't return. Her husband has told
the police he's very worried about her because she has severe
mental health problems and unpredictable behaviour. He
said she's unstable and a danger to herself and others. She
needs to be found and taken back home to safety.*

Ring me on this number if you hear anything.

Bye.

I was astonished to learn what Malik had told the police.

'Well, what do you think of that?' said Sally.

'It's a pack of lies!' I said, fighting my indignation. 'How
dare he?'

'Yes, though it wouldn't be at all surprising if your traumas
hadn't given you a degree of mental health problems – it would
be the same for anyone in that situation. But you certainly don't
match his description of you. And is he your husband?'

'No, he told the hospital as well that he was my husband
and at that time I was underage so he couldn't have married me
without my parents' permission, could he?'

'You're right.' She paused as we sat down to talk it through.
'Anyway, even if he was your husband, you would still have the
right to leave him if you wanted to, like anyone else.'

We talked and talked that evening. I didn't want Sally to let
her boss or the police know where I was – I was still wracked
with the fear that the family might track me down and kidnap
me all over again.

'Well, I'll have to ring Mike in the morning and tell him something,' said Sally. 'I can't ignore his message; that would be too suspicious.'

'Yes, I see what you mean. But I don't want the police coming round here,' I told her.

Even more pressing was the question of where I could go. Sally needed me out by Monday morning at the latest. I felt very vulnerable, but she didn't seem aware of all the dangers I might be in… and I couldn't tell her too much. I couldn't see any alternative other than to ask my mother if I could stay there for a bit, at least until I found my feet. I dreaded to think what her reaction would be.

I had a lot on my mind when I snuggled down on Sally's comfy sofa that Saturday night, but I don't remember thinking much at all. I must have fallen asleep quite quickly and didn't wake up until nearly lunchtime.

'Thank goodness you're awake at last,' Sally smiled. 'I was just about to wake you up. We have some decisions to make.'

'OK,' I said, sitting up and stretching. 'I suppose you'd better call your boss and say whatever you think best. But maybe pretend you're just going out for the rest of today, so you won't be able to talk to the police until later, or tomorrow. Could you do that?'

'Yes, I suppose. But what about you, do you know where you want to go?'

'To be honest, I don't have anywhere to go where I'd be wanted. I think I just have to go to my mother's. It will be harder for her to turn me away if I turn up with nothing.'

'Oh, I feel awful at having to ask you to leave.'

'Don't worry. It's not your fault.'

'Do you know where your mum lives?' asked Sally.

'I know where she used to live.'

We had some lunch, then Sally drove me over to my mother's old address that Sunday afternoon. I hoped she still lived there. Sally stayed in the car while I went up to the front door. Taking a deep breath, I rang the bell. I had to ring twice before I could hear somebody coming. As the door opened I steeled myself.

The woman standing there, in her glamorous outfit and painted nails, was my mother. I recognised her immediately, but it took three or four seconds before she realised who I was.

'You'd better come in,' she said in a surly voice.

No hug, not even a smile, but I hadn't expected it. In fact, I had feared she would simply slam the door in my face. This was better than I thought.

I turned to signal that Sally could go, then went in.

'Where have you been?' my mother asked as we sat on separate chairs in her lounge. 'You're so thin,' she added. 'What have you been doing to yourself?'

I started to tell her about Malik and the kidnapping and being locked into the room, the abuse and everything. She was listening, though I couldn't tell whether she believed any of it.

I think Sally must have rung her boss as soon as she got back to the flat and one of them rang the police to say she had delivered me to my mother's house and that's where I would stay. I can't blame Sally for that – she had to cover herself and she'd been kind to me.

It wasn't her fault that the police must have passed this information straight on to Malik – but what were they thinking? Did they want me to be kidnapped again?

* * *

Within an hour of my arrival, while I was still talking to my mother, Malik's taxi pulled up outside the house and almost the entire family clambered out. There was Malik, Eshrat, Farhat, Bushra, Surayya and several of the children and they all stood on my mother's front doorstep, urging me to get in the car.

I was petrified. Even my mother could see the effect just their presence had on me. She must have been alarmed but she put on her bolshie 'don't mess with me' face as she opened the door.

Malik pushed his way in and everyone else followed. I wanted to hide, but I knew it was no use; I was convinced I was doomed. Just two days of freedom, then a lifetime of severe and continuous punishment. I froze where I stood, a trembling wreck.

Malik marched into the lounge and started shouting at me in Punjabi. There were a lot of swear words, but in between he was plain enough.

'You're mine and I'm not leaving without you so get a move on! Get into that f***ing taxi and get back where you should be! You're a disgrace to the family.'

For once I stood my ground and shook my head, still trembling.

He raised his hand to give me a backhander. I flinched.

That's when my mother stepped in.

'You touch her and I'll call the police! I'll have you for assault,' she told him.

For the first time in my life she had stood up for me and helped me. I don't know where I got the strength from, but I spoke up too. 'Get out of this house,' I shouted at him. 'I'm not coming back and I never want to see you again!'

His face went apoplectic, and I knew then we'd won … this round at least.

'Out!' ordered my mother bravely. 'You heard her – there's the door. Get out, all of you. Go to hell!'

Turning to leave, Malik had one parting shot: 'If you ever leave this house, I'll have you knee-capped.'

After they'd gone, I realised it wasn't so much me they wanted, but the money they could no longer claim or earn from me. As for the threat, I was in no shape to go out anyway. I was by now so anorexic if I'd even tried to eat, I started coughing up blood – as I first discovered at Sally's flat. I needed to be under medical supervision.

* * *

What I hadn't realised was my mother was having an affair with a policeman, so he came round and had a chat with me. He seemed quite fatherly, as if he wanted to help. He asked me what had been going on and I told him as much as I felt able. Of course, there was a lot more I didn't say, and that I didn't feel able to tell anyone, but what I said was enough. The police wanted me to help them prosecute Malik, but I needed to regain my strength first. In the meantime, they placed me under police protection, which meant they kept a watch on the house, with 24/7 patrols.

Sally must have found out my mother's number from the police or from her work, and she rang me after a couple of days to find out how I was. I told her about Malik and the family coming to get me and my mother standing up for me, as well as what I'd said. Then she told me she had been sacked.

'All because of me,' I said, shocked. 'That's so unfair. I'd never have got out without your help.'

'According to the rules I shouldn't have helped you, but I had to. I don't regret a thing, so you mustn't feel bad. I expect I'll find a new job,' she told me.

But I did feel bad about Sally losing her job. She had been my saviour and I hoped one day I'd be able to thank her properly.

* * *

Gradually, my mother began to accept my presence in her house, though I always knew I wasn't wanted. At least she could now claim benefits for me being there, as her dependent, so that helped financially. But her tolerance didn't last long and one day she sat me down.

'I want to talk to you,' she began. 'I've got something to tell you.'

Well, I thought, *she's not drunk so it must be something interesting.*

'Do you know why I hate you so much?'

'So, you're telling me you hate me?'

'Well, wouldn't you hate a child when you were raped to conceive it?'

'You mean …'

'Yes, your father raped me – he forced sex on me. That's how you were conceived, and that's why I hate you so much.'

Gobsmacked, I couldn't believe she'd told me that. Clearly she had said it deliberately; she must have wanted to hurt me. It made me think back to my own children, all conceived out of rape, but I loved them all. We were very different, my mother and me. Although astonished she told me, I was not surprised by what she said – I had always known she didn't love me.

From then on we only ever spoke to each other when we had to.

* * *

Five days after I escaped, I heard the doorbell ring. My mother answered it.

'It's someone for you,' she called.

I couldn't think of anyone who would want to see me, except Malik and his family, or the police, or maybe Sally, but my mother would have said who they were. And if it was someone bad, surely she wouldn't have called me?

'Who is it?'

'Come and see,' she told me.

I went out to the hall. The front door was ajar, so I opened it a bit further and peeked out. There on the doorstep was a young man in uniform with a familiar face.

It was the boy in the photo.

'Hi Anna,' said Jamie with a grin. 'Somebody told me you'd come back.'

EPILOGUE

I was reborn on 21st April 2000 – the day I thought I would never see. It was a new beginning in every sense, but my past continues to haunt me.

The young man on the doorstep was the boy in the photo, the one treasured possession I'd managed to keep hidden all those years, then smuggled out with me when I finally escaped.

'Do you want to come out for a drink?' he asked.

We picked up from there almost as if the years hadn't gone between. Jamie soon moved in with me at my mother's – extra rent for her. But the atmosphere was so bad that often we ate our meals at his mother's or grandmother's houses nearby. Sadly they didn't have enough room for us to stay with them, but they always made us both welcome. Indeed, Jamie's mother became the mother I'd never had since Nana died. I still wear his grandmother's wedding ring every day.

The police continued to provide round-the-clock protection for quite a few years and several times tried to persuade me to help them convict Malik and his accomplices for their crimes against me, but I have never yet felt strong enough to give evidence. Writing this book is the first time I have revealed any of the details of what happened to me in those stolen years.

Even Jamie didn't know, and I could never bring myself to tell him – I was too ashamed.

In the months following my escape, Malik and his brothers were in the local newspapers for a number of fights and attacks involving drugs, weapons and violence. He was convicted of a number of these crimes and sent to prison for several years. But still the police haven't been able to persuade me to bring my case to court. They tell me another underage victim has also come forward, but will only give evidence in court if I do too. Maybe one day I will feel brave enough to provide the evidence that could put him away for much longer.

Meanwhile, although no longer under police protection, mainly because I refused to go into hiding and take on a new identity, I have been given a 24-hour hotline to the police in case I or any of my family are ever threatened or in danger from any of them. If I press the red button on my phone, a squad car will come round immediately.

One police officer recently asked why I didn't 'say anything' when his colleagues came to Malik's family home following a neighbour's concern on hearing my screams.

'Well,' I said, 'you try telling someone you're being beaten up and sexually abused and you've had your babies stolen when you've got 13 of your abuser's family in the room, making sure you don't even lift your head, let alone speak.'

What was I supposed to say? What if the police hadn't believed me? It would have been one against 13. As soon as they'd gone, the family mafia would have killed me for sure. I couldn't speak.

'What could I say?' Here, I paused to reflect before adding somewhat bitterly, 'Why didn't the police think it odd that I didn't speak? Didn't it occur to them that I wasn't allowed to answer, that something might be wrong? Why didn't they send in a squad to rescue me?'

I might have said similar things to the NHS and social services, but nobody cared, it seemed... except for Sally. Somebody told me she did get another job as a health visitor in a nearby town.

* * *

I'm now settled with my loyal and loving partner Jamie and our four (yes, *four*) lively, much-wanted and much-loved children. When the eldest was born, I wouldn't let him go. I just wanted to hold him forever. That was the moment when I truly had hope for the future – for him and for all the other firsts I would experience in freedom.

I still suffer mental health issues due to the lasting effects of my ordeals, including Complex Post-Traumatic Stress Disorder (C-PTSD). Some internal injuries remain, and made my births more complicated, but they were all worth it. A close physical relationship has also been challenging, but we are still working through that and I am trying hard to accept that love can be without violence.

My past continues to haunt me in many other ways, too. Jamie tells me I often speak Punjabi in my nightmares and lash out at him. He has had a lot to put up with, and still does. He is amazing.

When I have those nightmares, which I often do, I'm there. I can hear them shouting at me … I can feel the punches … I can feel the kicks … I can feel them pulling my hair. Then I wake up sweaty, in a panic attack, my heart racing. But I also sense the relief of the reality that I am not there any more.

I fear leaving the safety of our house, so rarely go out except for therapy or hospital appointments – I can't even take the bins out to the gate. And I have an abiding terror of male taxi drivers. My greatest fear is of being kidnapped again, or one of my children being harmed.

I have a number of NHS doctors and support workers from various departments who continue to work with me and I've been through a variety of therapy programmes, few of which have helped me much, yet, but I really feel that at last some of these specialists do finally believe that I've been through the most relentless and severe traumas, even if they don't know what they are, and I am more optimistic now that there may be a better future out there for me. If the NHS allows, I would love to start on a cognitive behavioural therapy (CBT) course as soon as possible, which I hope may help me to learn strategies to deal with my feelings of shame and all my other living nightmares and fears. I know I won't ever rid myself of them, but learning how to cope would be a great step forward.

In the meantime, I still have eating disorders – principally bulimia. I take prescribed medication for my depression and mental health issues and I also have a long-term addiction to paracetamols for the physical pains I still suffer. My kidney and liver were both damaged in captivity, as were other parts of my body. Although I'm trying my best to cut down, I still take far too many painkillers. I understand now this has become a ritual and I do need help to prevent further damage.

One therapist suggested that I write down some notes about what happened to me to help me understand and come to terms with it all. For the first time, through doing this, I have been able to start speaking openly to a close confidante about my traumatic experiences and this has opened a new door for me. I have shared things I have never told anyone before and this has been a great release, almost as if I were giving them to someone else. At first, it was extremely hard, but the writing of this book has been the best therapy and has opened up for me the possibility of a future, with some hope of a more 'normal' and outgoing life with my favourite people, my family.

There were two things that had always worried me. Did I have to be a Muslim, after they had made me one? But when I asked people, they all said no, which was a great relief. My other fear was that Malik had somehow made me marry him without my knowing. A solicitor looked into that for me and reassured me that we had never married.

There was a time, a few weeks after I escaped, when I received a solicitor's letter, requesting me to go to my own choice of solicitor and sign a document. When I went there, he explained that Malik wanted me to sign this document to pass all my parental responsibility over to him, for the four children I had given birth to whilst in captivity.

'What does that mean?' I asked him.

'That you agree never to seek any involvement in the children's lives – you won't ask to see their school reports, medical records or any other information about them, and you won't every try to trace or look for them.'

I felt a great weight of sadness ... but I knew I could be putting myself in too much danger if I ever did any of that, so I had no choice. I had to sign. I would have done anything, signed any document, to cut off all contact with Malik and his family. I have not been in touch with my mother since she and her lawyer served an eviction notice on Jamie and me and we were offered a council house, where he and I have settled and made a permanent home together. A couple of years ago, I spotted her across a health-centre waiting room – I know she saw me too, but she ignored me. I never heard from my father again and I don't even know whether he is still alive. My grandfather and the rest of the family continue to shun me, without knowing the truth. Uncle Jack is the one I'd still love to see, but he's probably retired from the army now and I have no idea where he could be.

As far as I know, Val, who kindly took me in when I ran away, has moved on. I have no idea whether she ever knew about Malik kidnapping me. I recently tried to get in touch with Sally, the health visitor who rescued me, but her manager would not let her speak to me. Perhaps one day ...

But I have a new 'mum' now – Jamie's mother, who accepts me as I am and never judges me. She has been, and still is, a wonderful help and support to us all.

Now that my eldest son is growing up, he sometimes asks me difficult questions, like most teenagers do. But these are especially hard for me.

'What did you do for your sixteenth birthday, Mum?' or 'What was your school prom like?' or even 'What GCSEs did you do?' It saddens me that I cannot answer him truthfully. I can't bring myself to tell him how I missed all those landmarks, and so much else that happened in the outside world. Whenever I'm at my lowest, I still 'talk' to Nana and repeat those prayers to comfort me.

Despite the many issues that still remain, and the horrific memories that I cannot erase, I've been told that I'm now beginning to regain some of my original confidence and feistiness. I'd like to think I may feel strong enough soon to take up some training and part-time work as an assistant at our local hospice – that's what I would love to do. And I am at last prepared to consider the possibility, one day, of making a statement to the police and giving evidence in court.

I still have the dog-eared photo of Jamie that I had with me to keep me company all those years, but now I have the real Jamie as well, and he continues to give me amazing love and support. Perhaps I will agree to marry him one of these days.

If ever my nightmares wake me, as they do most nights, I go downstairs and check I can open a door to the outside world. Freedom is a precious gift to me and I treasure it alongside my beloved family.

ACKNOWLEDGEMENTS

A big thank you to Jacquie Buttriss for helping me to write this book and also for everything she's done for me, and how she's made my life easier to live.

Thank you to Clare Hulton, my agent, for believing in me and helping me to get this book published. I really appreciate your caring approach.

Thanks to Kelly Ellis, the editorial director, and everyone involved at Blink Publishing, an amazing team – kind, thoughtful and caring. They understood and they didn't judge me.

Thank you very much to Jamie for your enormous support and love throughout these years, and for bringing me happiness, which I never thought could happen. Thank you for staying with me, looking after me and our children through all my problems, and understanding me more now through the process of writing this book. I couldn't have done any of it without your love and loyalty.

HELPLINES

If you have suffered any kind of abuse and would like to talk to someone, the following 24-hour freephone helplines will help you.

Samaritans helpline: 116 123 (across UK and Ireland.) Look up your local number on their website.

National Domestic Violence helpline: 0808 2000 247.

The Survivors' Trust website: www.thesurvivorstrust.org. It also lists other relevant helplines and websites.